Oh My Goddess!

ああっ女神さまっ

31

STORY AND ART BY
Kosuke Fujishima

TRANSLATION BY
Christopher Lewis and Dana Lewis

LETTERING AND TOUCH-UP BY
Susie Lee and Betty Dong
WITH Tom2K

DARK HORSE MANGA™

CHAPTER 195

Love You to Death

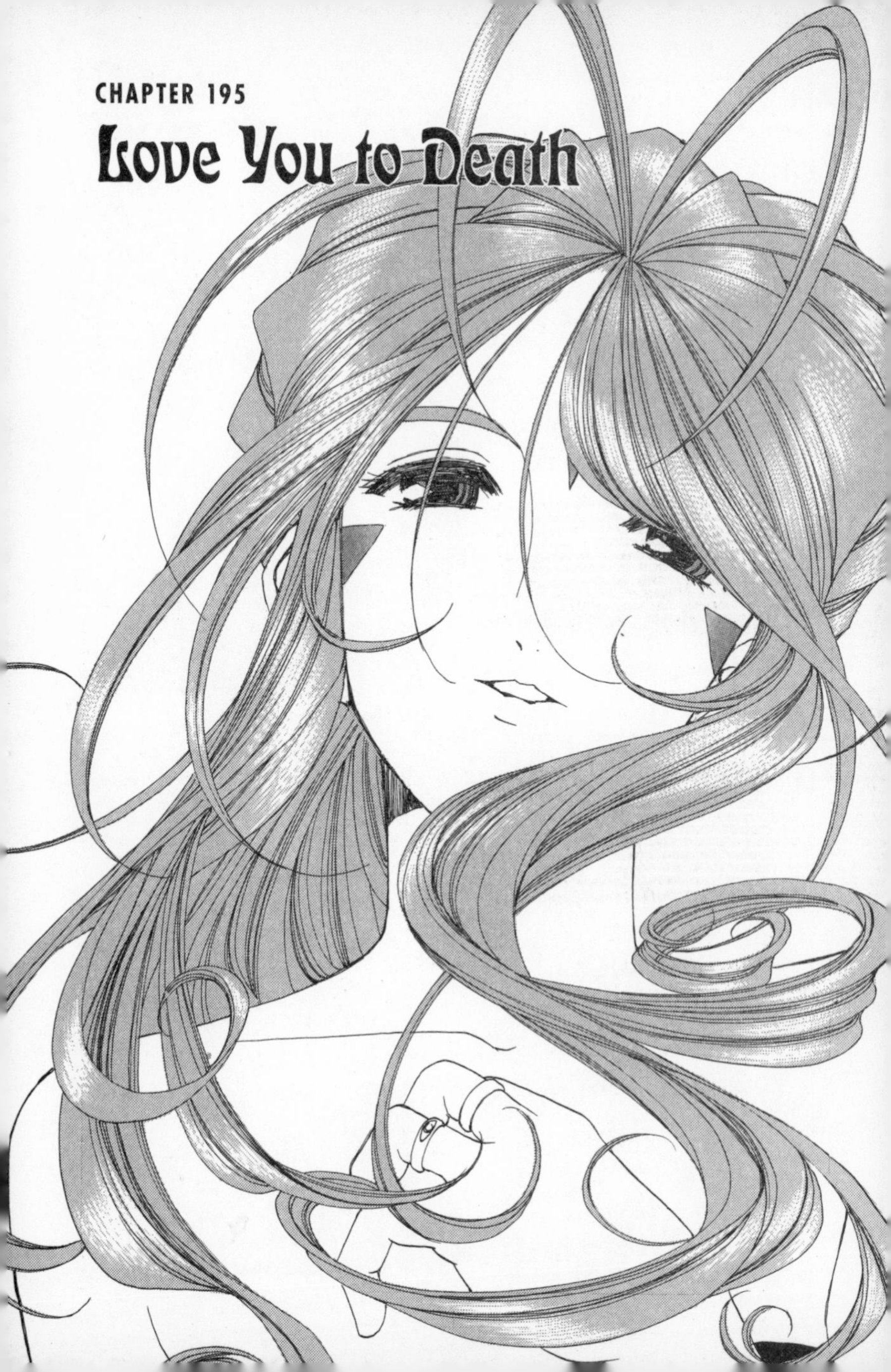

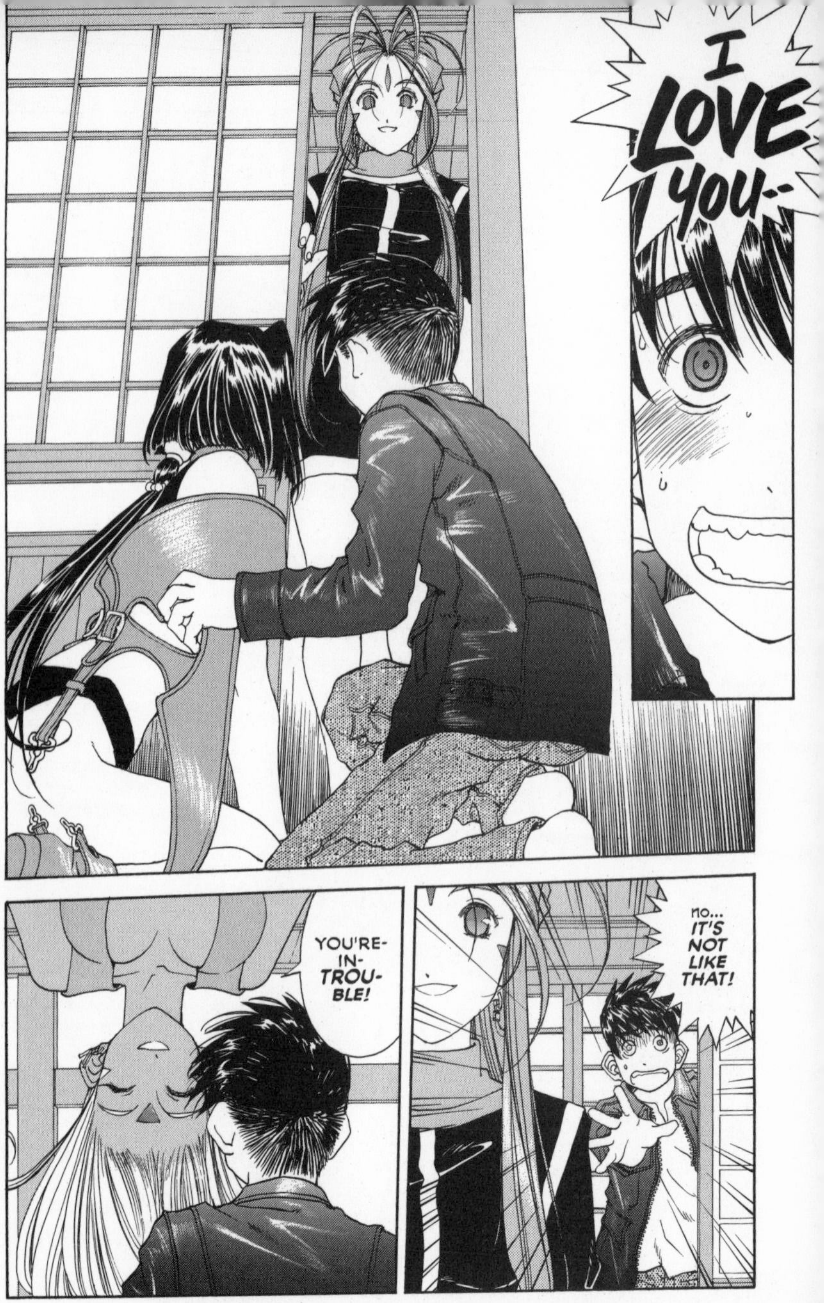
I LOVE you--
no... IT'S NOT LIKE THAT!
YOU'RE-IN-TROUBLE!

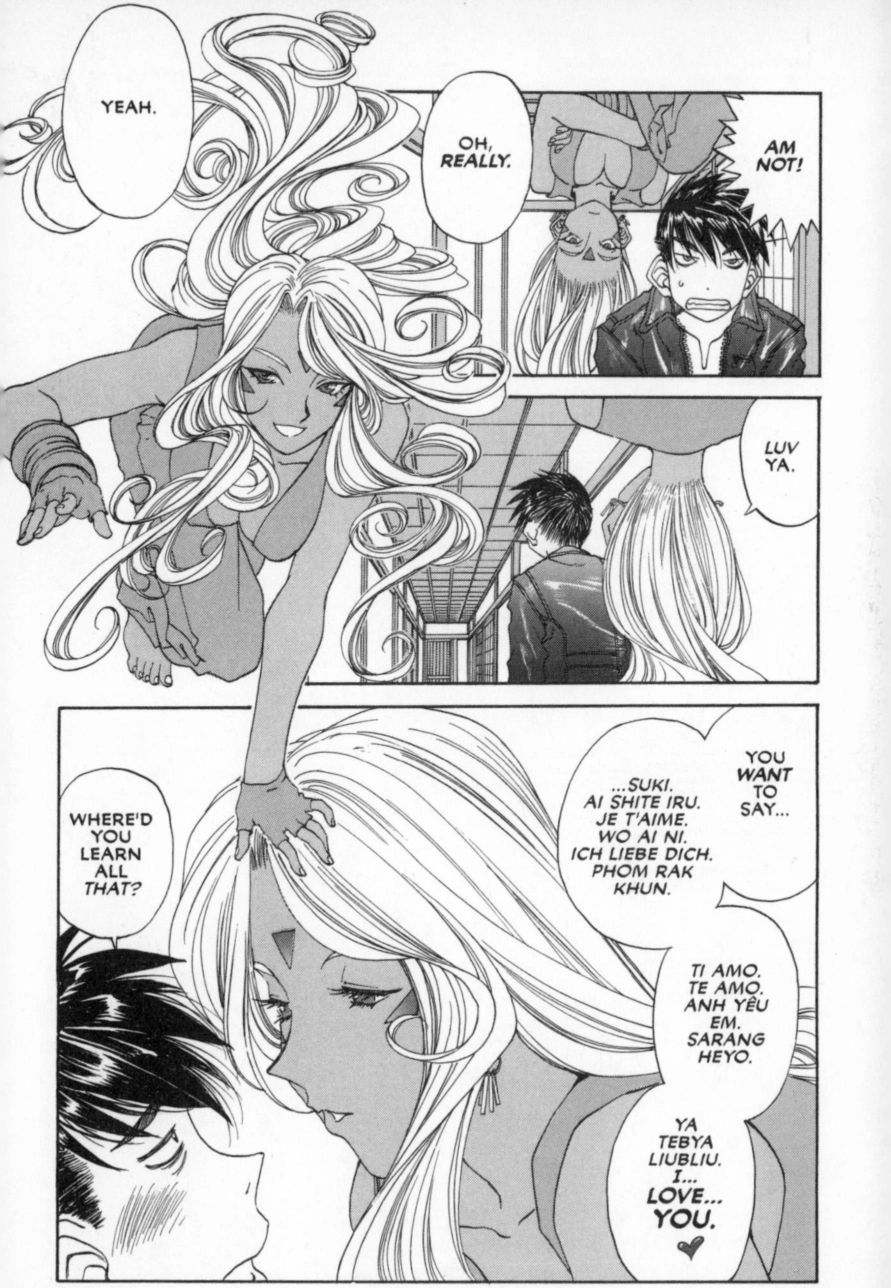
AM NOT!
OH, REALLY.
LUV YA.
YEAH.
YOU WANT TO SAY...
...SUKI. AI SHITE IRU. JE T'AIME. WO AI NI. ICH LIEBE DICH. PHOM RAK KHUN.
WHERE'D YOU LEARN ALL THAT?
TI AMO. TE AMO. ANH YÊU EM. SARANG HEYO.
YA TEBYA LIUBLIU. I... LOVE... YOU.

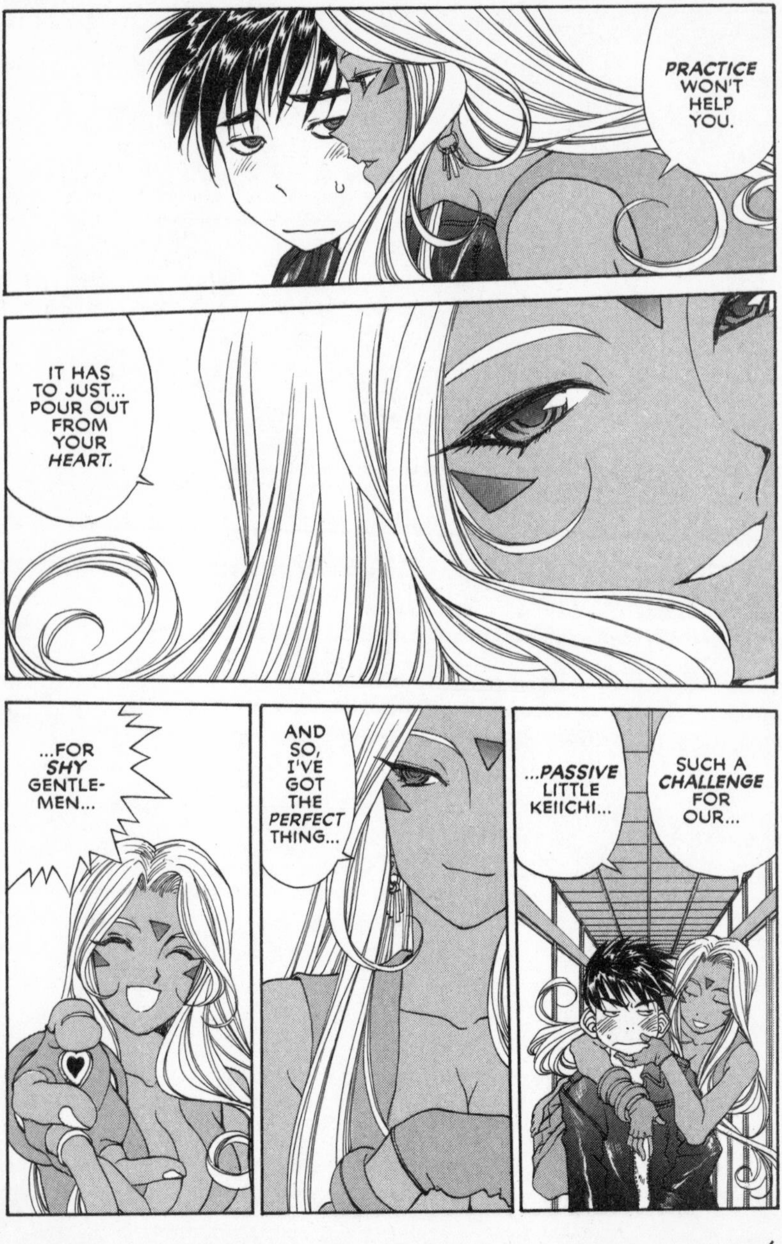
PRACTICE WON'T HELP YOU.
IT HAS TO JUST... POUR OUT FROM YOUR HEART.
SUCH A CHALLENGE FOR OUR...
...PASSIVE LITTLE KEIICHI...
AND SO, I'VE GOT THE PERFECT THING...
...FOR SHY GENTLE-MEN...

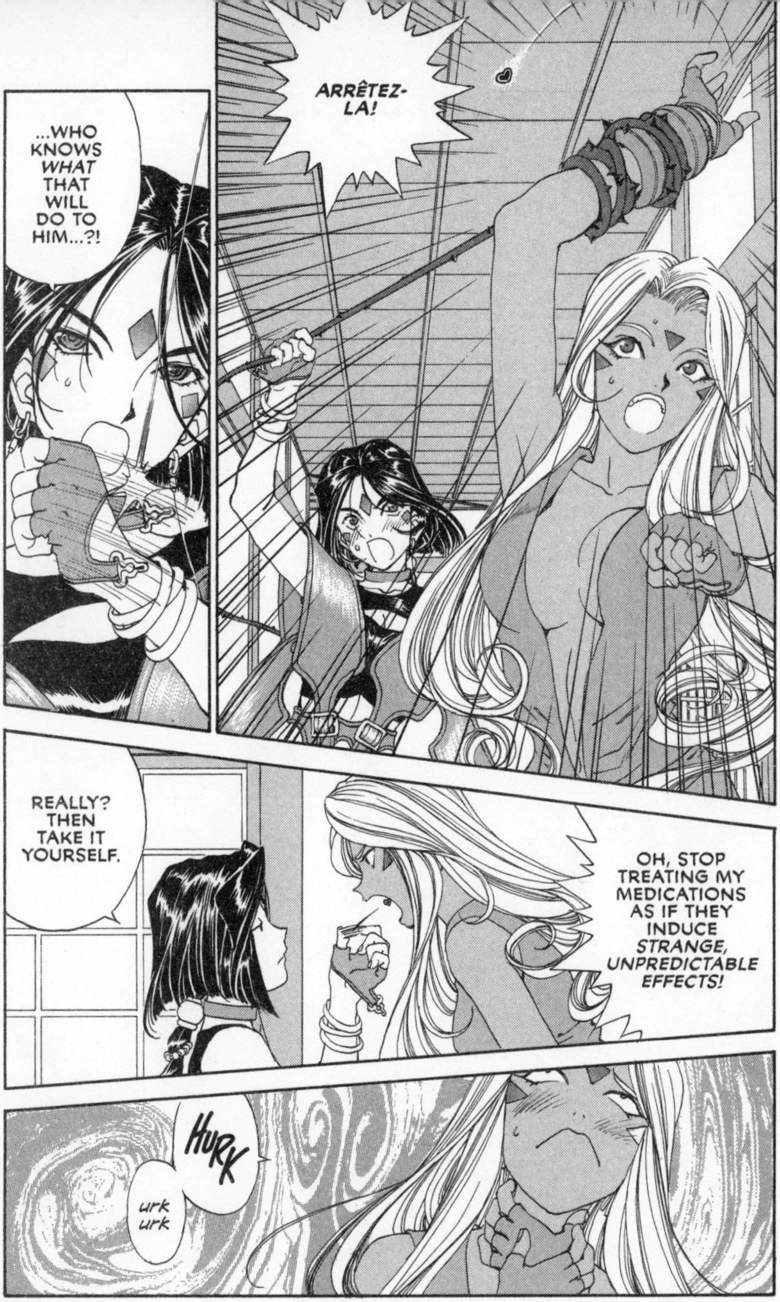
ARRÊTEZ-LA!
...WHO KNOWS *WHAT* THAT WILL DO TO HIM...?!
OH, STOP TREATING MY MEDICATIONS AS IF THEY INDUCE *STRANGE, UNPREDICTABLE* EFFECTS!
REALLY? THEN TAKE IT YOURSELF.
HURK
urk urk

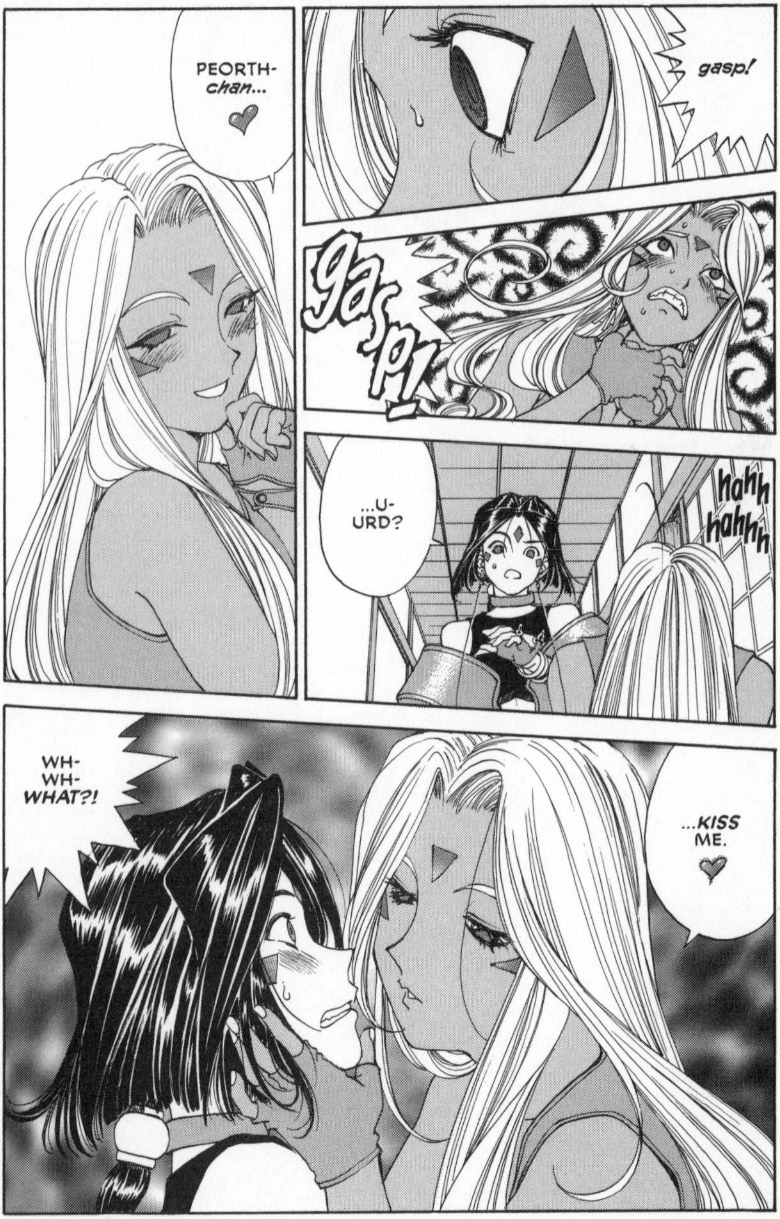
gasp!
gasp!
hahh hahhh
...U-URD?
PEORTH-chan...
...KISS ME.
WH-WH-WHAT?!

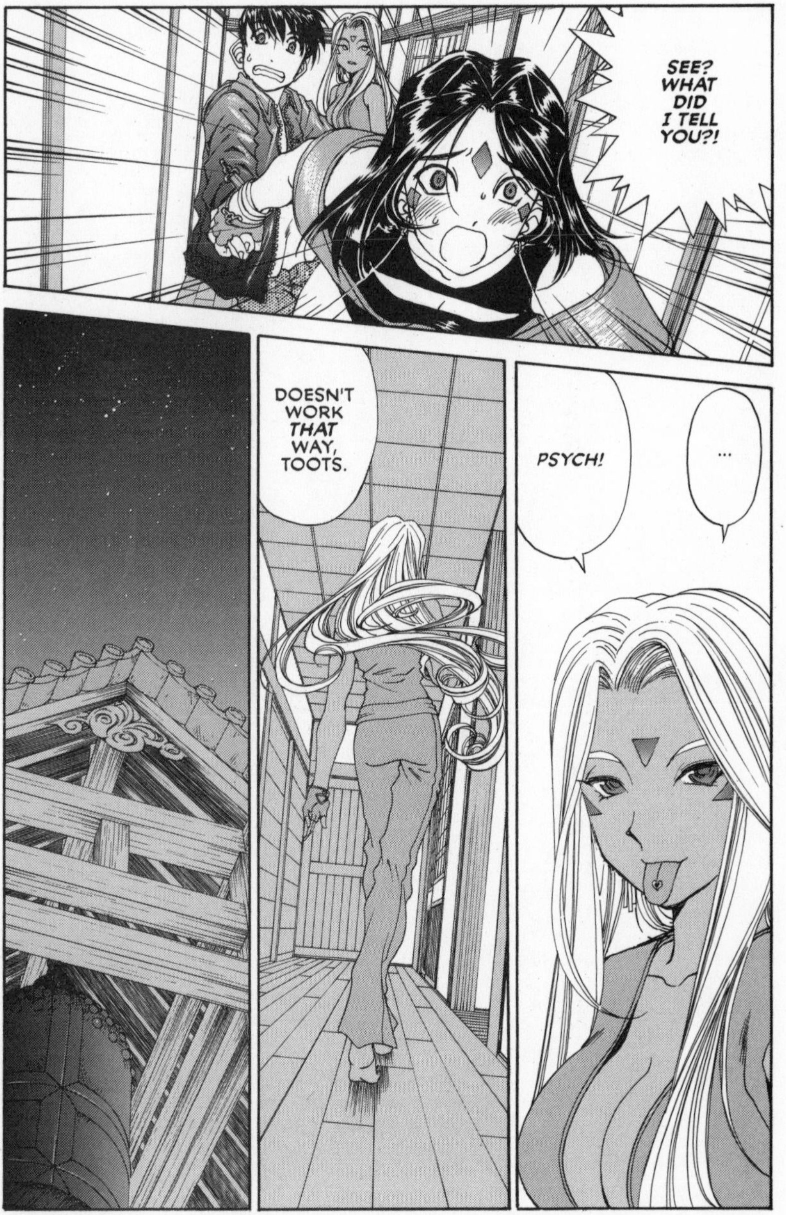
SEE? WHAT DID I TELL YOU?!
...
PSYCH!
DOESN'T WORK *THAT* WAY, TOOTS.

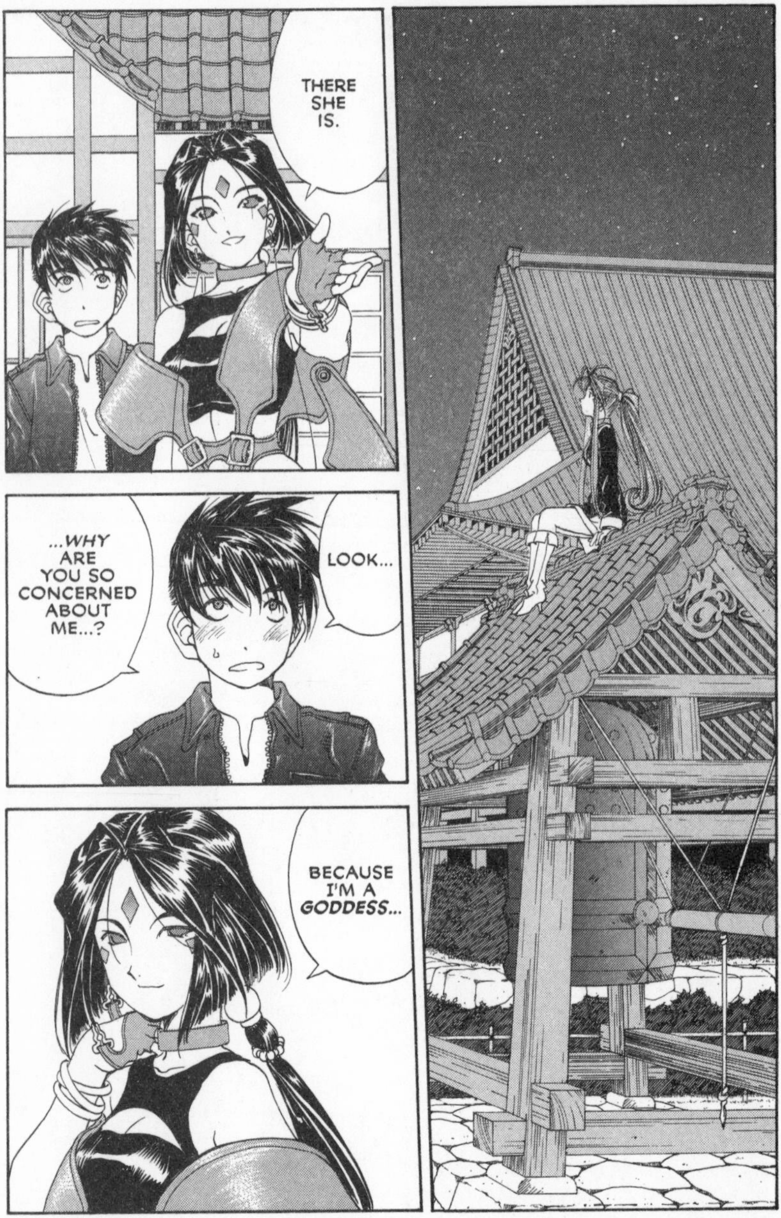
THERE SHE IS.
LOOK...
...*WHY* ARE YOU SO CONCERNED ABOUT ME...?
BECAUSE I'M A ***GODDESS***...

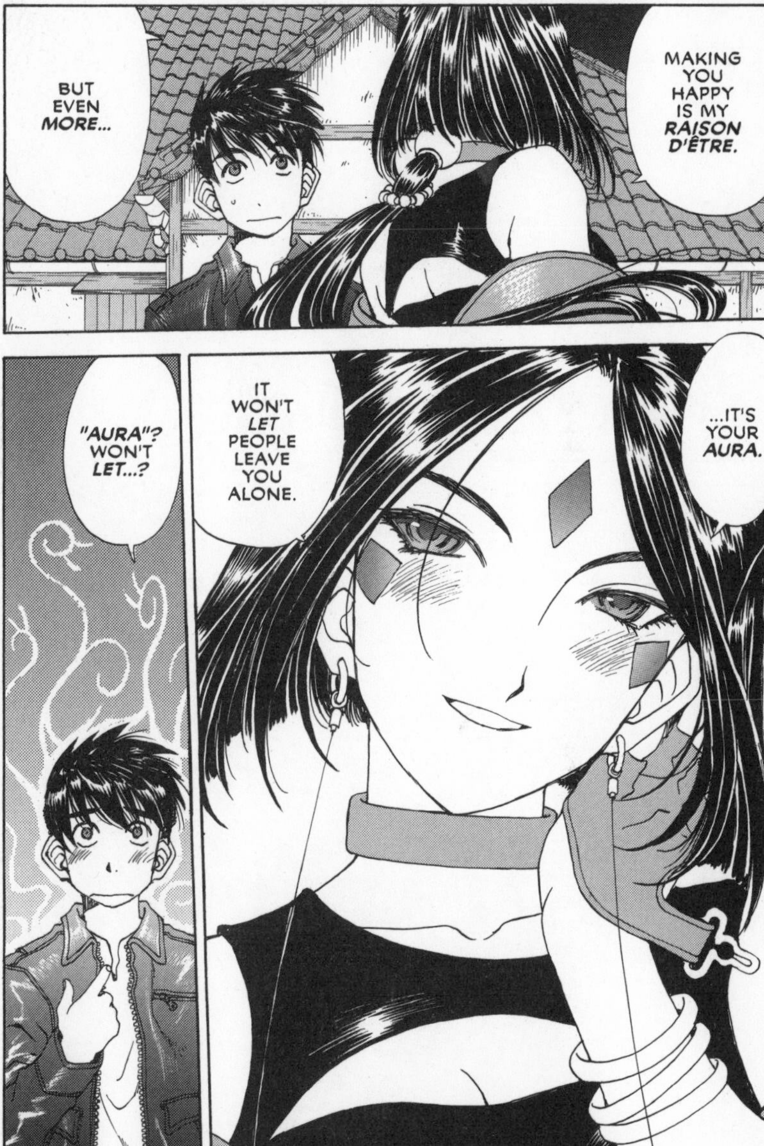
MAKING YOU HAPPY IS MY *RAISON D'ÊTRE.*
BUT EVEN *MORE...*
...IT'S YOUR *AURA.*
IT WON'T *LET* PEOPLE LEAVE YOU ALONE.
"AURA"? WON'T *LET...?*

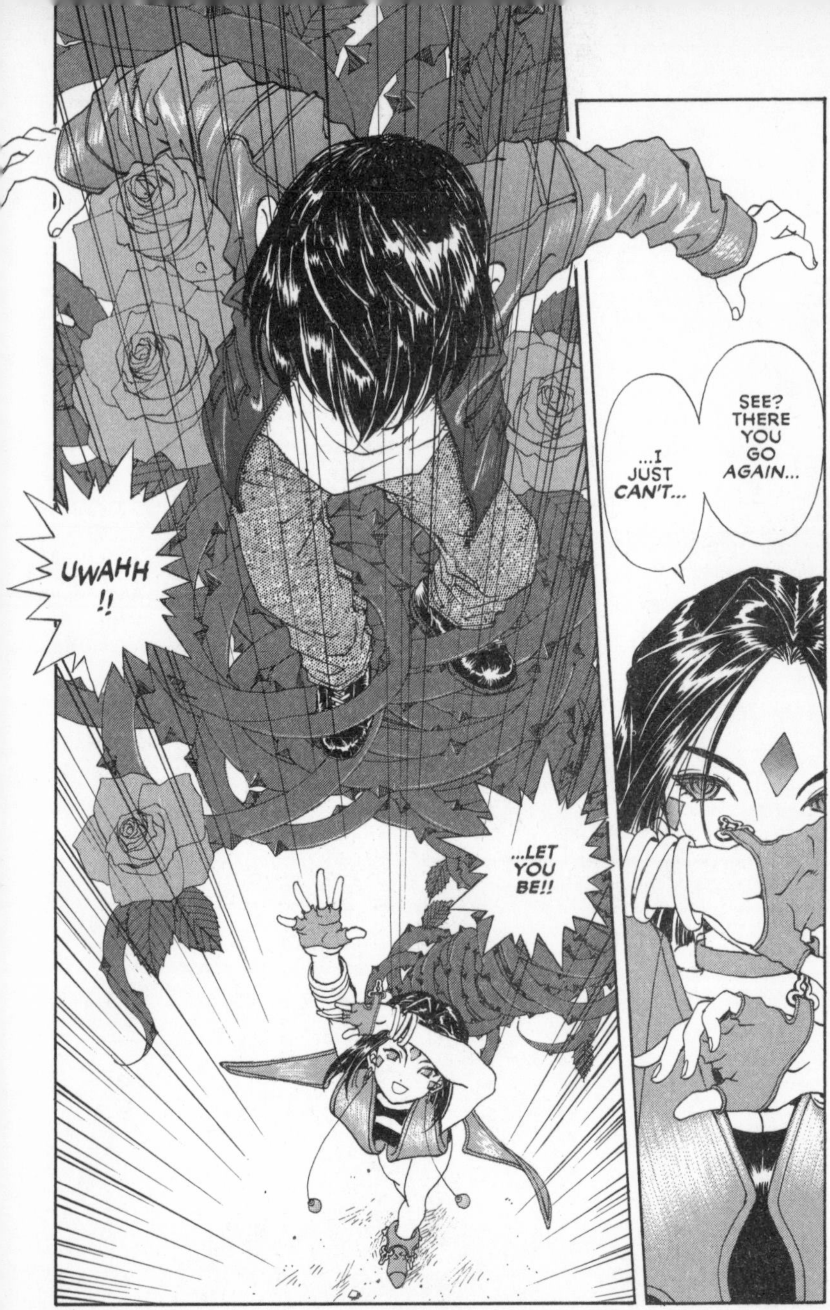
SEE? THERE YOU GO AGAIN...
...I JUST CAN'T...
UWAHH!!
...LET YOU BE!!

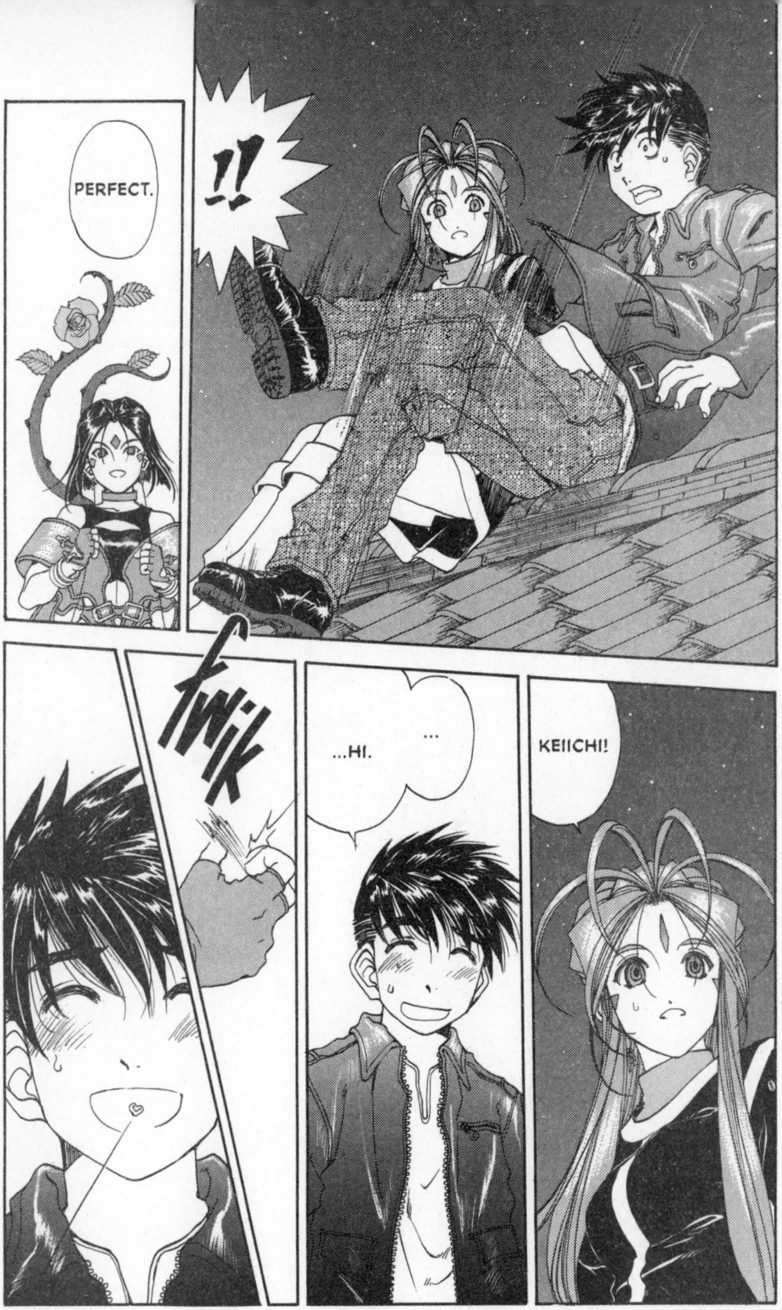
!!
PERFECT.
KEIICHI!
...
...HI.
fwik

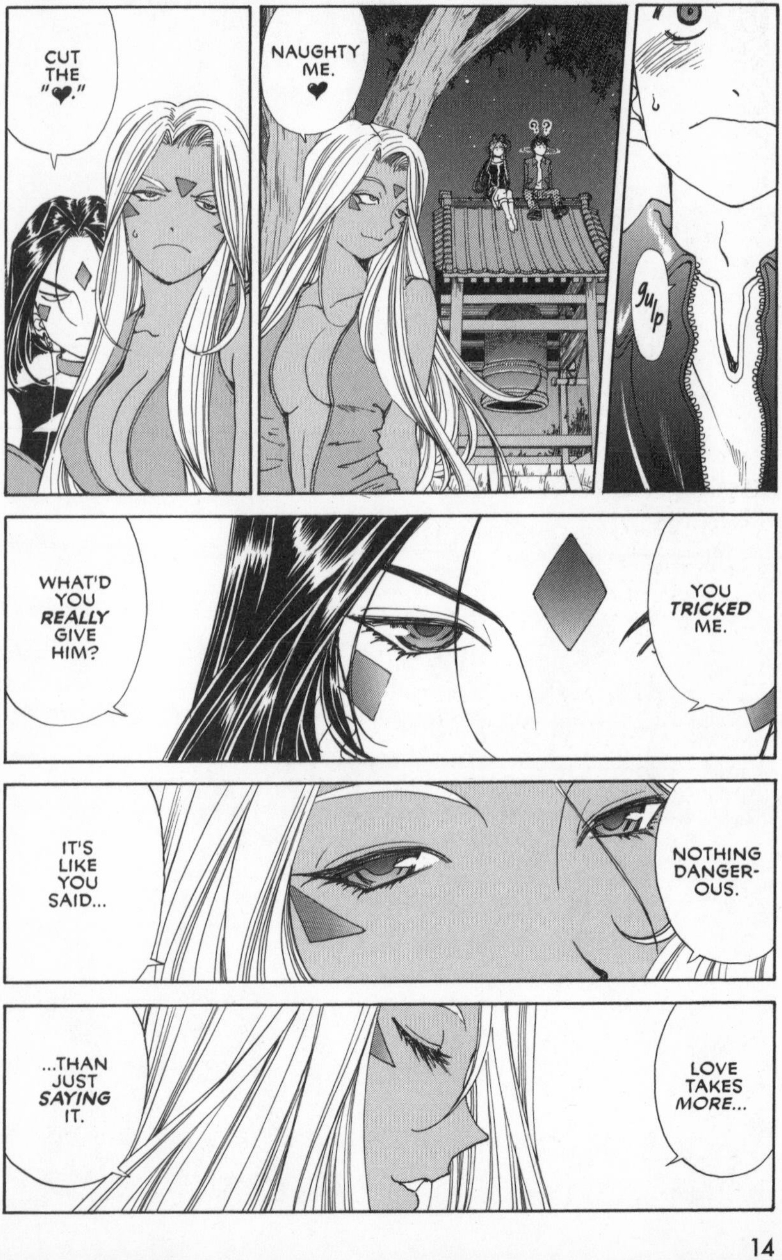
gulp
NAUGHTY ME. ❤
CUT THE "❤."
YOU *TRICKED* ME.
WHAT'D YOU *REALLY* GIVE HIM?
NOTHING DANGER-OUS.
IT'S LIKE YOU SAID...
LOVE TAKES *MORE*...
...THAN JUST *SAYING* IT.

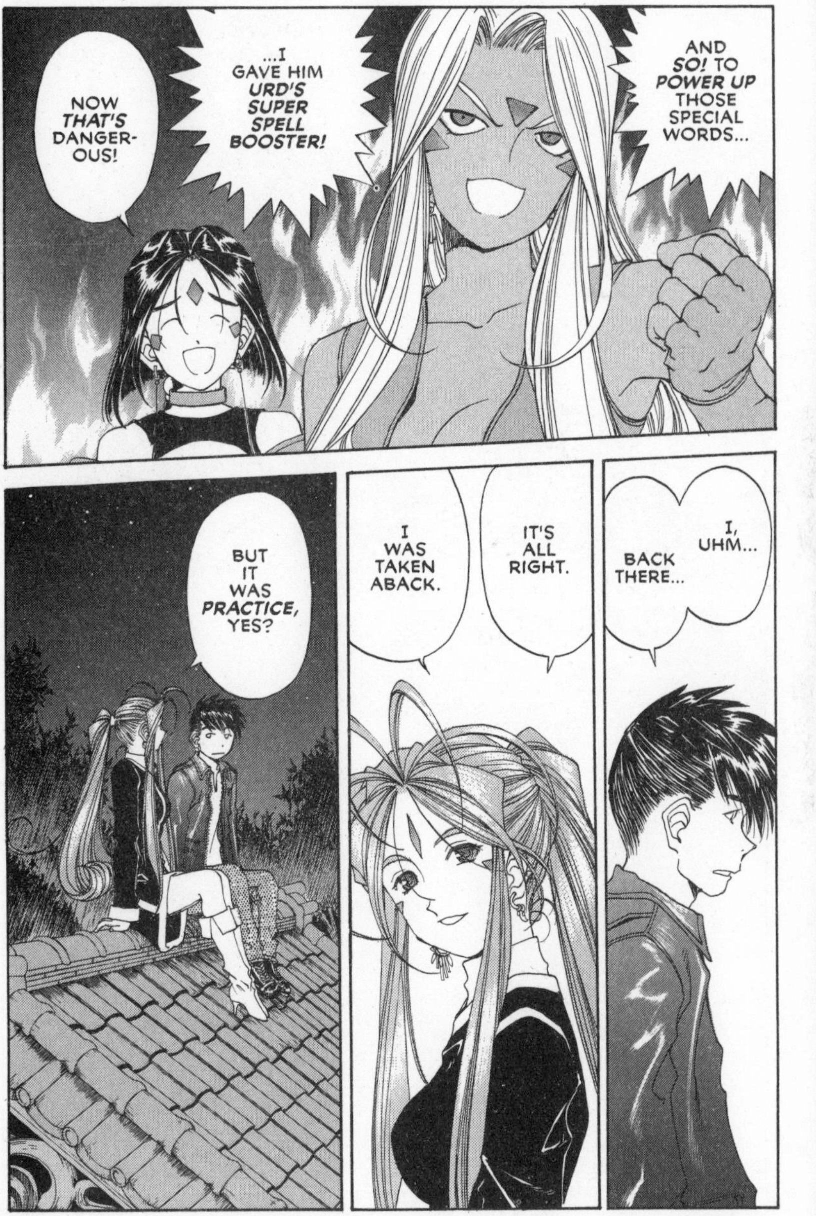
AND SO! TO POWER UP THOSE SPECIAL WORDS...
...I GAVE HIM URD'S SUPER SPELL BOOSTER!
NOW THAT'S DANGER-OUS!
I, UHM...
BACK THERE...
IT'S ALL RIGHT.
I WAS TAKEN ABACK.
BUT IT WAS PRACTICE, YES?

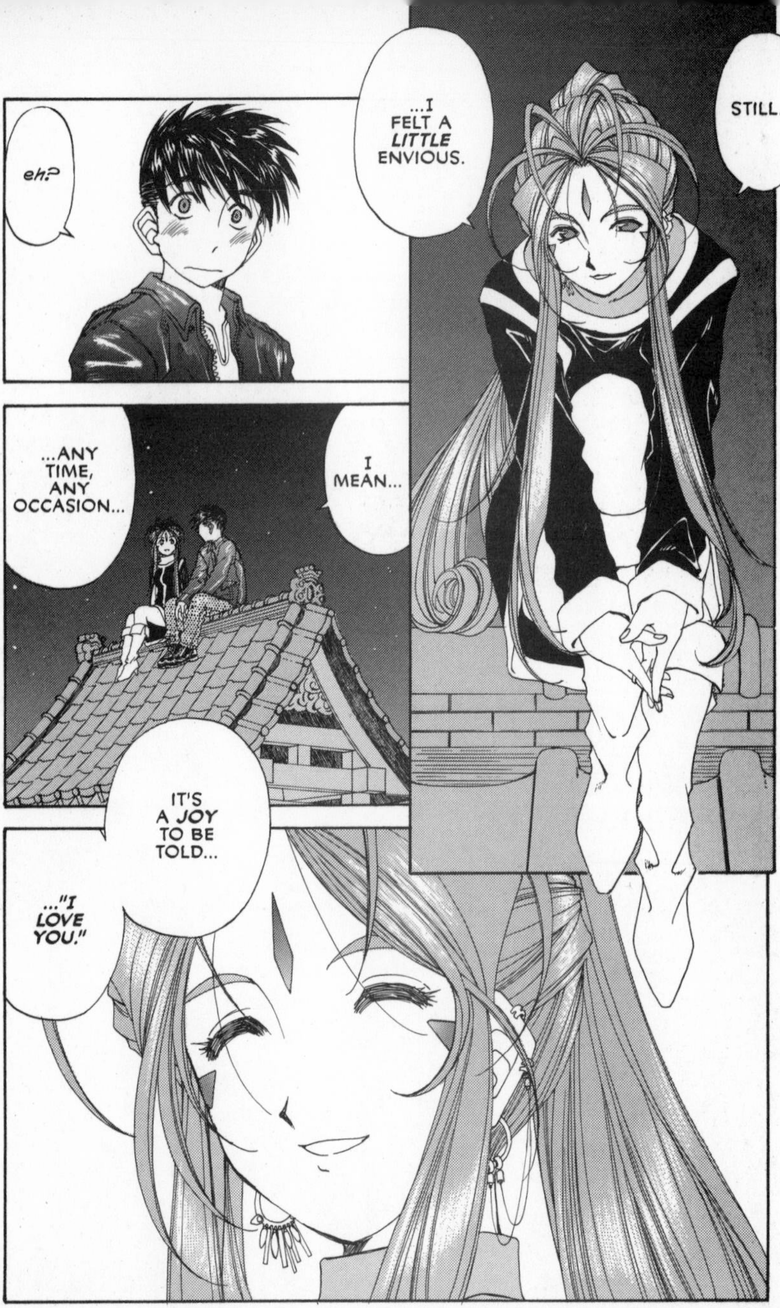
STILL...
...I FELT A *LITTLE* ENVIOUS.
eh?
I MEAN...
...ANY TIME, ANY OCCASION...
IT'S A *JOY* TO BE TOLD...
..."I LOVE YOU."

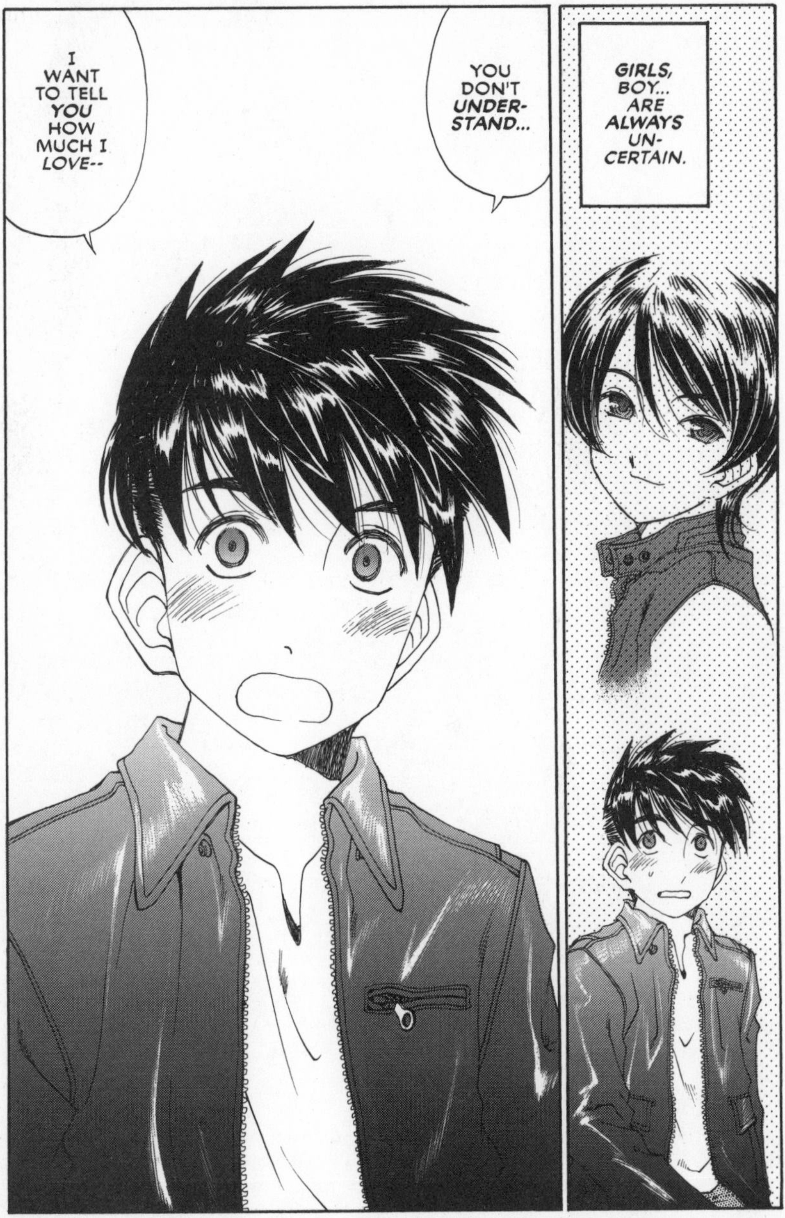
GIRLS, BOY... ARE ALWAYS UN-CERTAIN.
YOU DON'T UNDER-STAND...
I WANT TO TELL YOU HOW MUCH I LOVE--

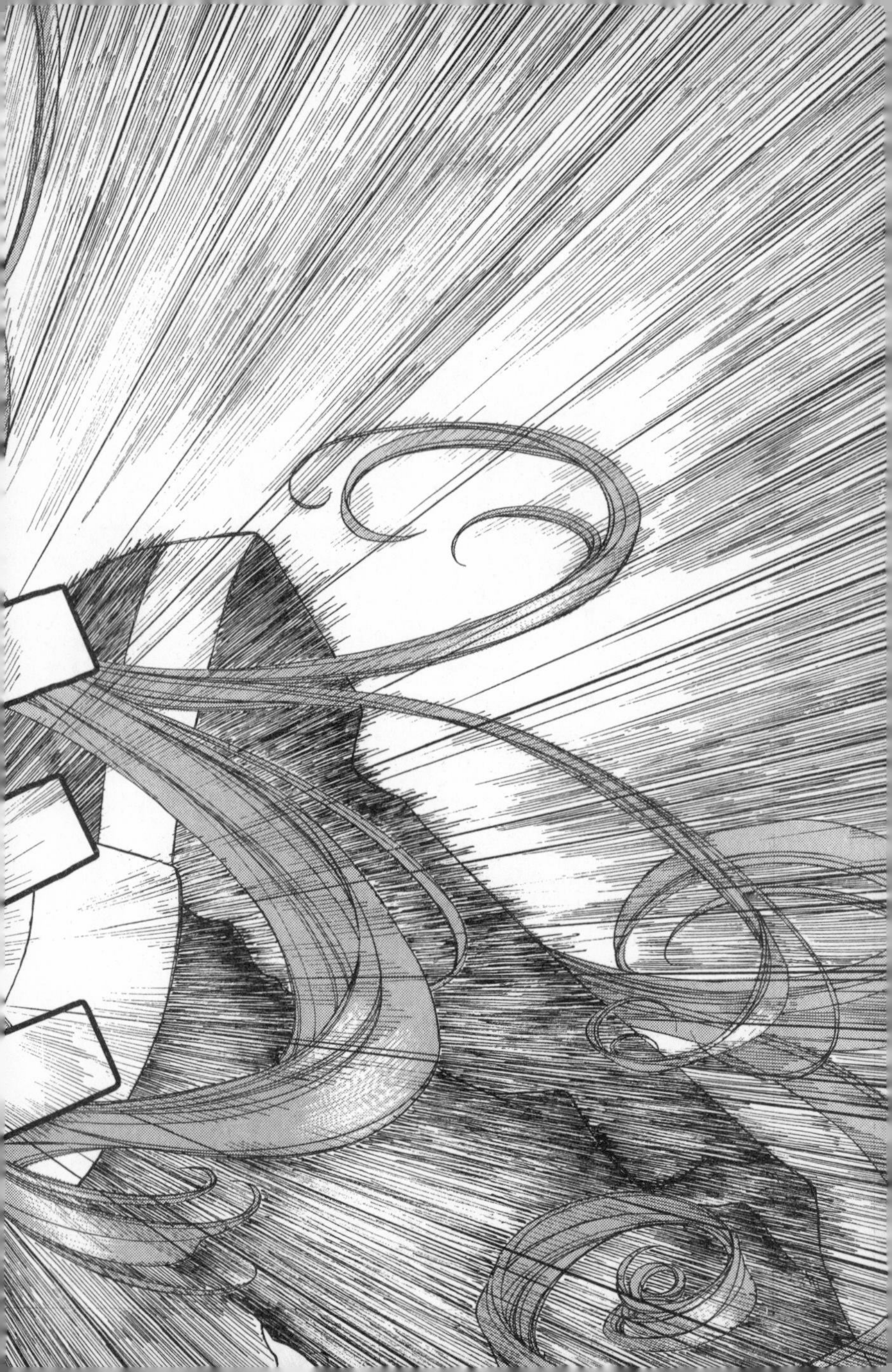

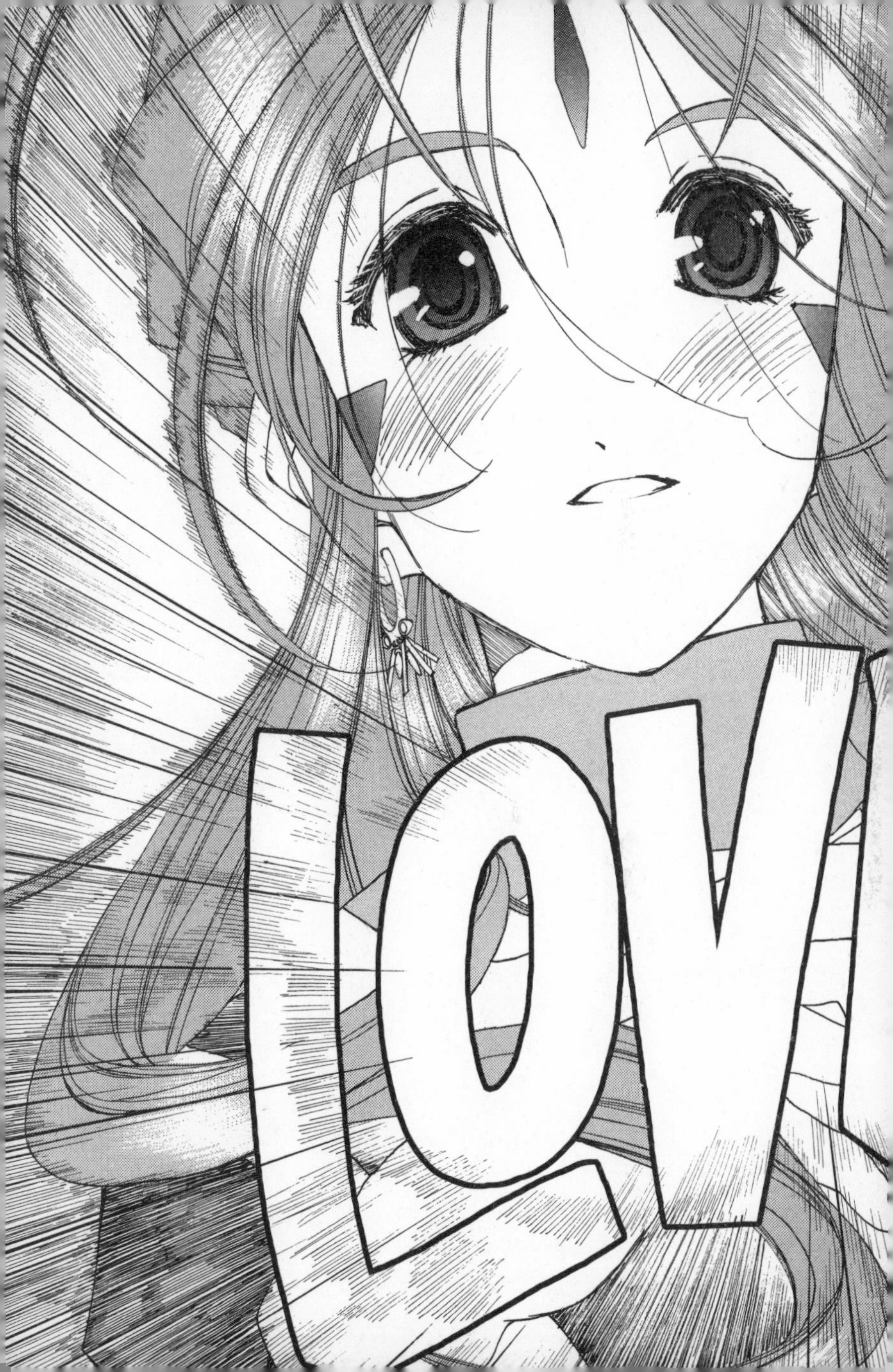
LOV

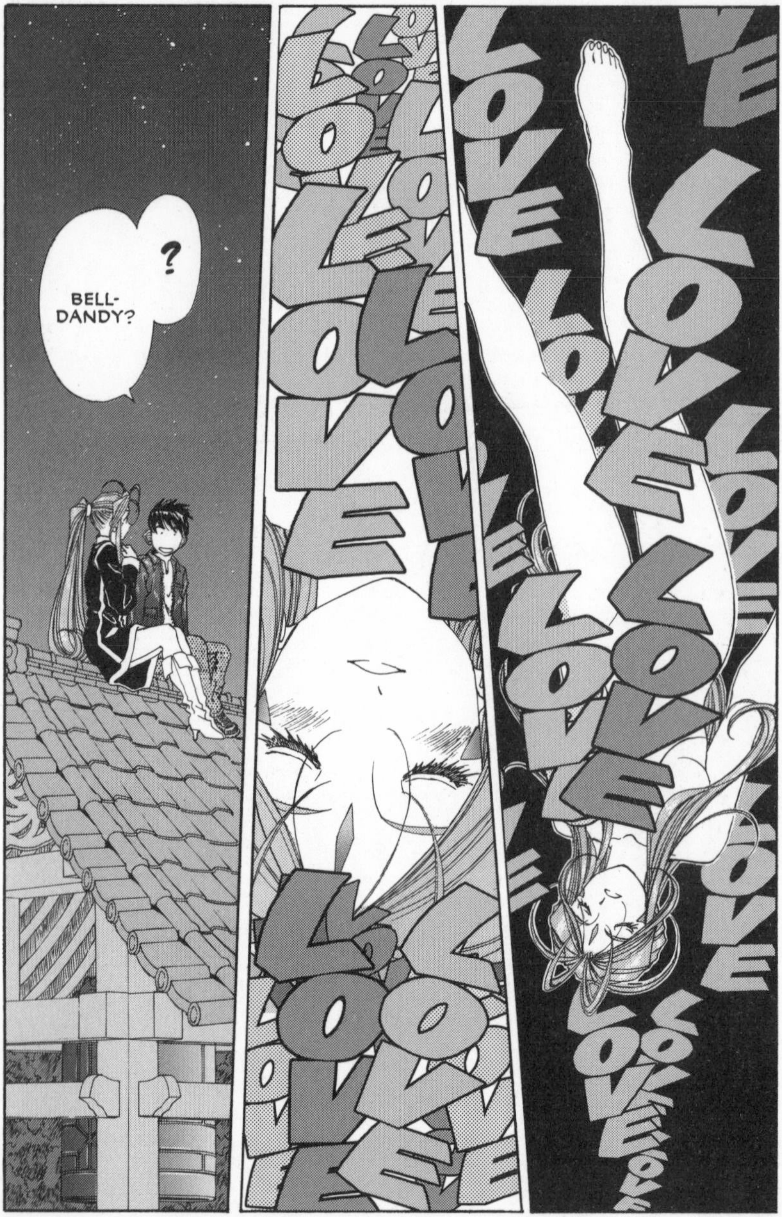
LOVE
LOVE
?
BELL-DANDY?

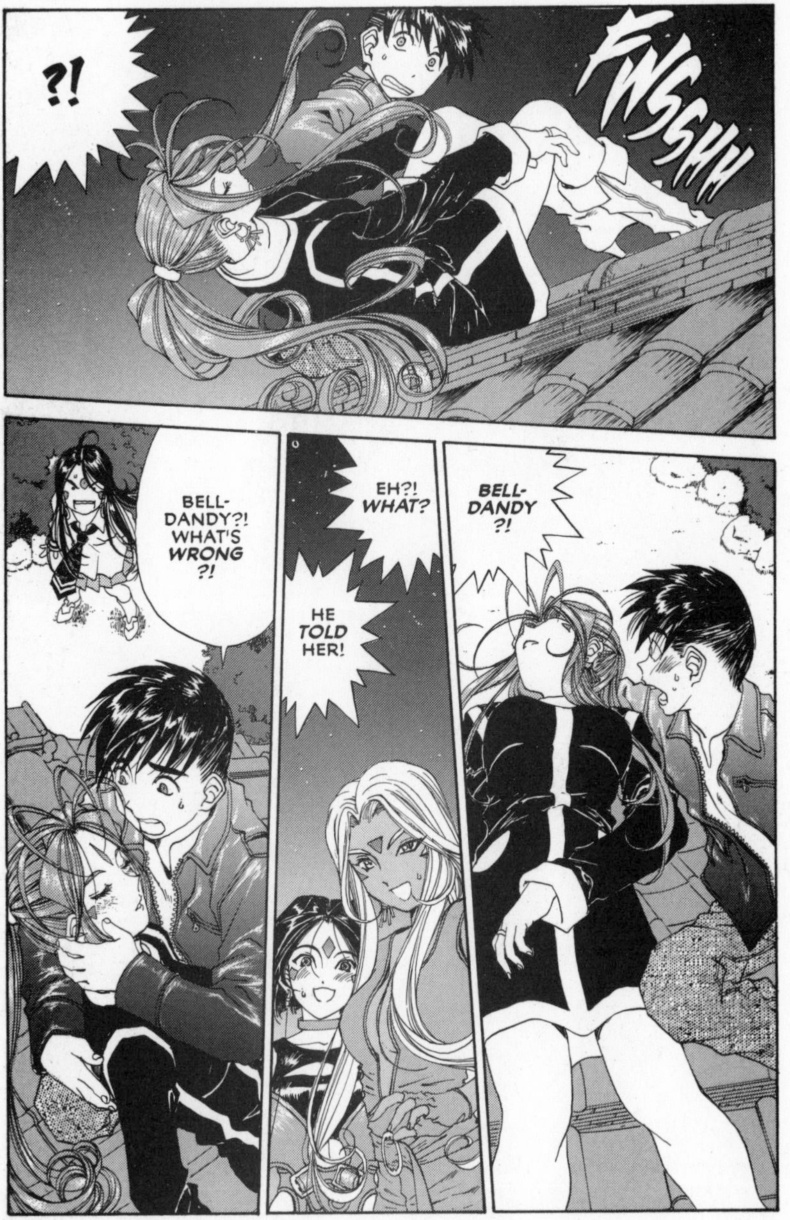
?!
FWSSHH
BELL-DANDY?!
EH?! WHAT?
HE TOLD HER!
BELL-DANDY?! WHAT'S WRONG?!

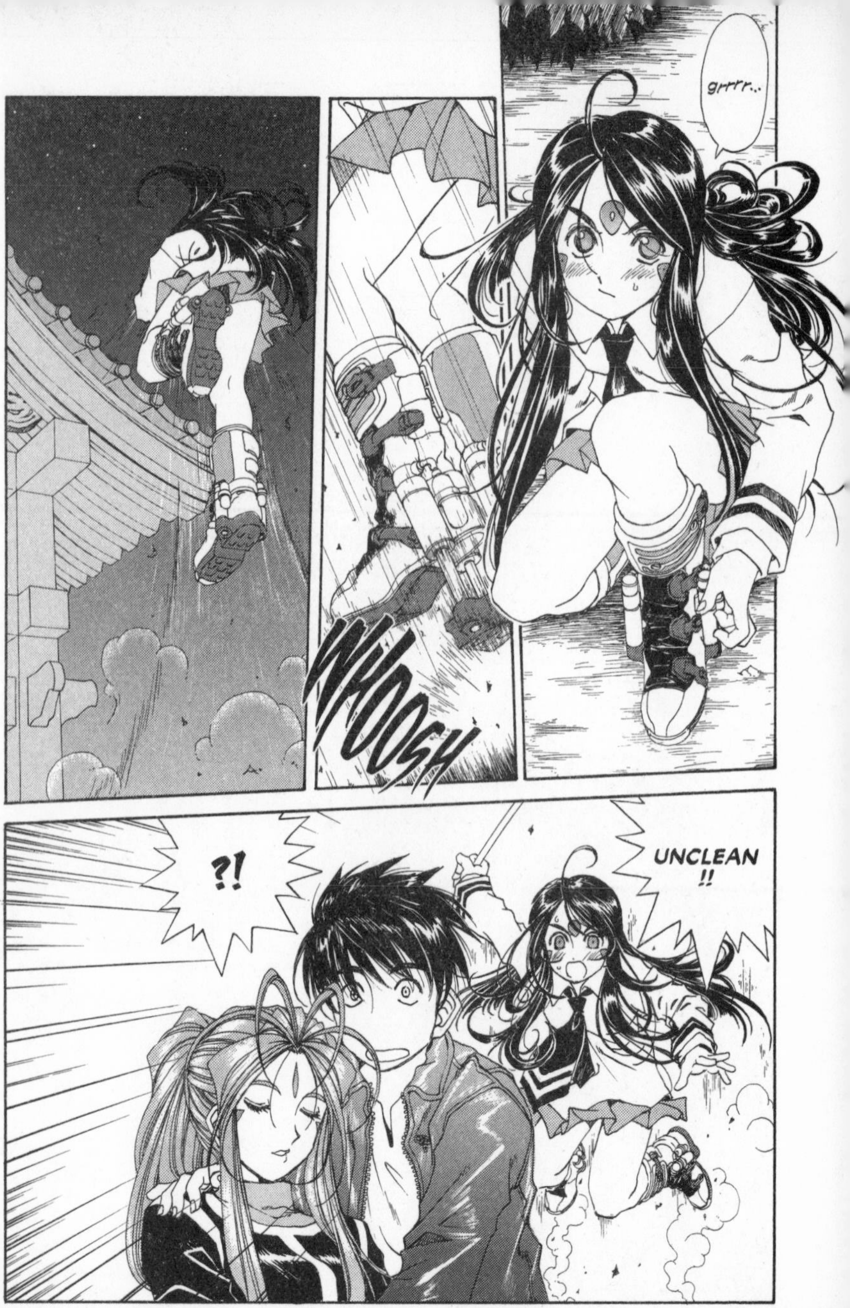
grrrr..
WHOOSH
UNCLEAN !!
?!

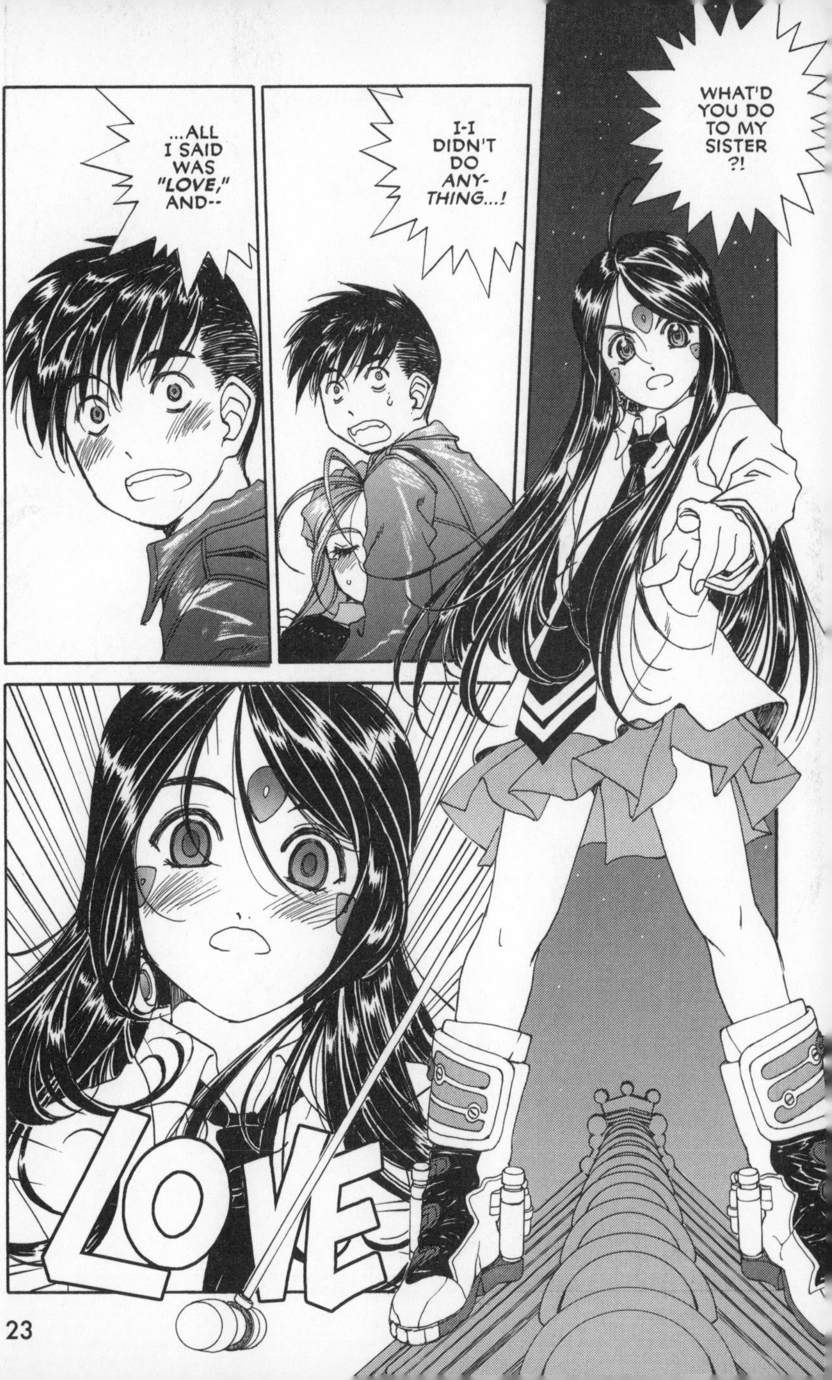
WHAT'D YOU DO TO MY SISTER ?!
I-I DIDN'T DO ANY-THING...!
...ALL I SAID WAS "LOVE," AND--
LOVE

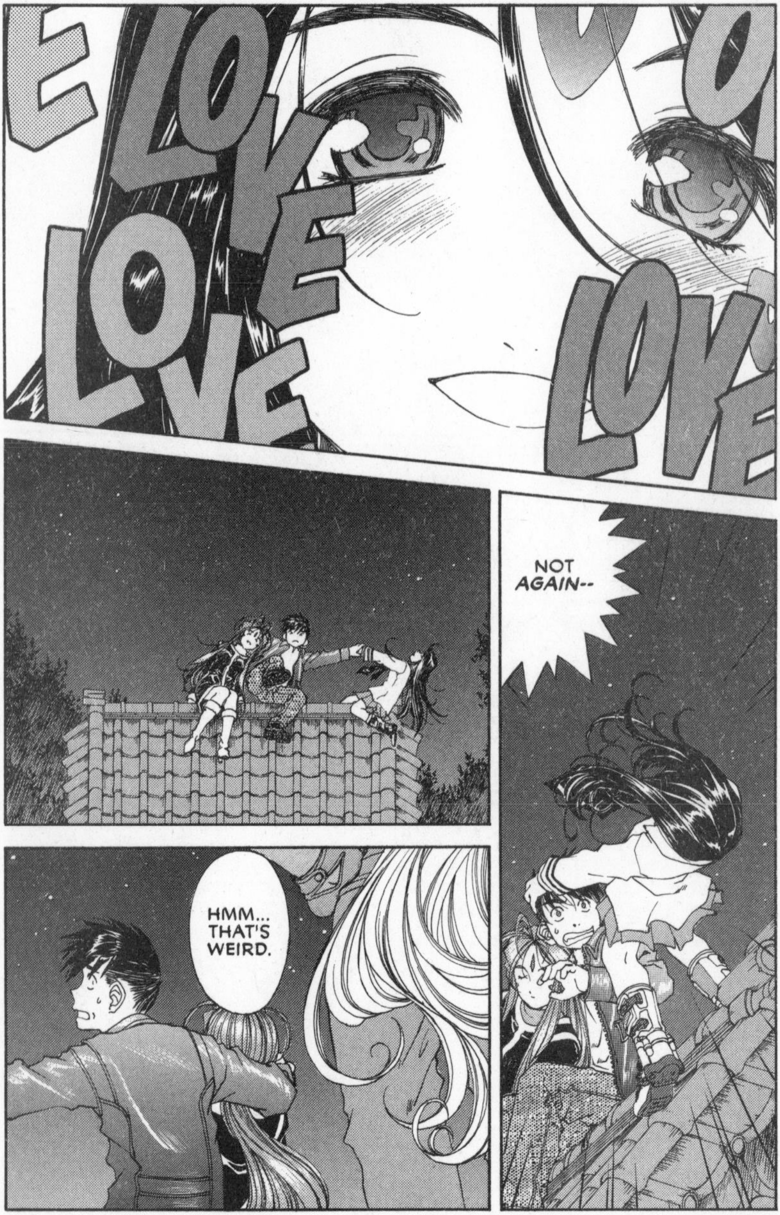
LOVE
LOVE
LOVE
LOVE
NOT AGAIN--
HMM... THAT'S WEIRD.

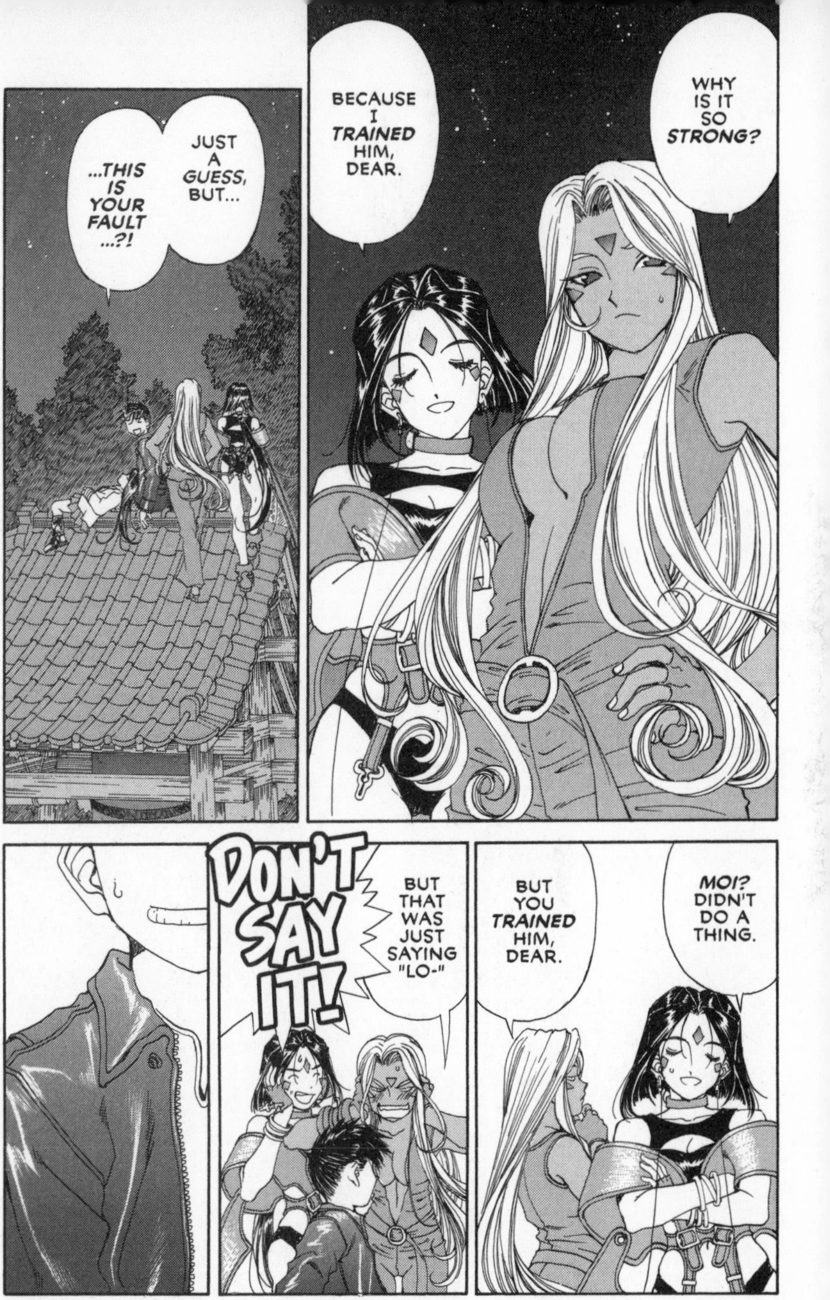
WHY IS IT SO *STRONG?*
BECAUSE I *TRAINED* HIM, DEAR.
JUST A GUESS, BUT...
...THIS IS YOUR FAULT ...?!
MOI? DIDN'T DO A THING.
BUT YOU *TRAINED* HIM, DEAR.
BUT THAT WAS JUST SAYING "LO-"
DON'T SAY IT!

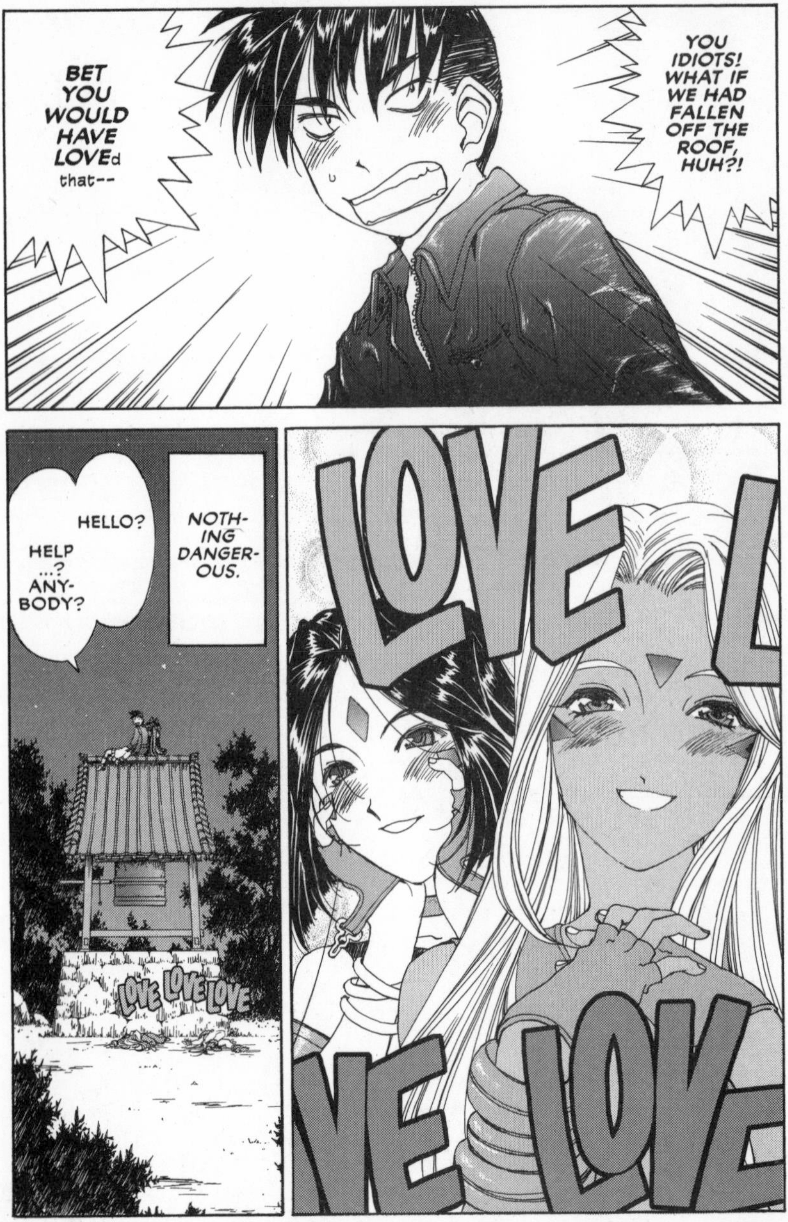
YOU IDIOTS! WHAT IF WE HAD FALLEN OFF THE ROOF, HUH?!
BET YOU WOULD HAVE LOVEd that--
LOVE
LOVE
NOTH-ING DANGER-OUS.
HELLO? HELP ...? ANY-BODY?
LOVE LOVE LOVE

CHAPTER 196

Return to Base

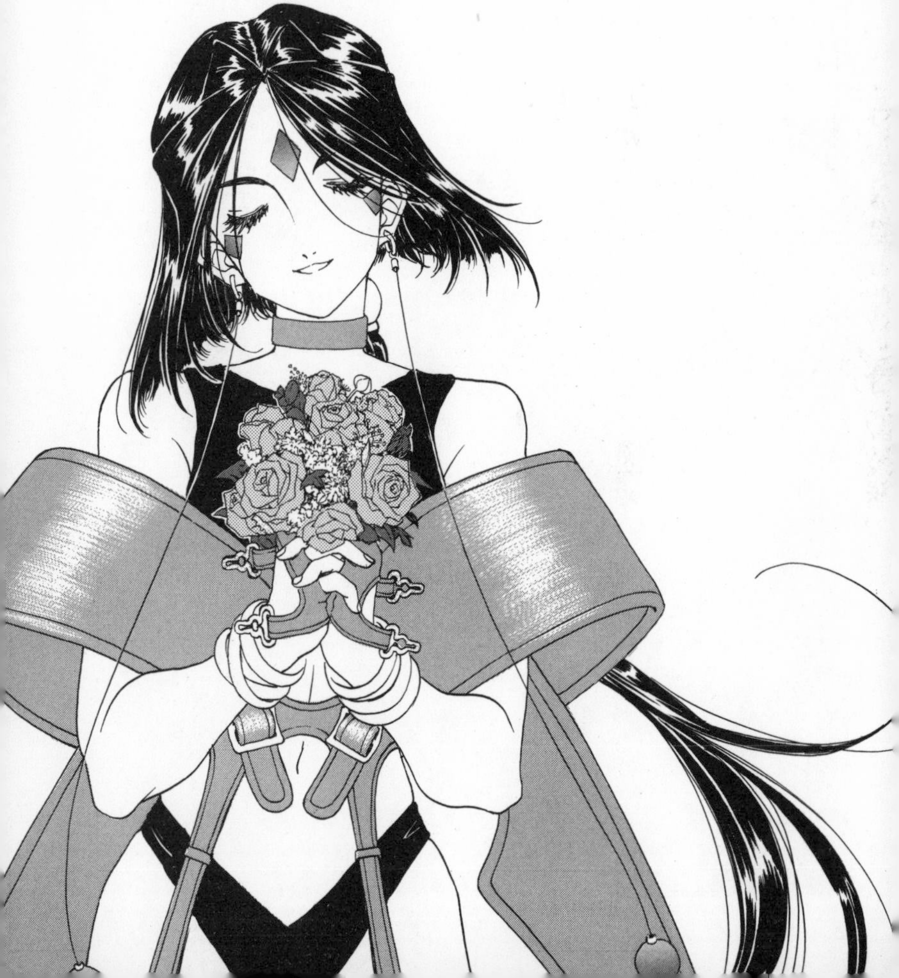

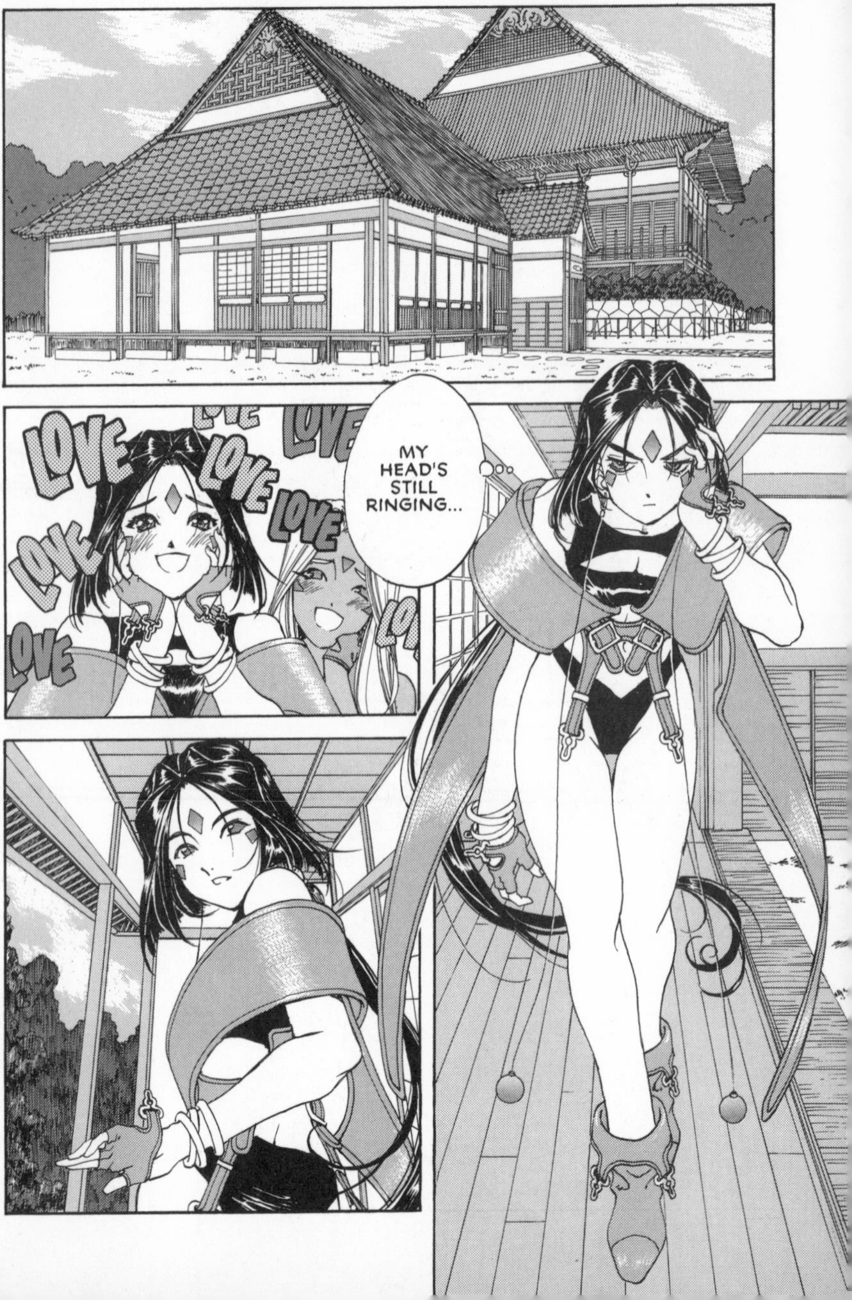
MY HEAD'S STILL RINGING...
LOVE
LOVE
LOVE
LOVE
LOVE
LOVE
LOVE

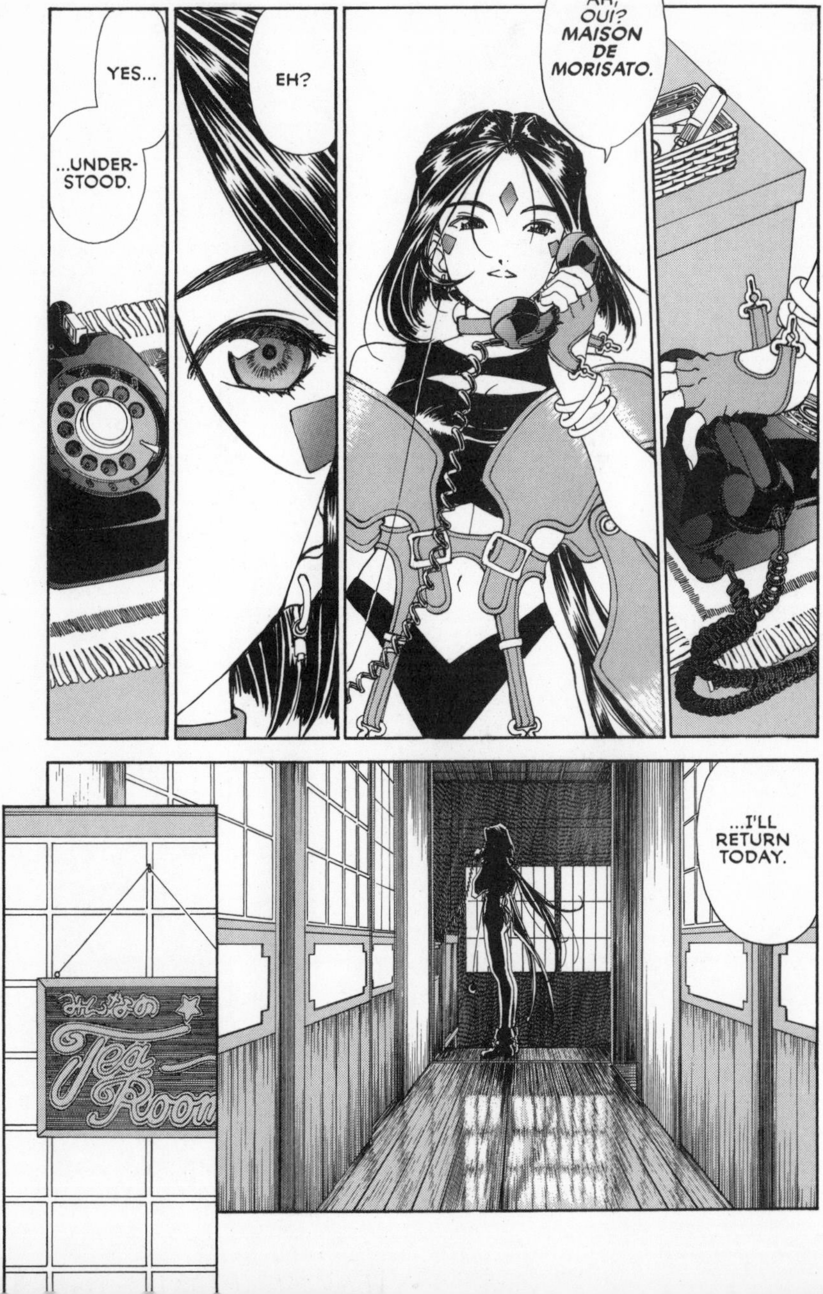
AH, OUI? MAISON DE MORISATO.
EH?
YES...
...UNDER-STOOD.
...I'LL RETURN TODAY.
みんなの
Tea-Room

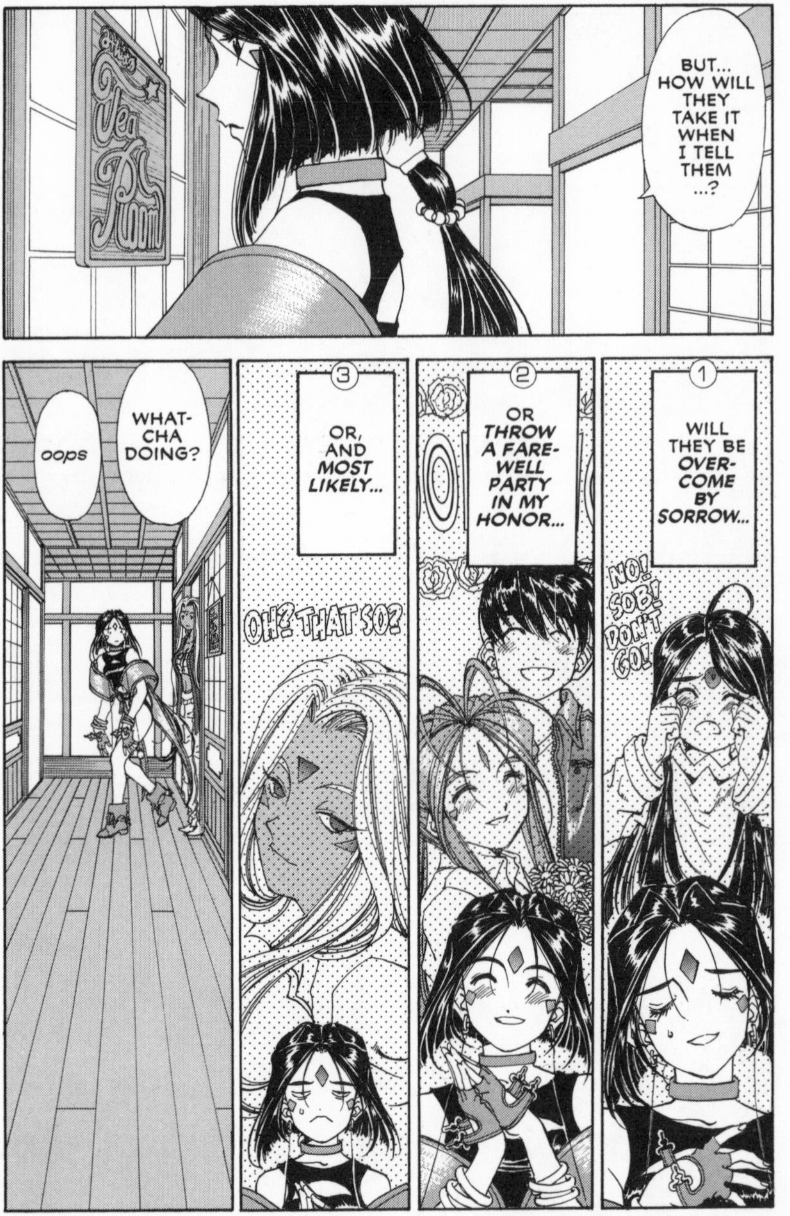
BUT... HOW WILL THEY TAKE IT WHEN I TELL THEM ...?
1
WILL THEY BE OVER-COME BY SORROW...
NO! SOB! DON'T GO!
2
OR THROW A FARE-WELL PARTY IN MY HONOR...
3
OR, AND MOST LIKELY...
OH? THAT SO?
WHAT-CHA DOING?
oops

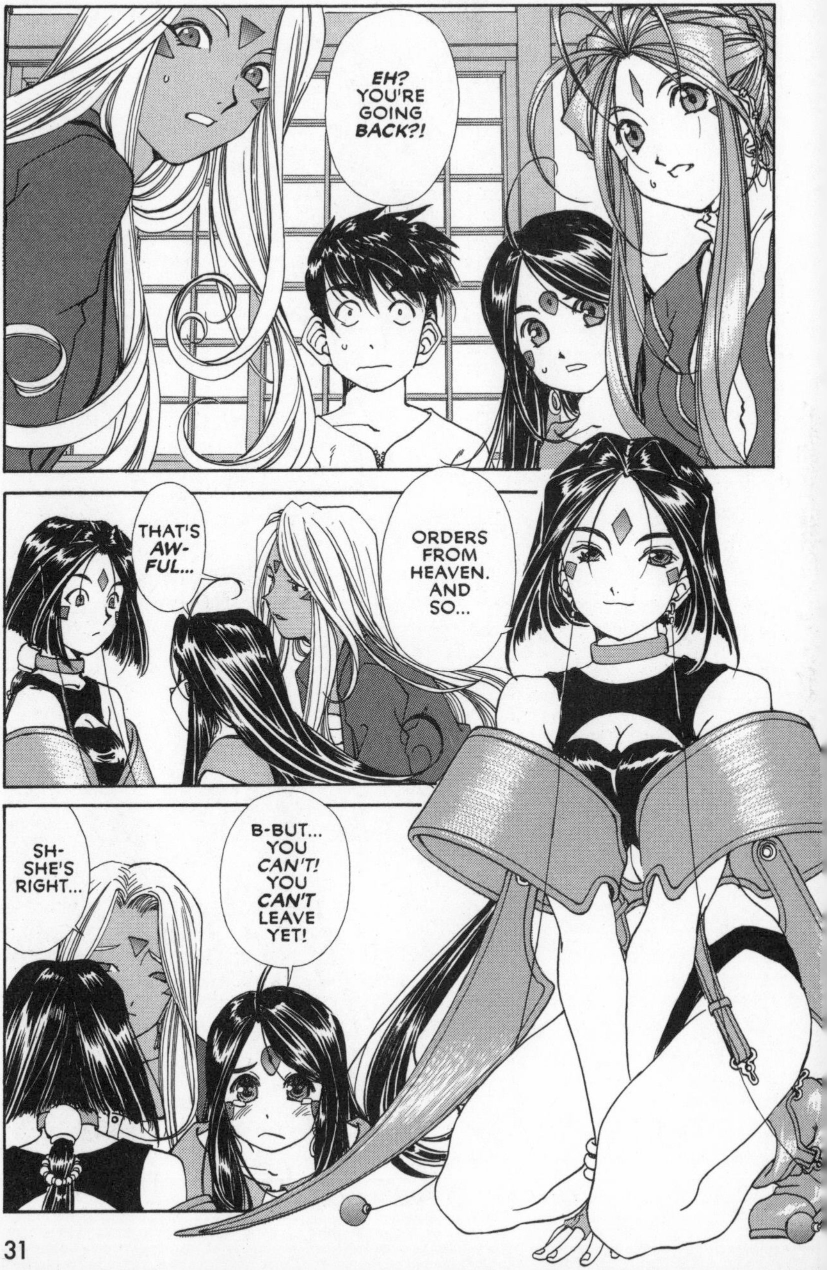
EH? YOU'RE GOING BACK?!
ORDERS FROM HEAVEN. AND SO...
THAT'S AW-FUL...
B-BUT... YOU CAN'T! YOU CAN'T LEAVE YET!
SH- SHE'S RIGHT...

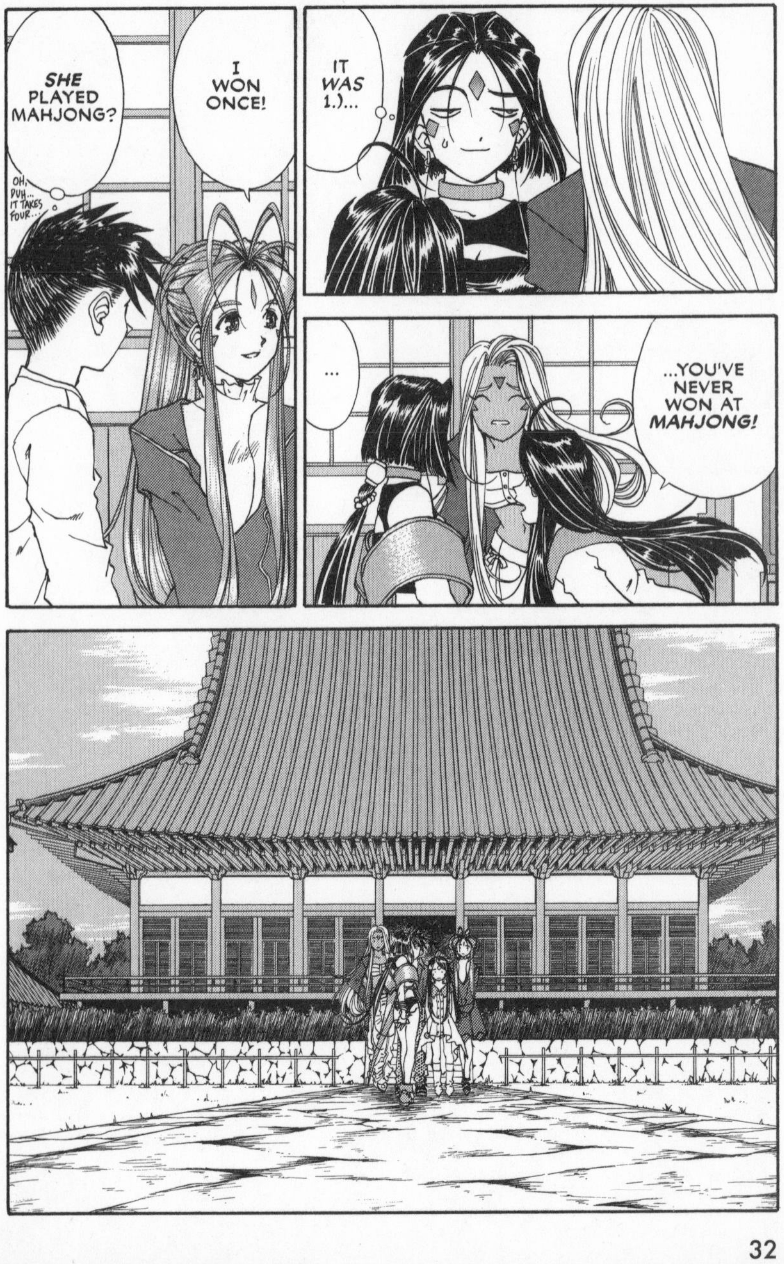
IT WAS 1.)...
...
...YOU'VE NEVER WON AT MAHJONG!
I WON ONCE!
SHE PLAYED MAHJONG?
OH, DUH... IT TAKES FOUR...

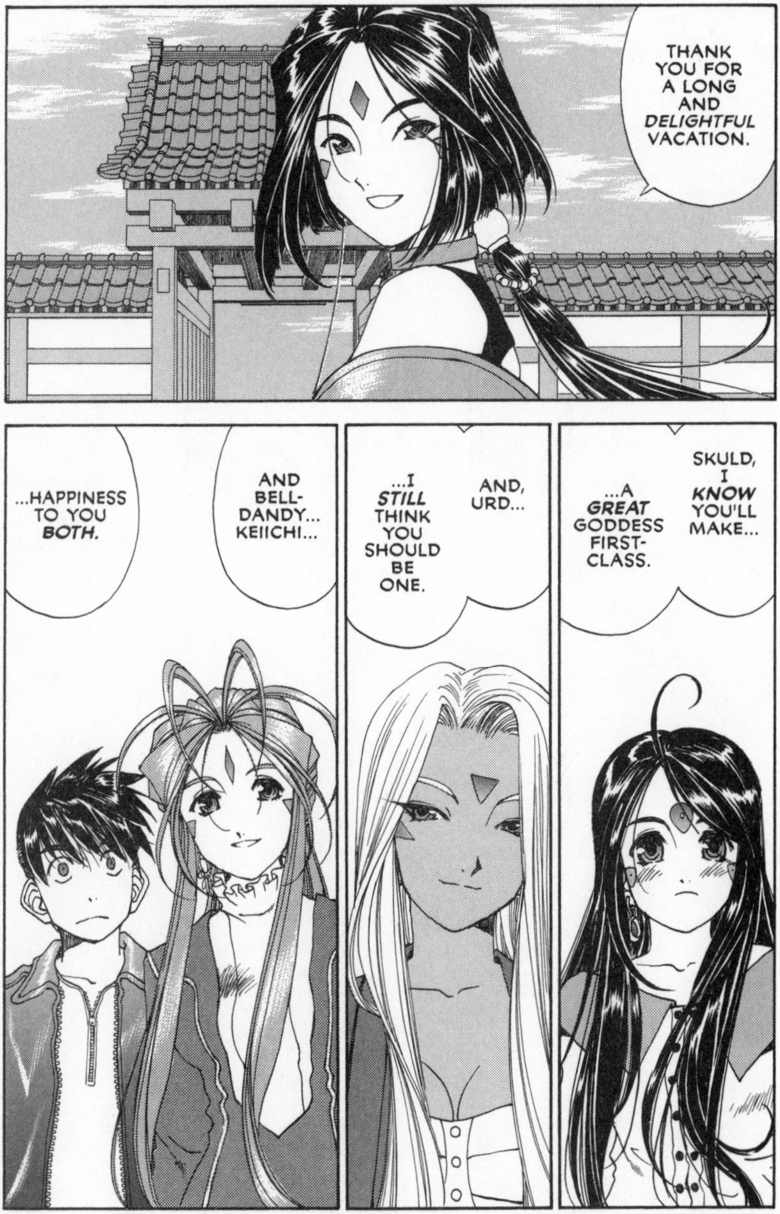
THANK YOU FOR A LONG AND *DELIGHTFUL* VACATION.
SKULD, I *KNOW* YOU'LL MAKE...
...A *GREAT* GODDESS FIRST-CLASS.
AND, URD...
...I *STILL* THINK YOU SHOULD BE ONE.
AND BELL-DANDY... KEIICHI...
...HAPPINESS TO YOU *BOTH.*

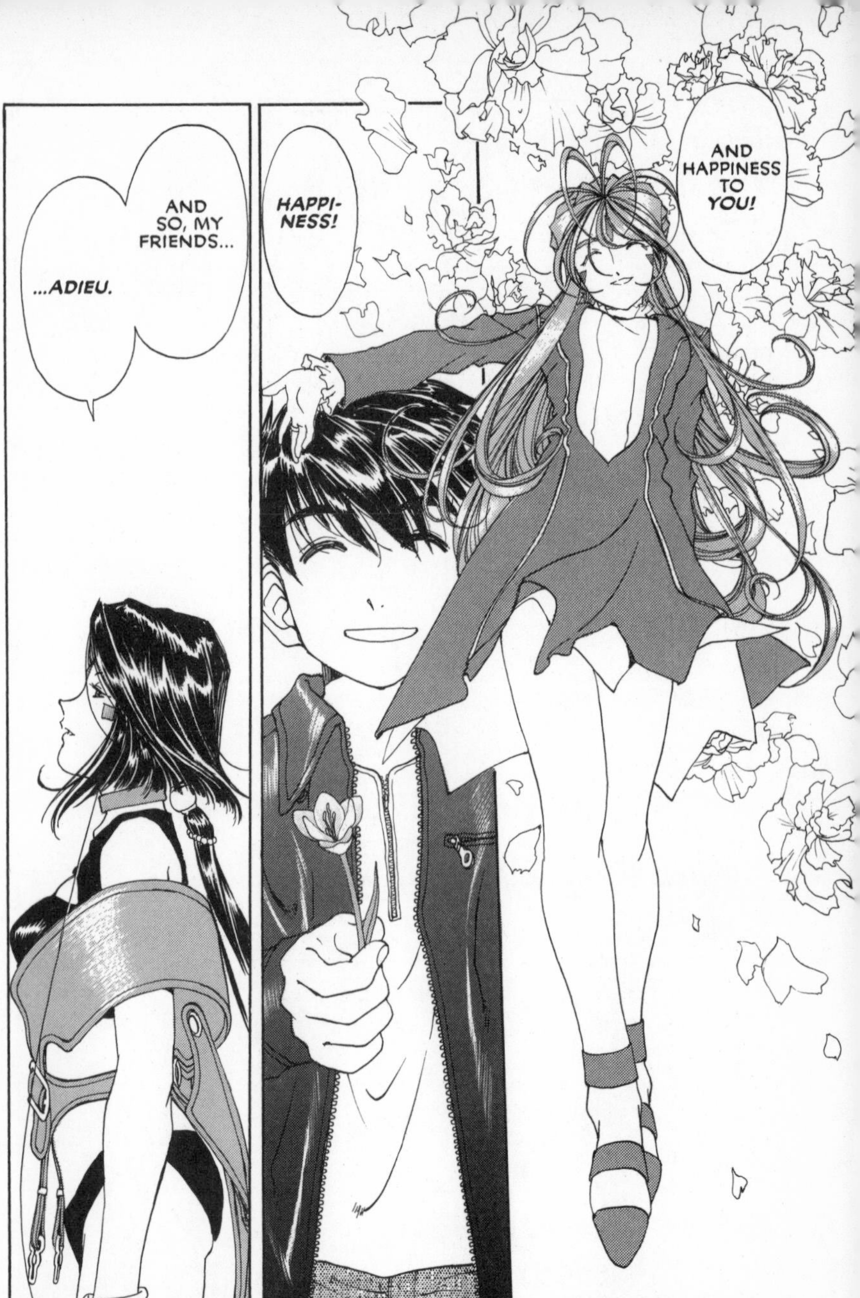
AND HAPPINESS TO YOU!
HAPPI-NESS!
AND SO, MY FRIENDS...
...ADIEU.

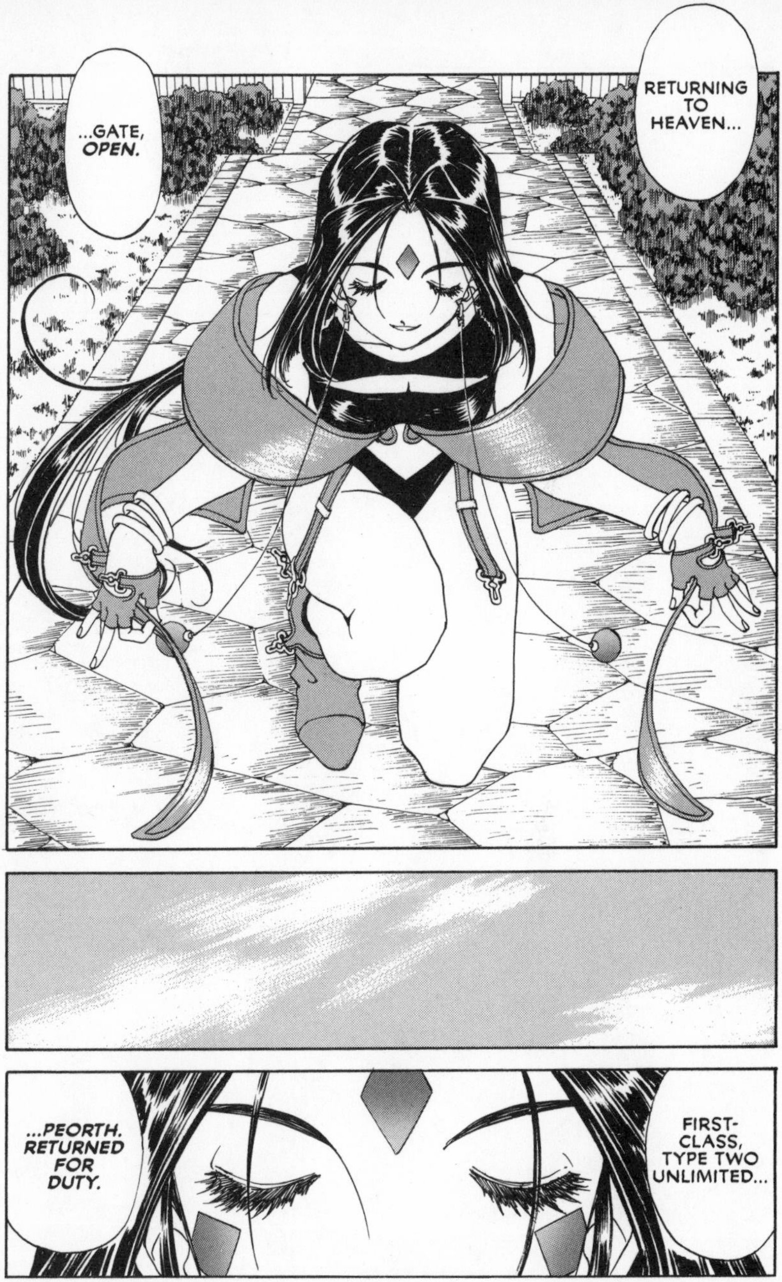
RETURNING TO HEAVEN...
...GATE, OPEN.
FIRST-CLASS, TYPE TWO UNLIMITED...
...PEORTH. RETURNED FOR DUTY.

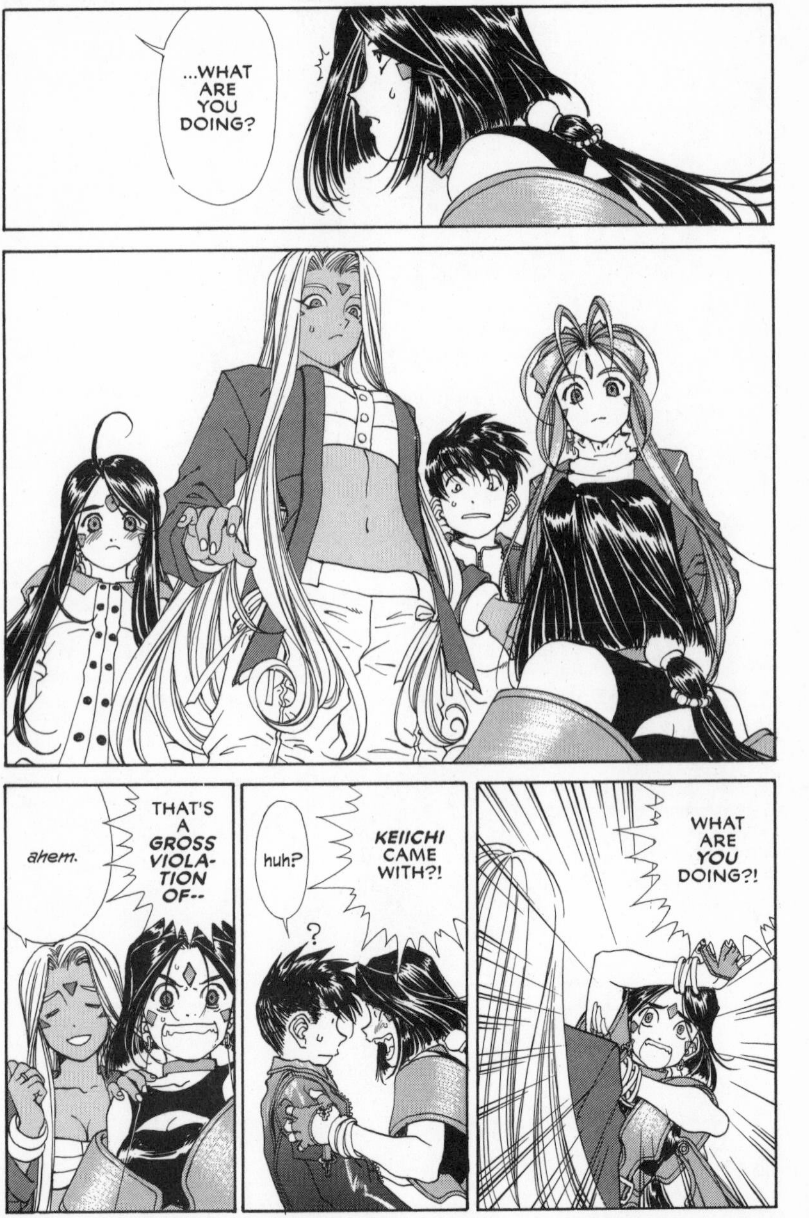
...WHAT ARE YOU DOING?
WHAT ARE YOU DOING?!
KEIICHI CAME WITH?!
huh?
?
THAT'S A GROSS VIOLATION OF--
ahem.

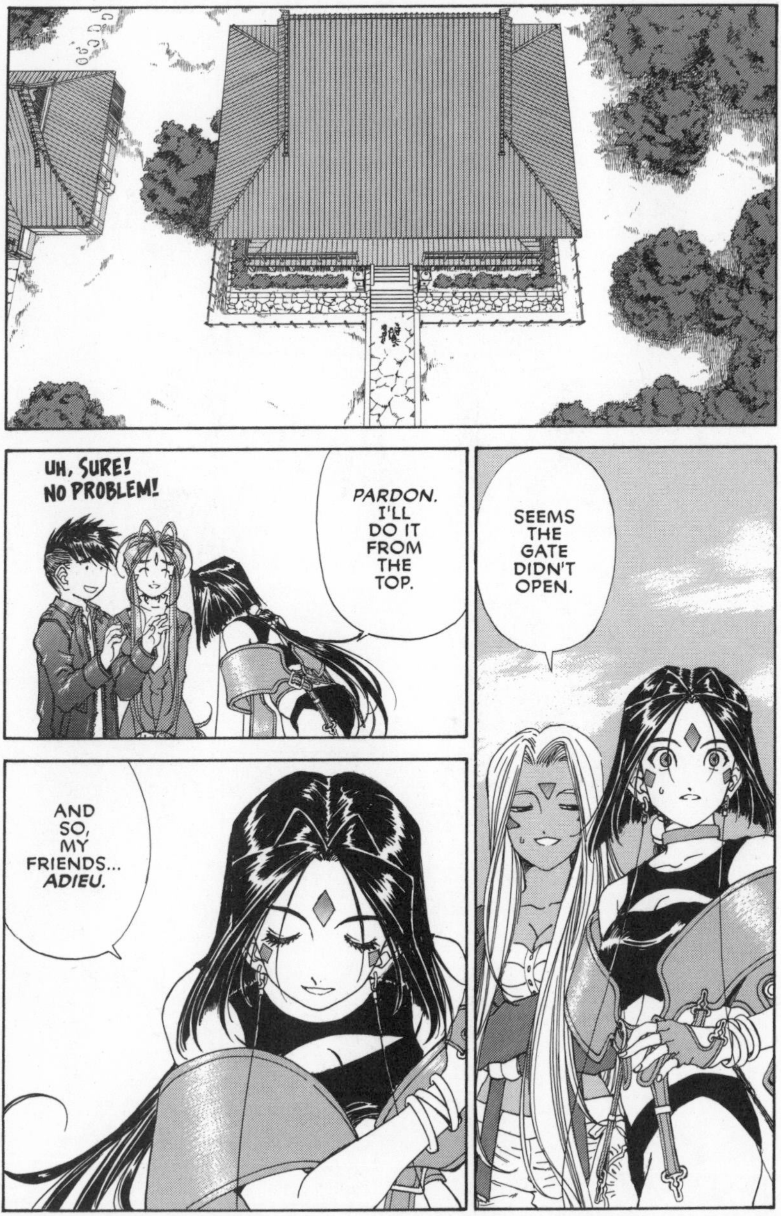
SEEMS THE GATE DIDN'T OPEN.
PARDON. I'LL DO IT FROM THE TOP.
UH, SURE! NO PROBLEM!
AND SO, MY FRIENDS... ADIEU.

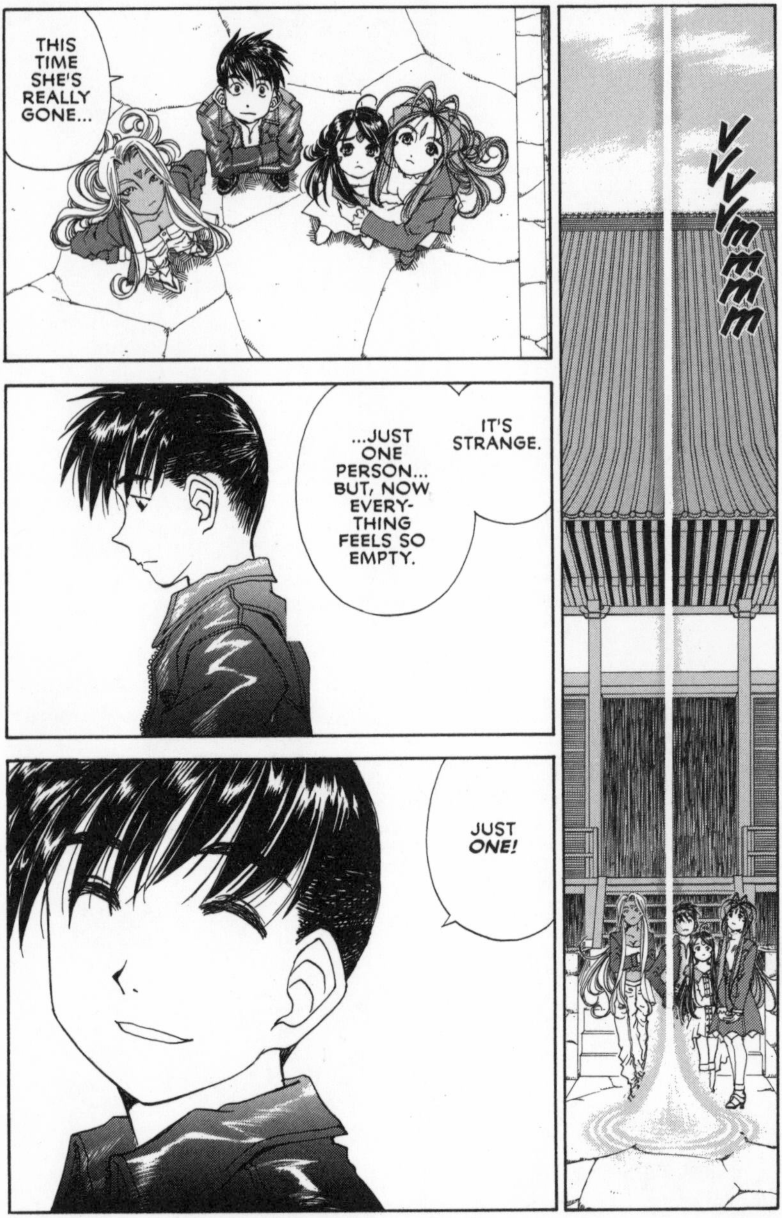
VVVVMMMM
THIS TIME SHE'S REALLY GONE...
IT'S STRANGE.
...JUST ONE PERSON... BUT, NOW EVERYTHING FEELS SO EMPTY.
JUST *ONE!*

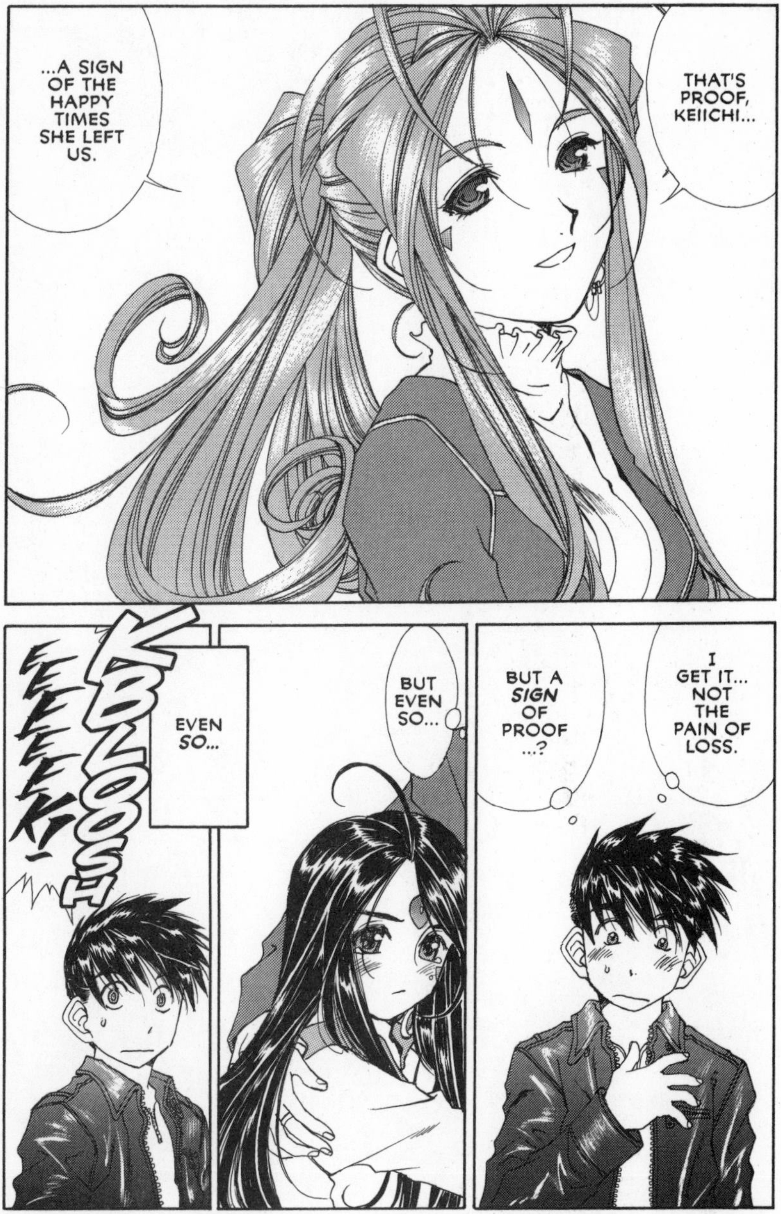
THAT'S PROOF, KEIICHI...
...A SIGN OF THE HAPPY TIMES SHE LEFT US.
I GET IT... NOT THE PAIN OF LOSS.
BUT A *SIGN* OF PROOF ...?
BUT EVEN SO...
EVEN *SO*...
KBLOOOSH
EEEEEK!

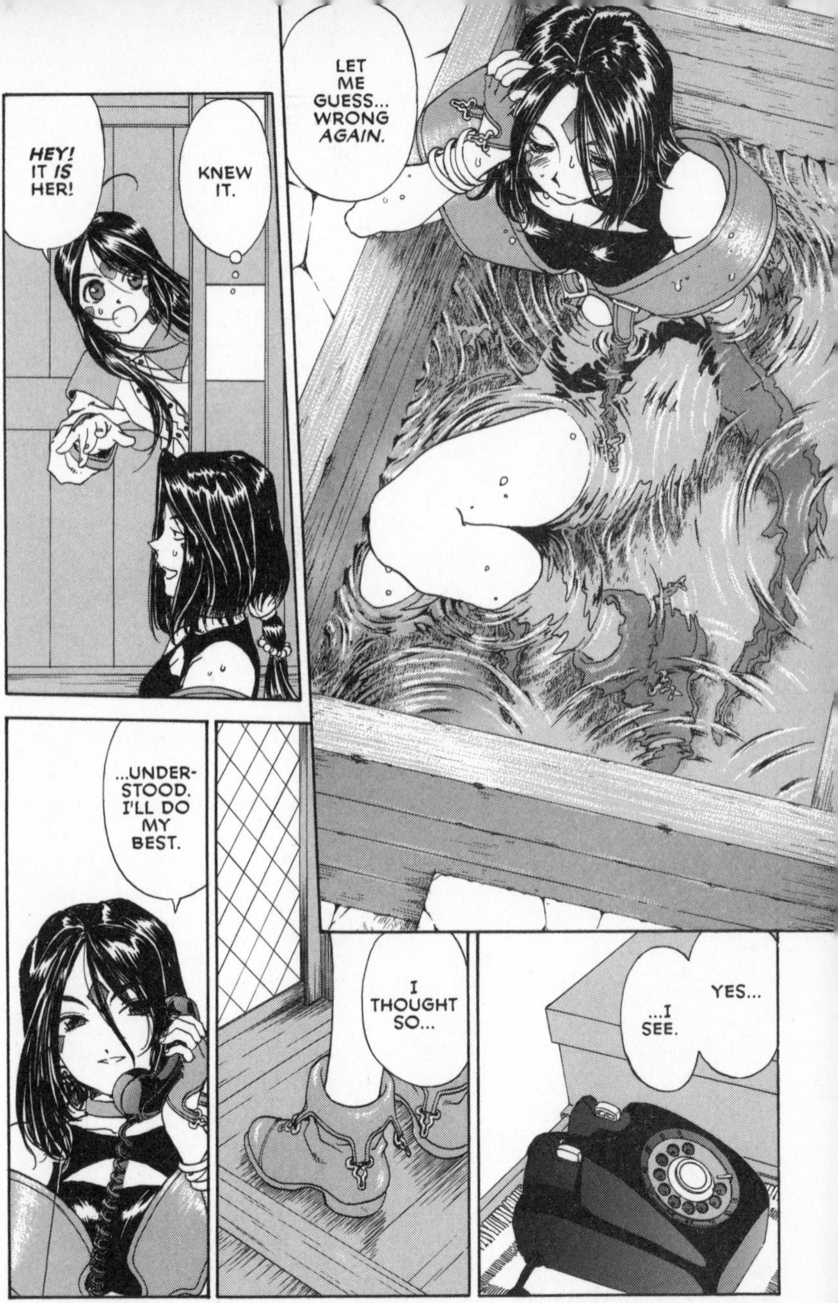
LET ME GUESS... WRONG *AGAIN.*
KNEW IT.
HEY! IT *IS* HER!
YES...
...I SEE.
I THOUGHT SO...
...UNDER-STOOD. I'LL DO MY BEST.

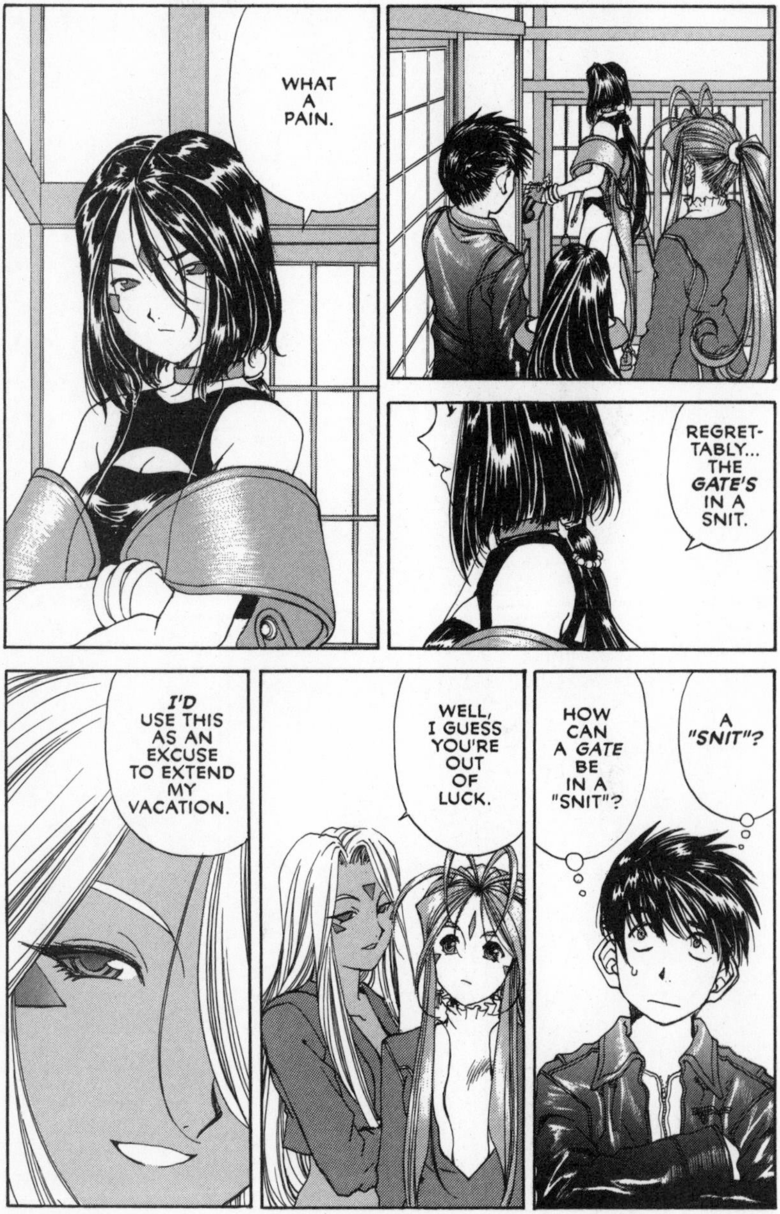
REGRETTABLY... THE *GATE'S* IN A SNIT.
WHAT A PAIN.
A *"SNIT"*?
HOW CAN A *GATE* BE IN A "SNIT"?
WELL, I GUESS YOU'RE OUT OF LUCK.
I'D USE THIS AS AN EXCUSE TO EXTEND MY VACATION.

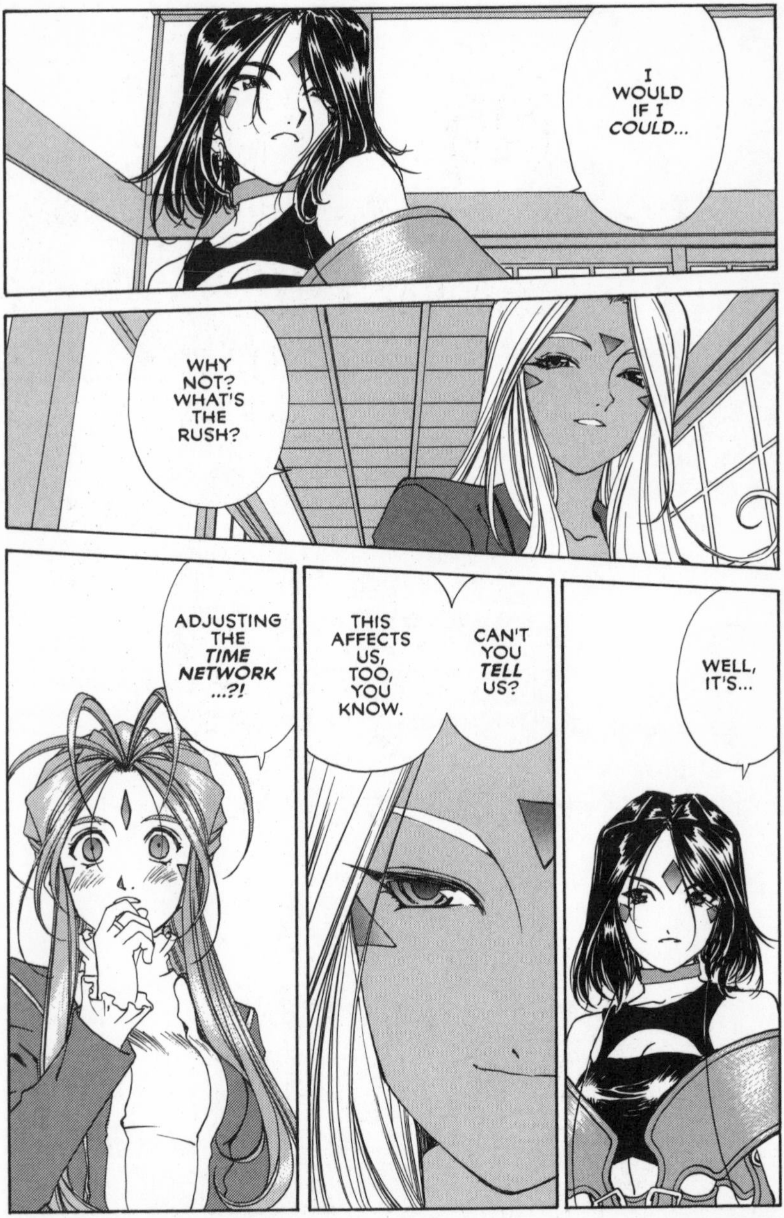
I WOULD IF I *COULD*...
WHY NOT? WHAT'S THE RUSH?
WELL, IT'S...
CAN'T YOU *TELL* US?
THIS AFFECTS US, TOO, YOU KNOW.
ADJUSTING THE *TIME NETWORK* ...?!

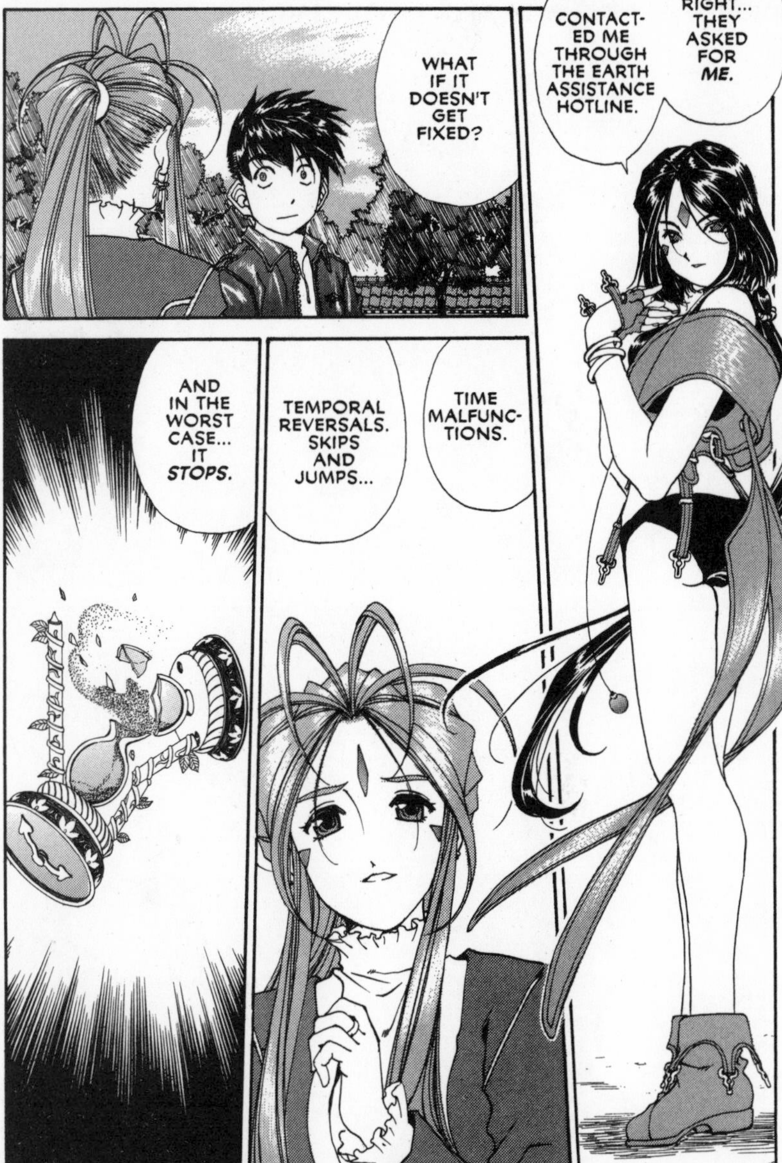
THAT'S RIGHT... THEY ASKED FOR *ME.*
CONTACT-ED ME THROUGH THE EARTH ASSISTANCE HOTLINE.
WHAT IF IT DOESN'T GET FIXED?
TIME MALFUNC-TIONS.
TEMPORAL REVERSALS. SKIPS AND JUMPS...
AND IN THE WORST CASE... IT *STOPS.*

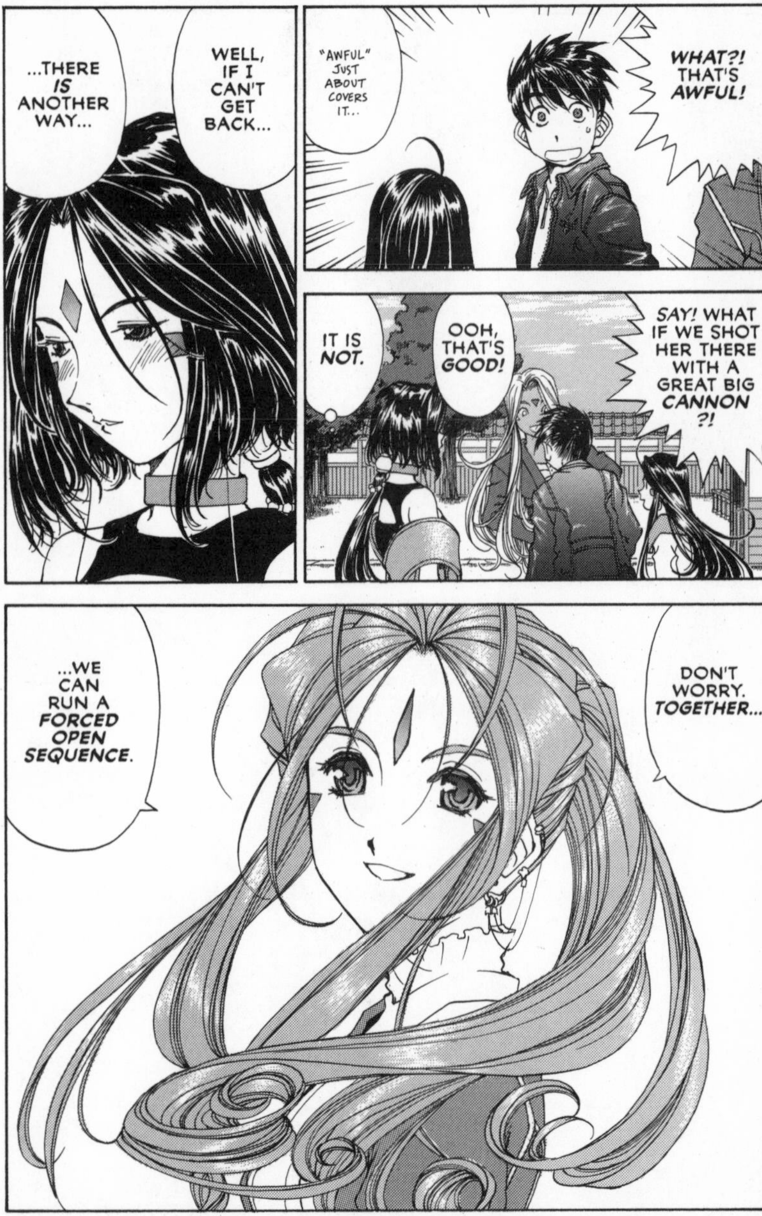
WHAT?! THAT'S AWFUL!
"AWFUL" JUST ABOUT COVERS IT...
SAY! WHAT IF WE SHOT HER THERE WITH A GREAT BIG CANNON?!
OOH, THAT'S GOOD!
IT IS NOT.
WELL, IF I CAN'T GET BACK...
...THERE IS ANOTHER WAY...
DON'T WORRY. TOGETHER...
...WE CAN RUN A FORCED OPEN SEQUENCE.

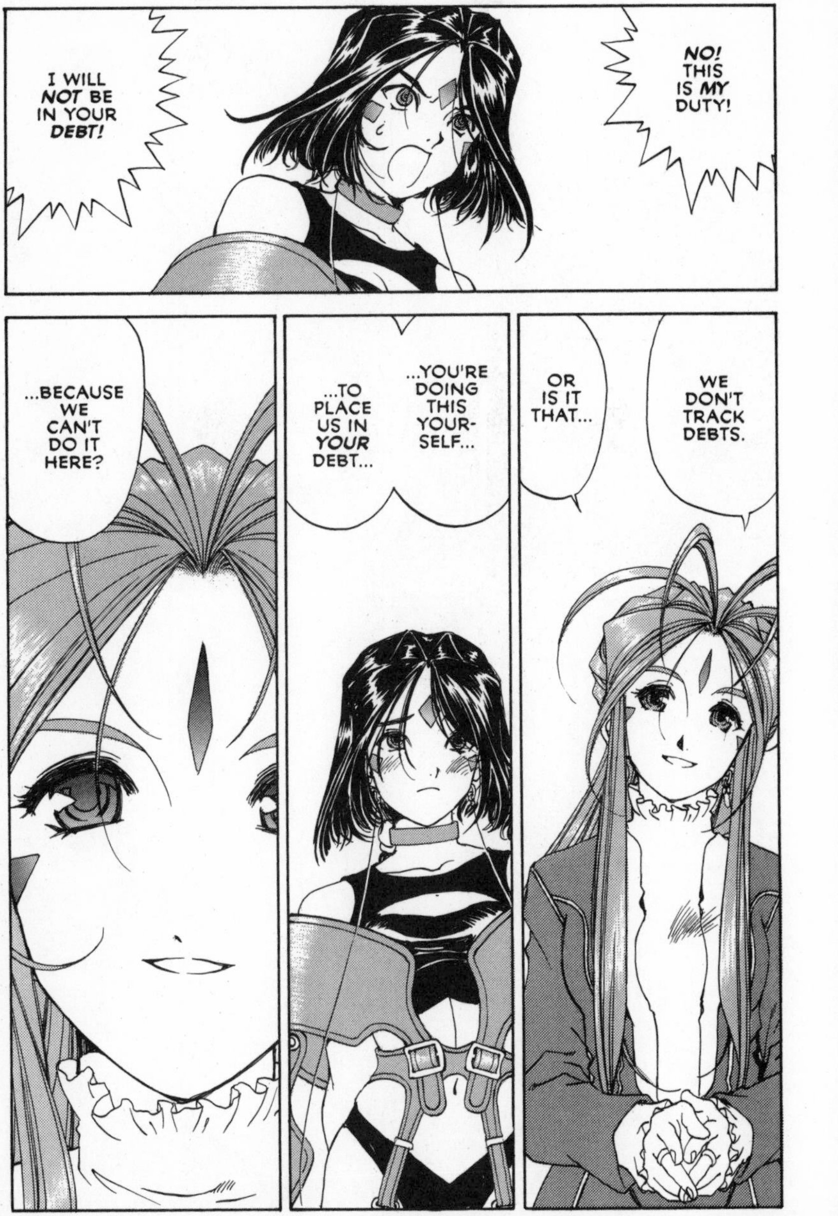
NO! THIS IS *MY* DUTY!
I WILL *NOT* BE IN YOUR *DEBT!*
WE DON'T TRACK DEBTS.
OR IS IT THAT...
...YOU'RE DOING THIS YOURSELF...
...TO PLACE US IN *YOUR* DEBT...
...BECAUSE WE CAN'T DO IT HERE?

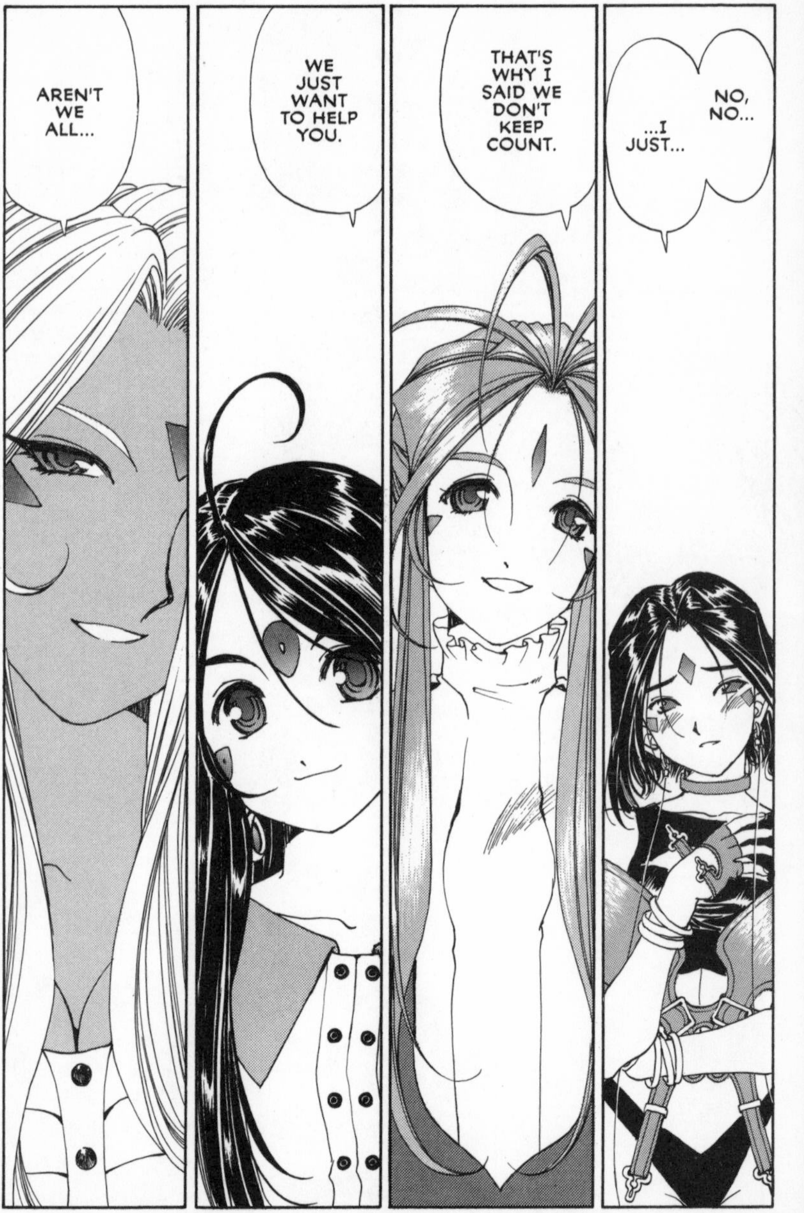
NO, NO...
...I JUST...
THAT'S WHY I SAID WE DON'T KEEP COUNT.
WE JUST WANT TO HELP YOU.
AREN'T WE ALL...

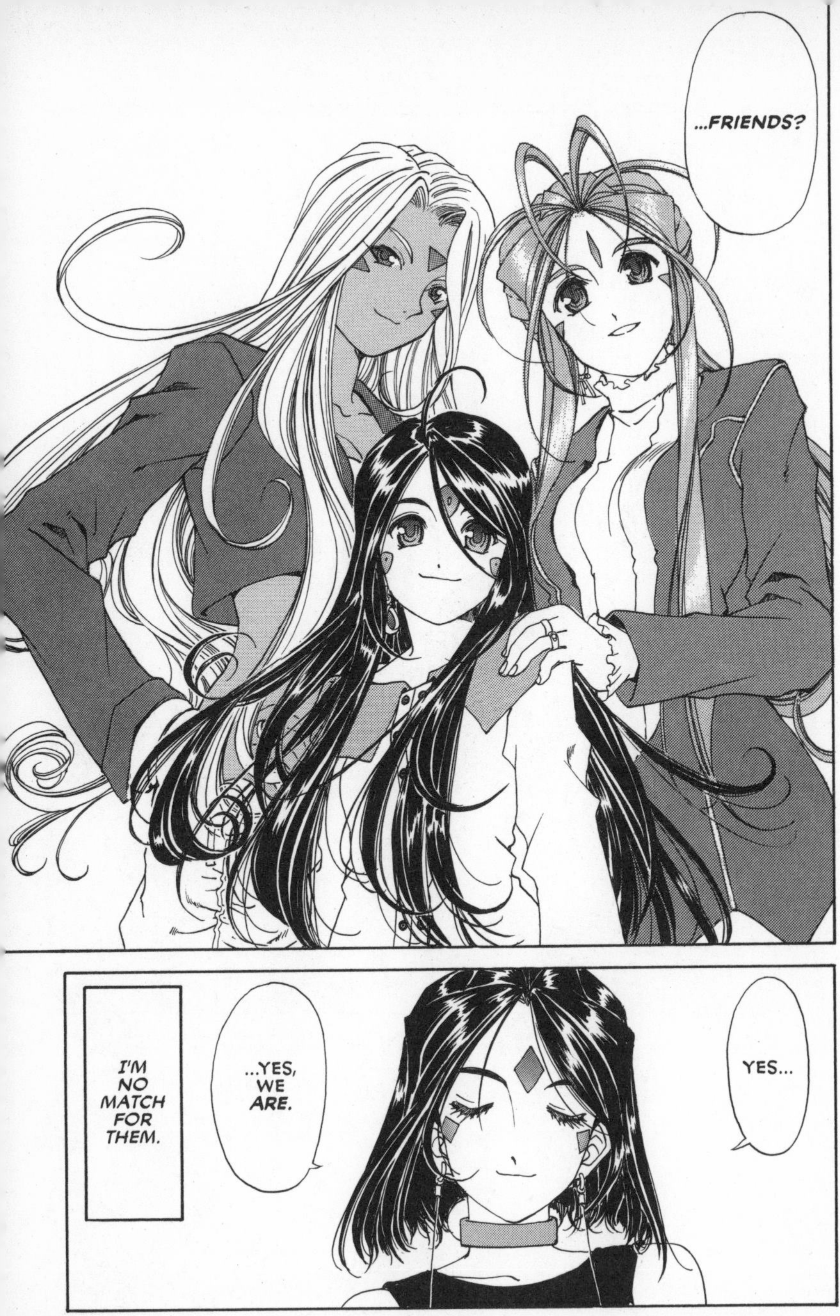
...FRIENDS?
YES...
...YES, WE ARE.
I'M NO MATCH FOR THEM.

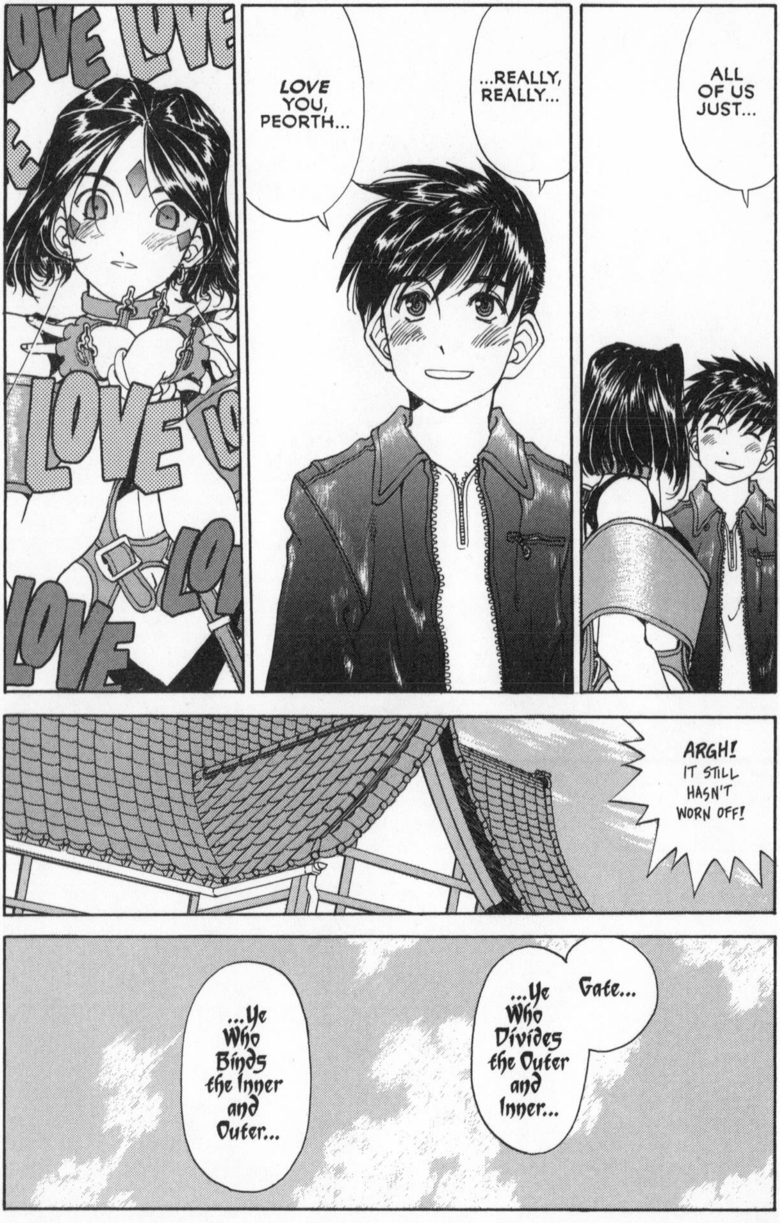
ALL OF US JUST...
...REALLY, REALLY...
LOVE YOU, PEORTH...
LOVE LOVE
LOVE
LOVE
ARGH! IT STILL HASN'T WORN OFF!
Gate... ...Ye Who Divides the Outer and Inner...
...Ye Who Binds the Inner and Outer...

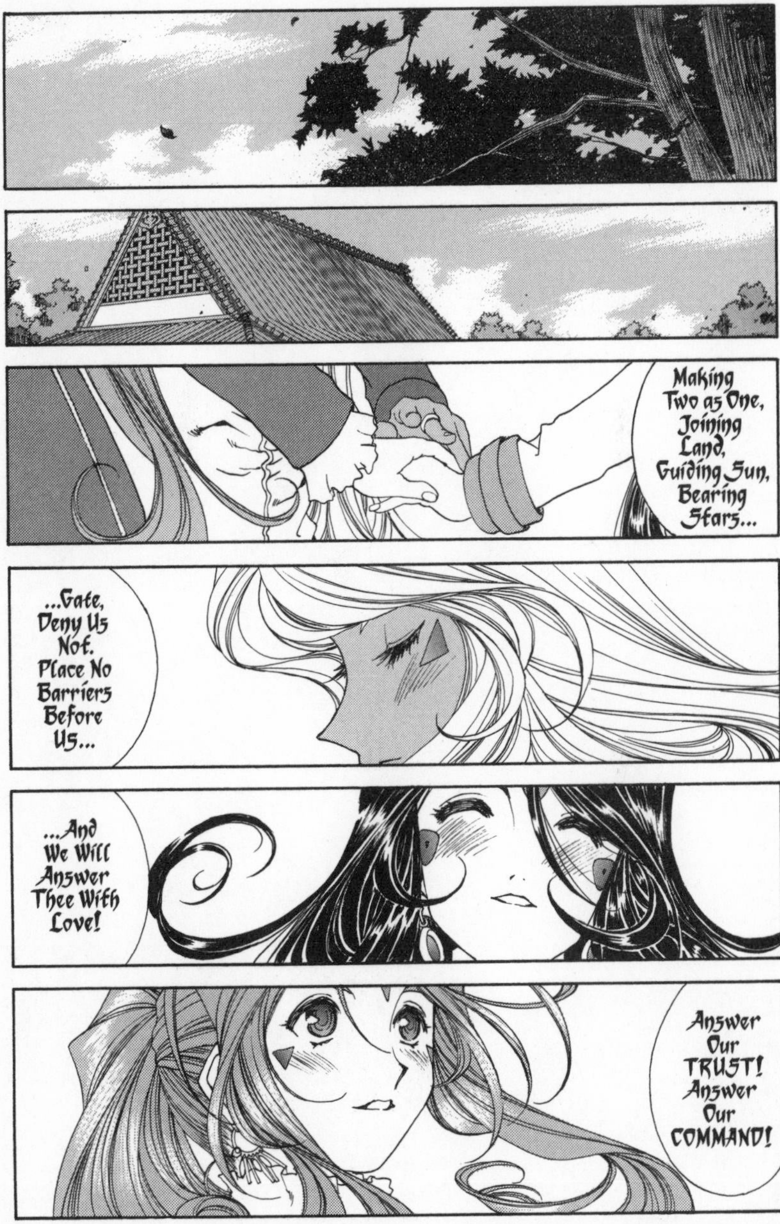
Making Two as One, Joining Land, Guiding Sun, Bearing Stars...
...Gate, Deny Us Not. Place No Barriers Before Us...
...And We Will Answer Thee With Love!
Answer Our TRUST! Answer Our COMMAND!

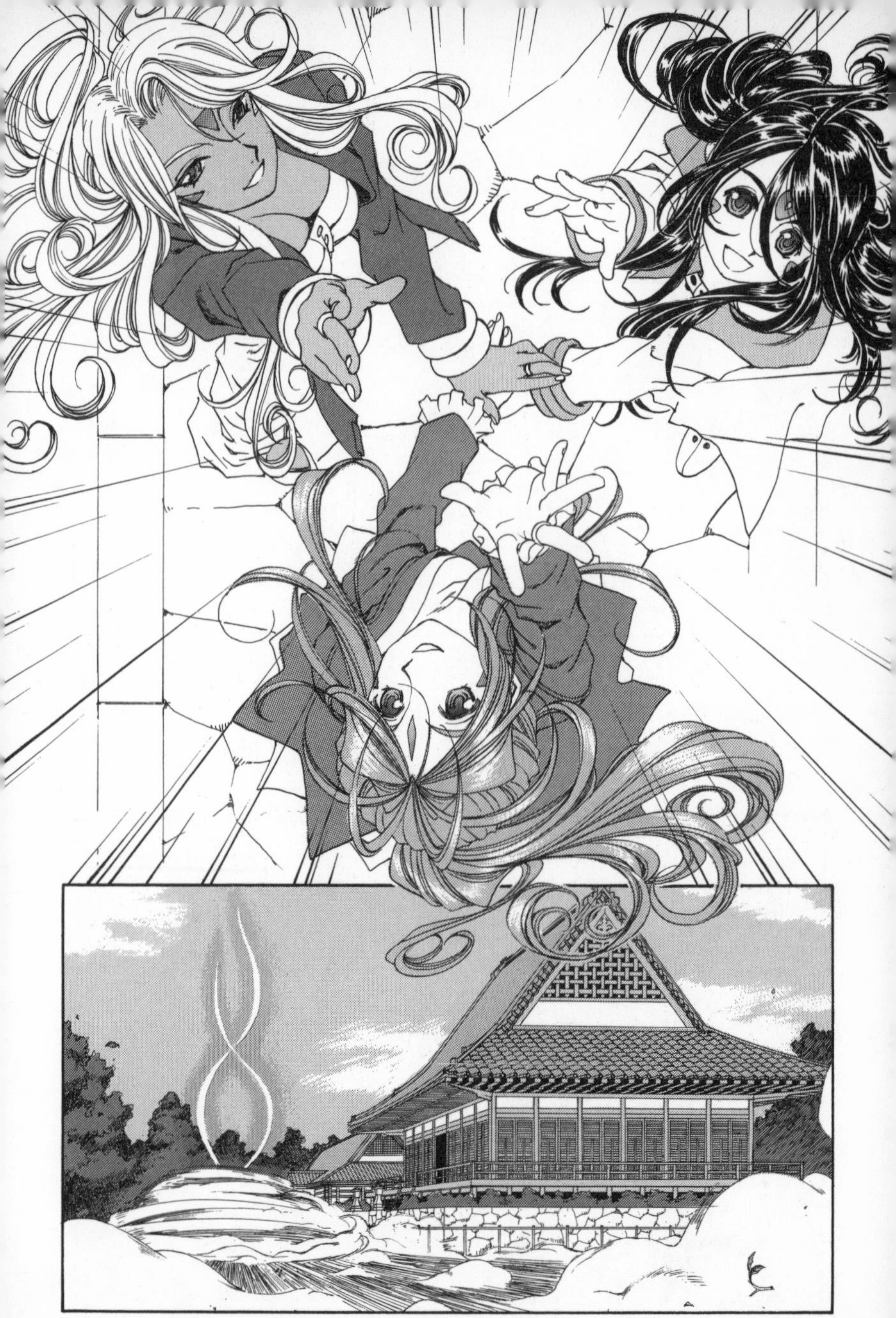

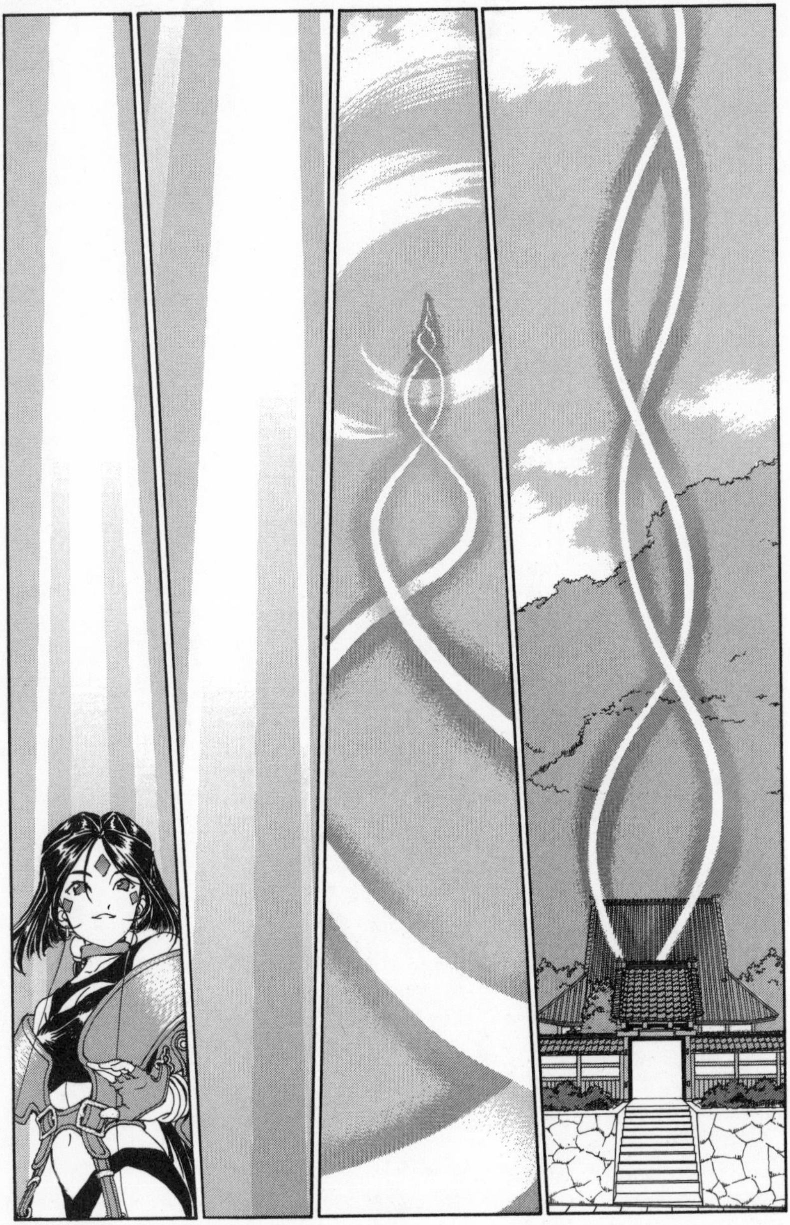

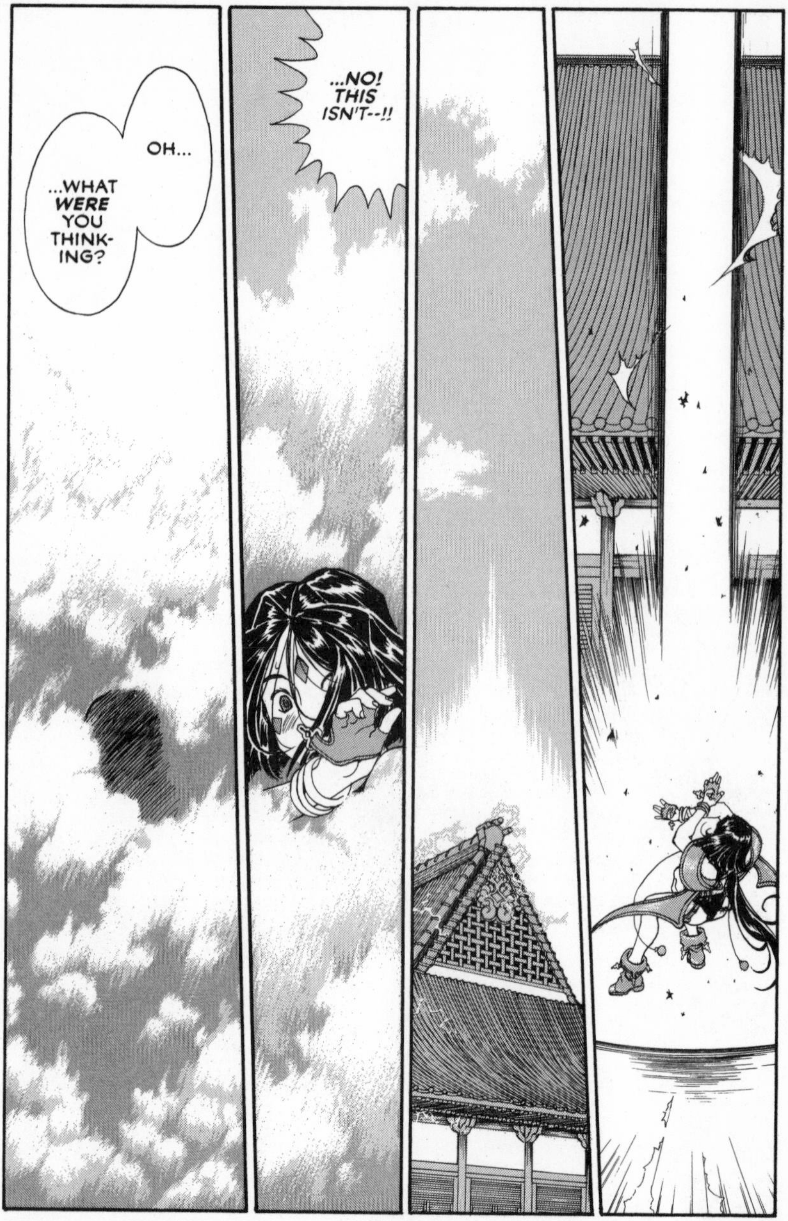
...NO! THIS ISN'T--!!
OH...
...WHAT *WERE* YOU THINKING?

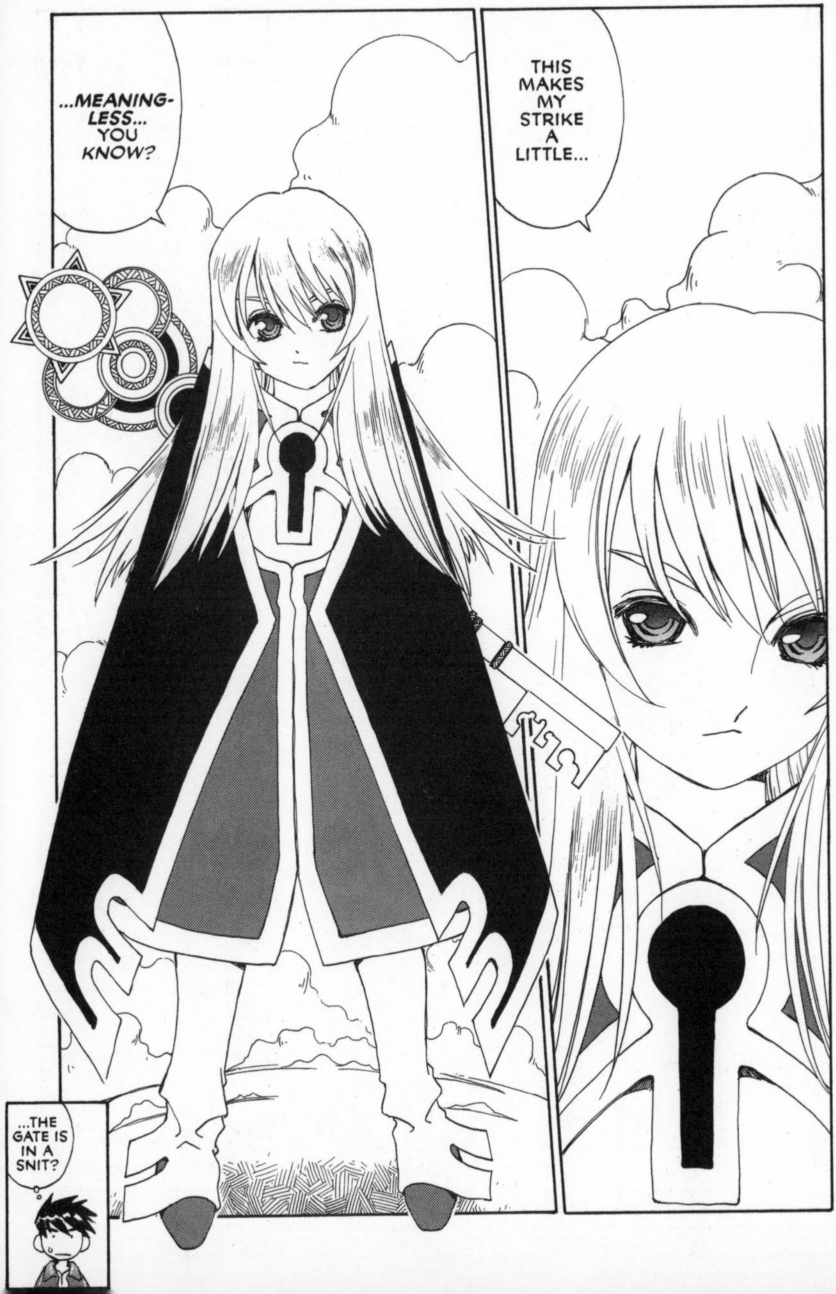
THIS MAKES MY STRIKE A LITTLE...
...MEANING-LESS... YOU KNOW?
...THE GATE IS IN A SNIT?

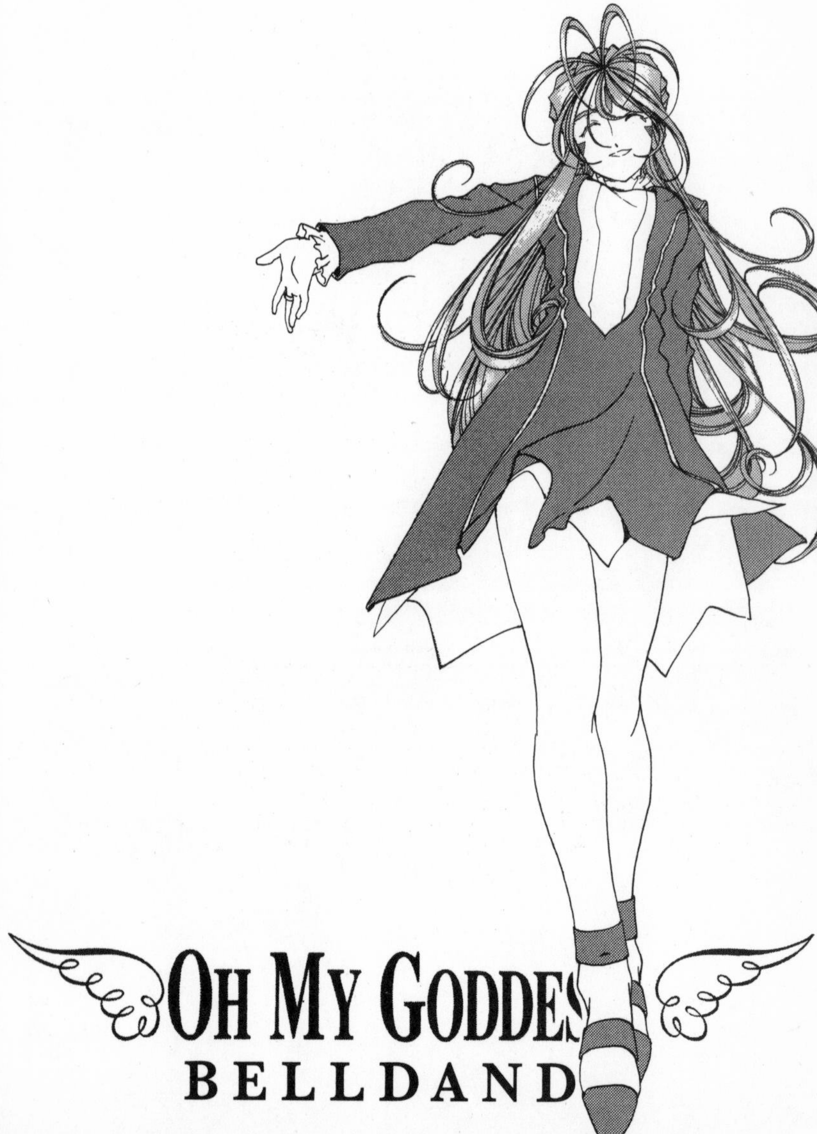
OH MY GODDES
BELLDAND

CHAPTER 197

The Forbidden Gate?!

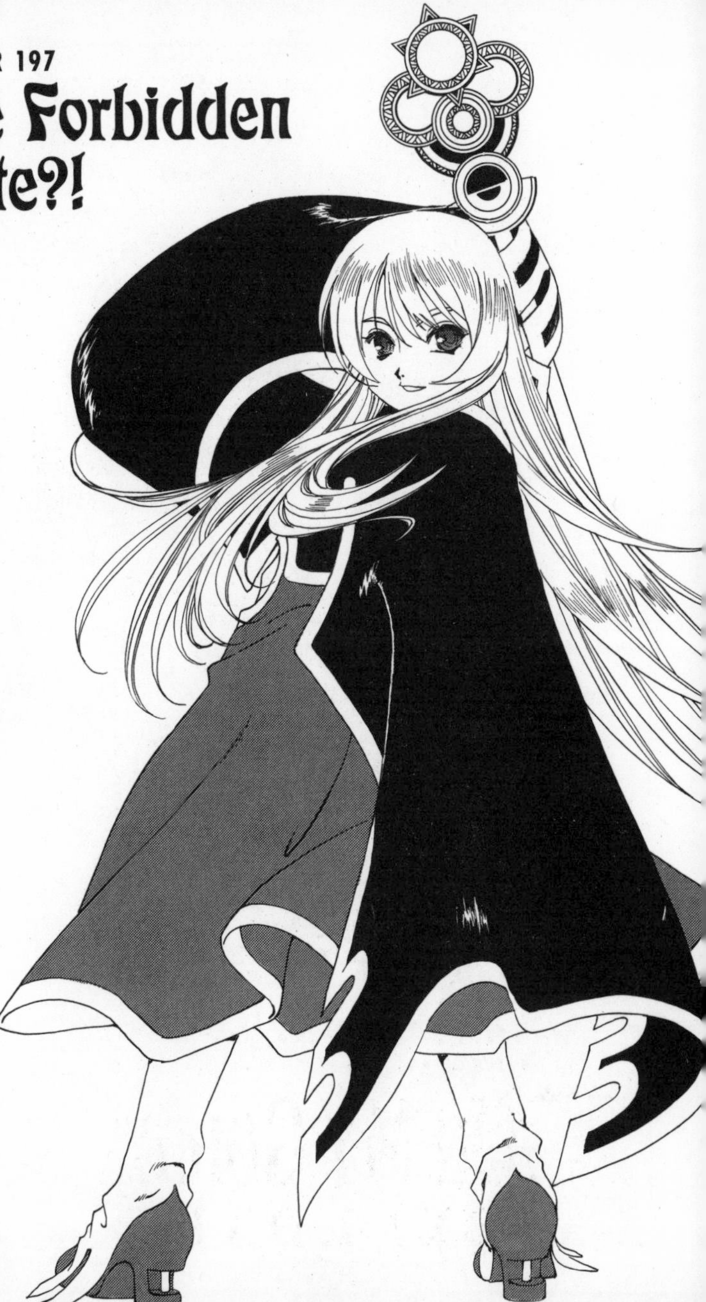

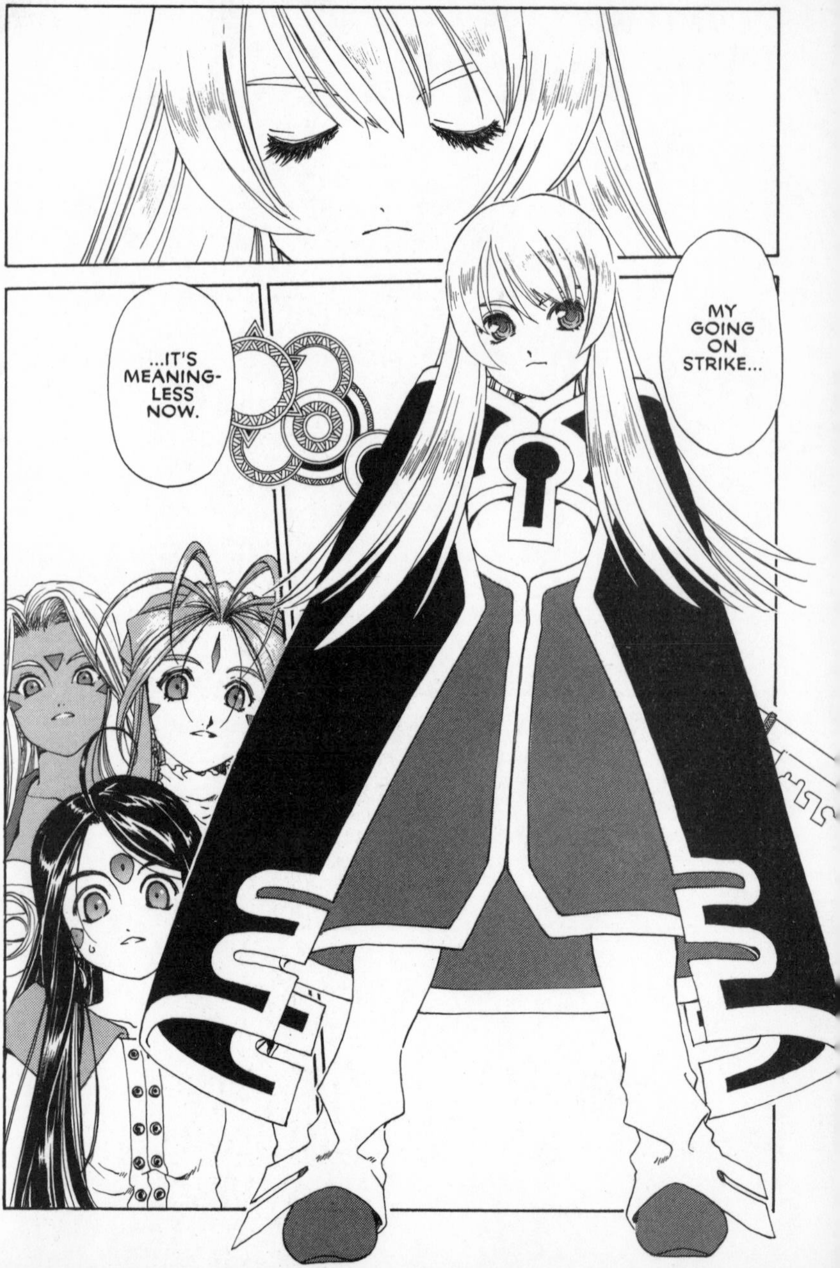
MY GOING ON STRIKE...
...IT'S MEANING-LESS NOW.

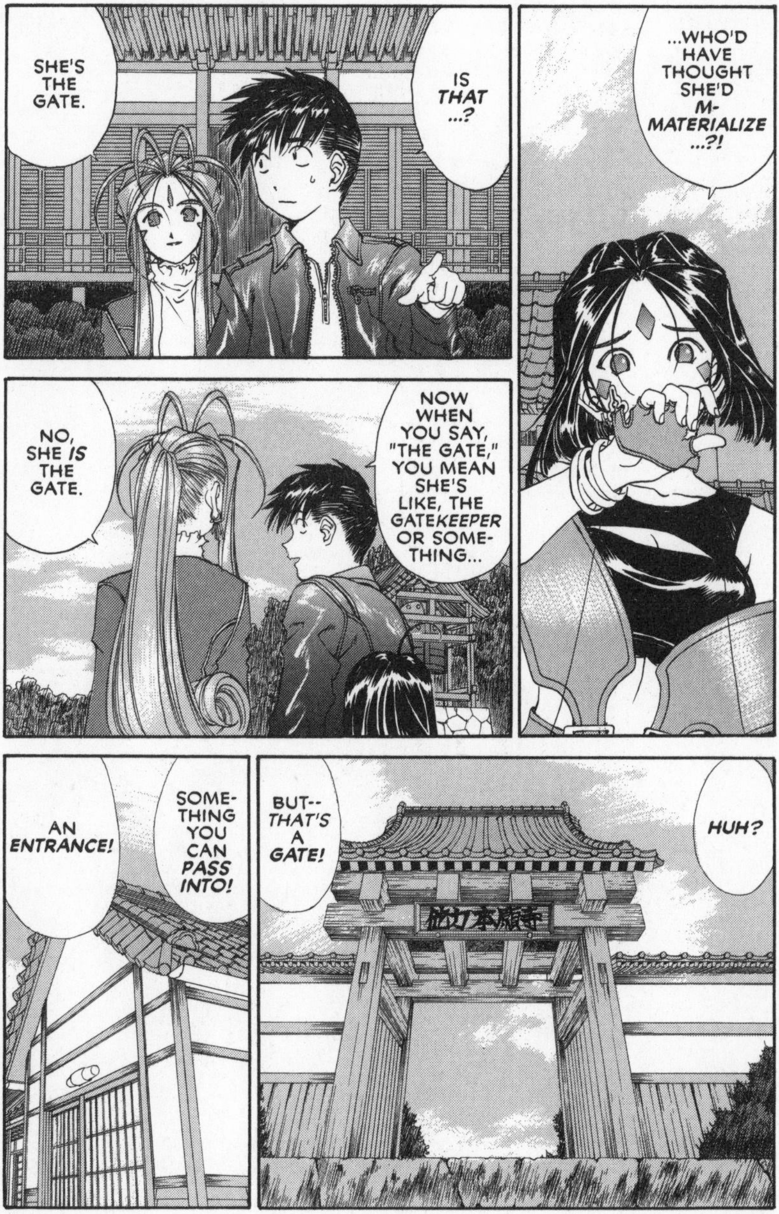
...WHO'D HAVE THOUGHT SHE'D *M-MATERIALIZE* ...?!
IS *THAT* ...?
SHE'S THE GATE.
NOW WHEN YOU SAY, "THE GATE," YOU MEAN SHE'S LIKE, THE GATE*KEEPER* OR SOME-THING...
NO, SHE *IS* THE GATE.
HUH?
BUT-- *THAT'S* A *GATE!*
SOME-THING YOU CAN *PASS INTO!*
AN *ENTRANCE!*

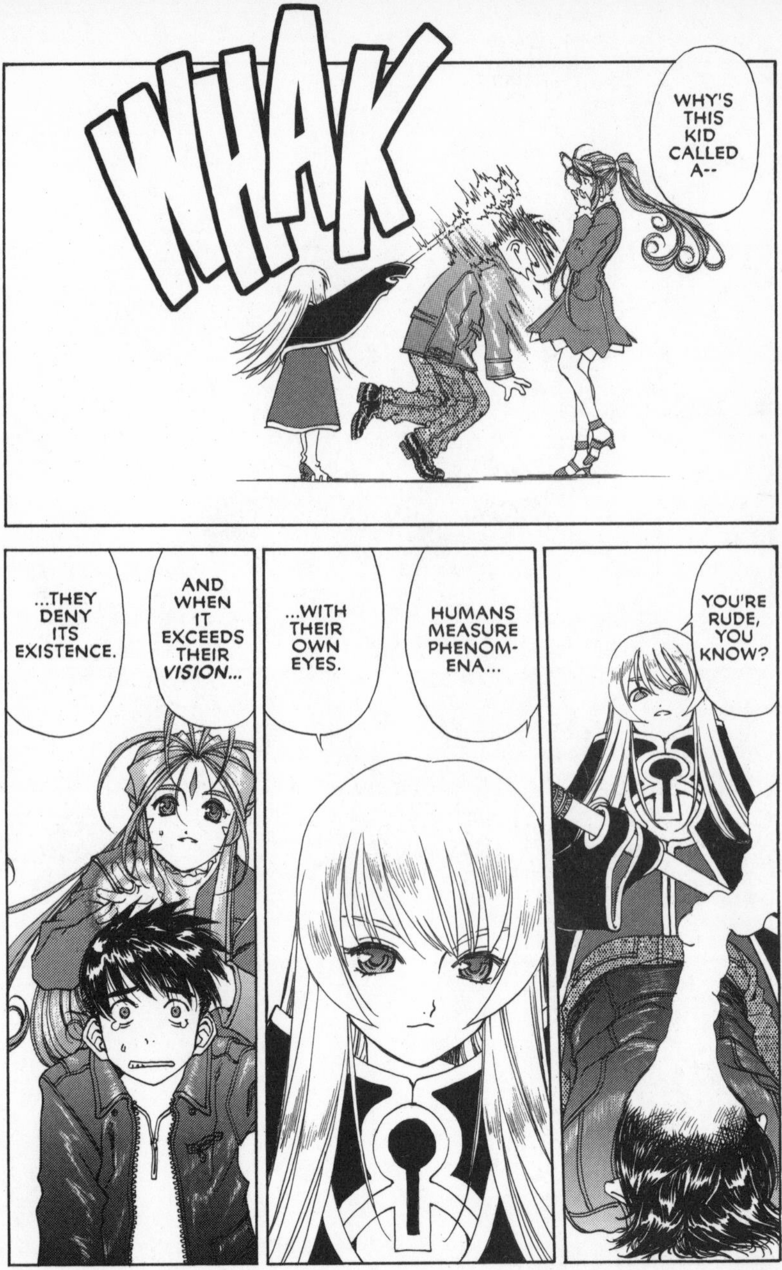
WHY'S THIS KID CALLED A--
WHAK
YOU'RE RUDE, YOU KNOW?
HUMANS MEASURE PHENOM-ENA...
...WITH THEIR OWN EYES.
AND WHEN IT EXCEEDS THEIR *VISION*...
...THEY DENY ITS EXISTENCE.

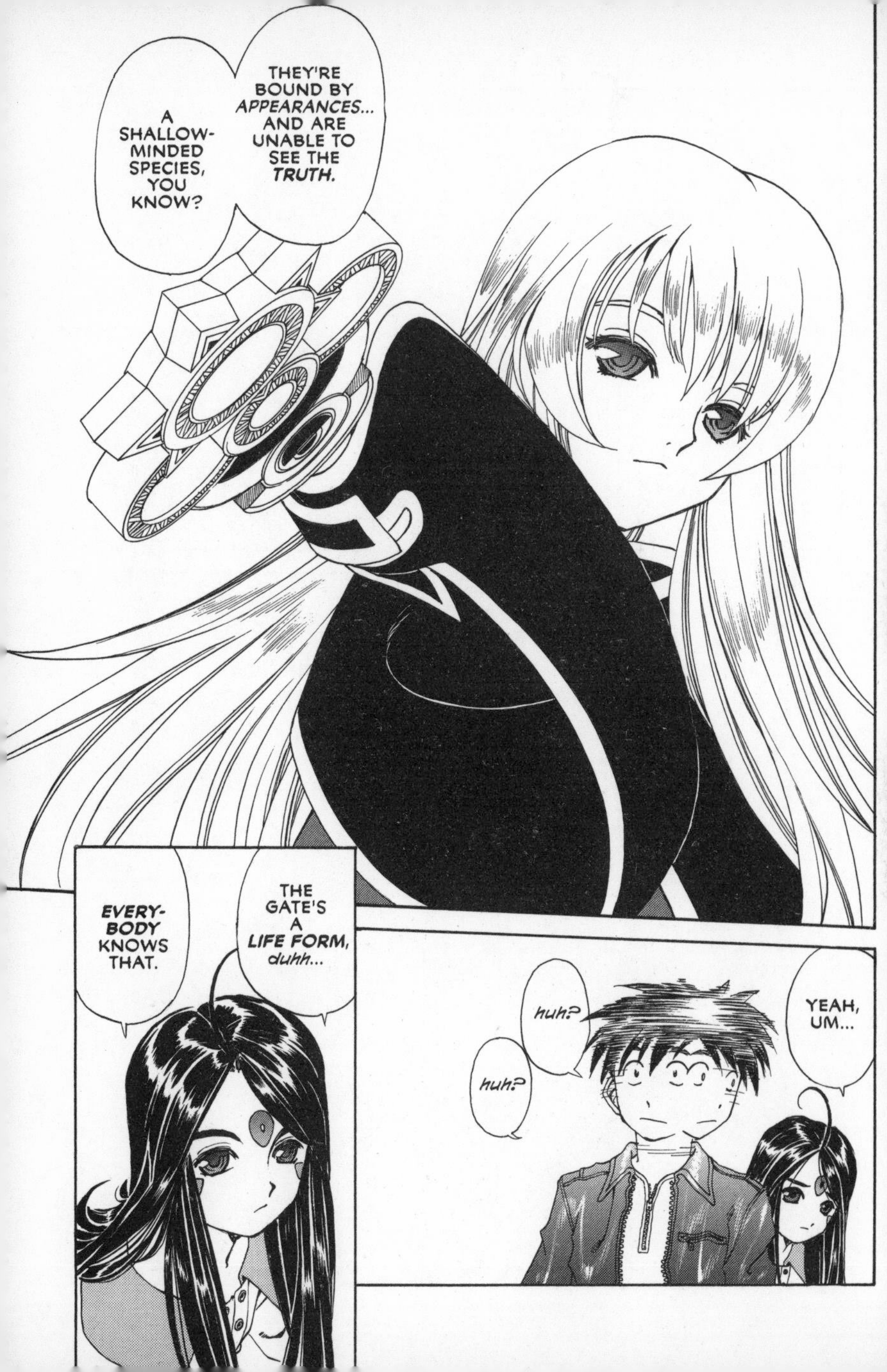
THEY'RE BOUND BY *APPEARANCES*... AND ARE UNABLE TO SEE THE *TRUTH.*
A SHALLOW-MINDED SPECIES, YOU KNOW?
YEAH, UM...
huh?
huh?
THE GATE'S A *LIFE FORM*, *duhh*...
EVERY-BODY KNOWS THAT.

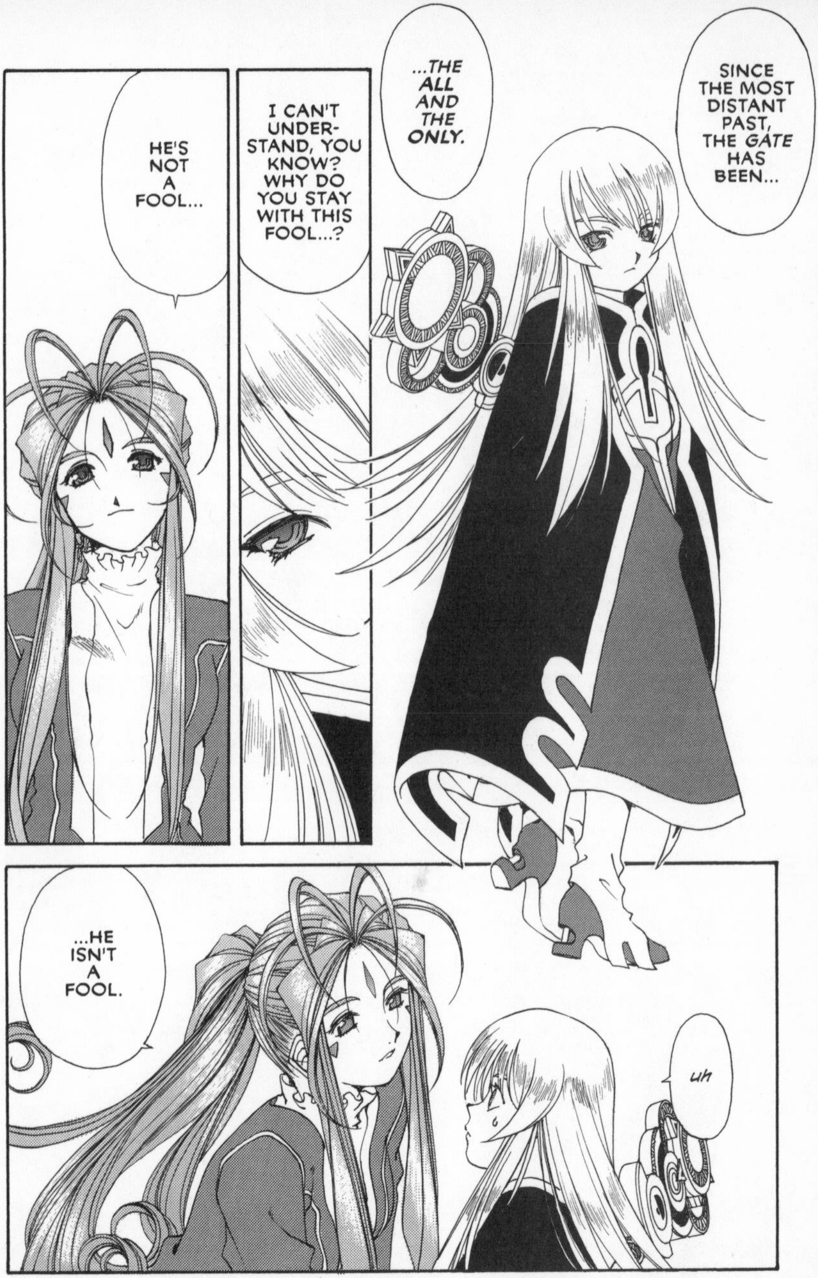
SINCE THE MOST DISTANT PAST, THE *GATE* HAS BEEN...
...*THE ALL AND THE ONLY.*
I CAN'T UNDER-STAND, YOU KNOW? WHY DO YOU STAY WITH THIS FOOL...?
HE'S NOT A FOOL...
...HE ISN'T A FOOL.
uh

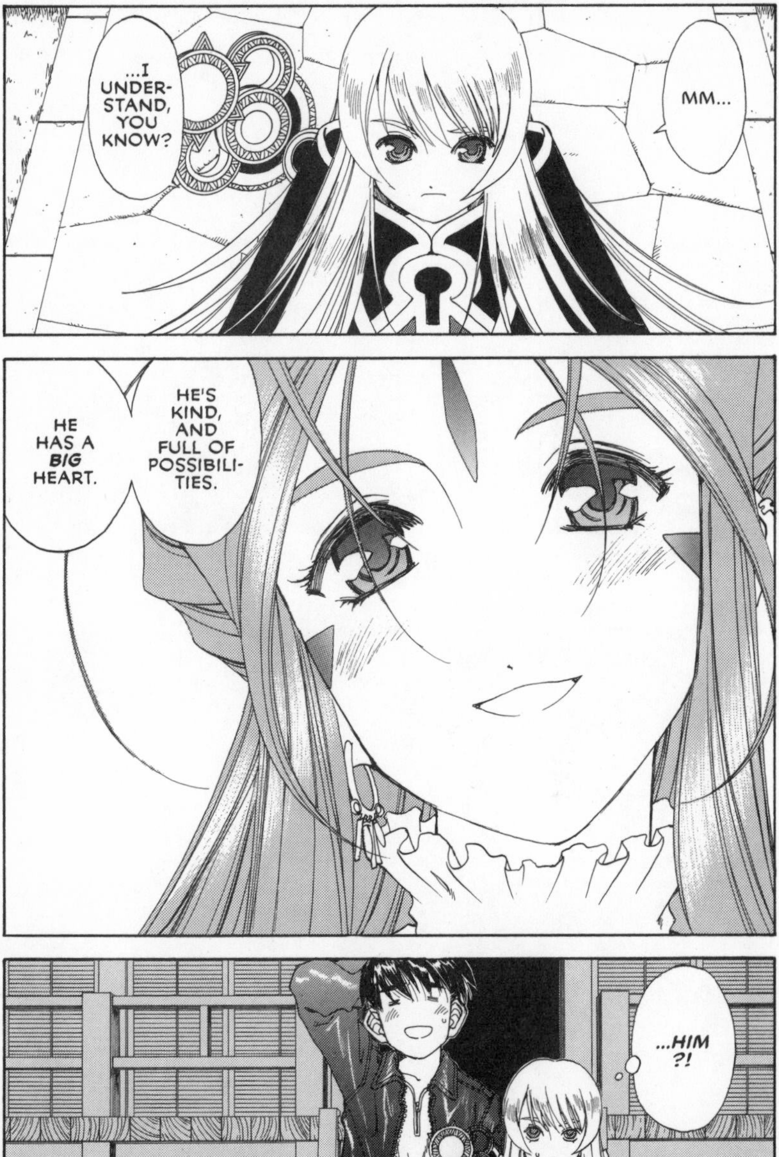
MM...
...I UNDER-STAND, YOU KNOW?
HE'S KIND, AND FULL OF POSSIBILI-TIES.
HE HAS A *BIG* HEART.
...HIM ?!

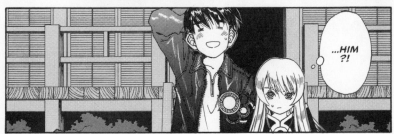

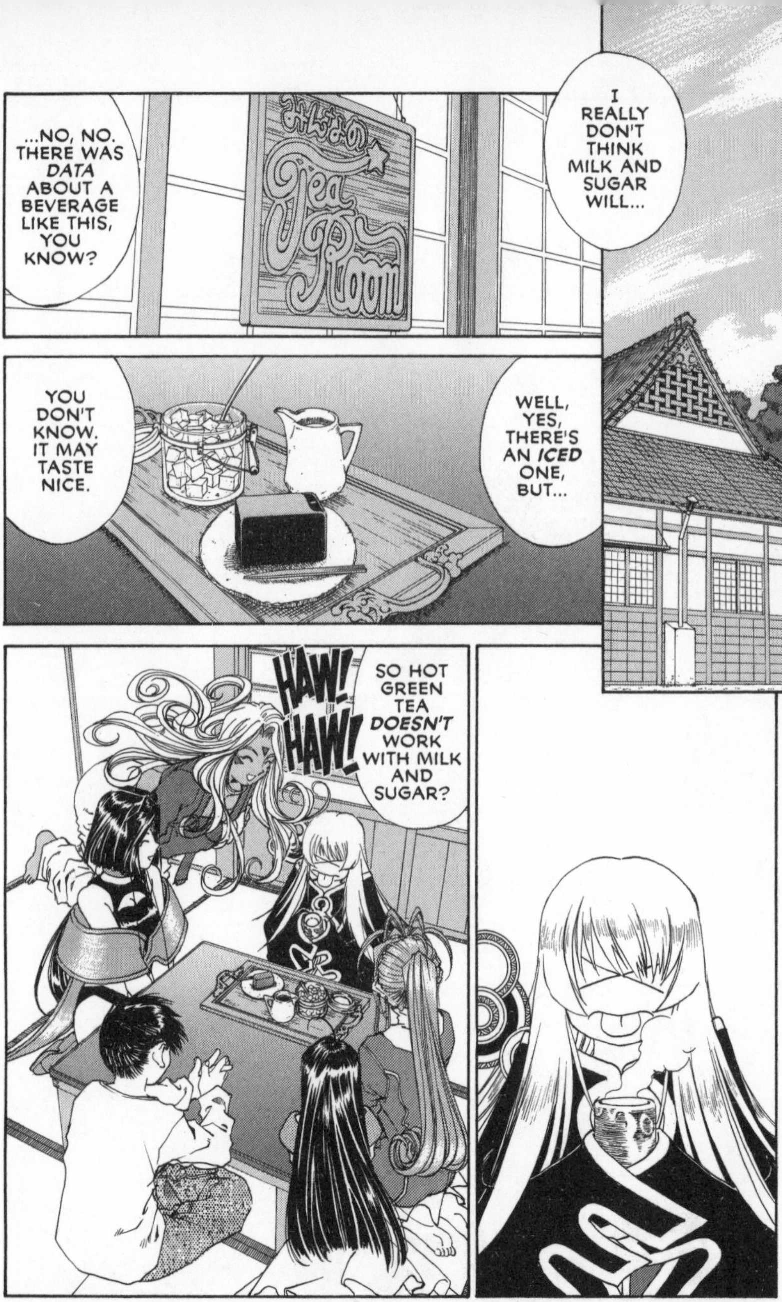
I REALLY DON'T THINK MILK AND SUGAR WILL...
...NO, NO. THERE WAS *DATA* ABOUT A BEVERAGE LIKE THIS, YOU KNOW?
Tea Room
WELL, YES, THERE'S AN *ICED* ONE, BUT...
YOU DON'T KNOW. IT MAY TASTE NICE.
SO HOT GREEN TEA *DOESN'T* WORK WITH MILK AND SUGAR?
HAW! HAW!

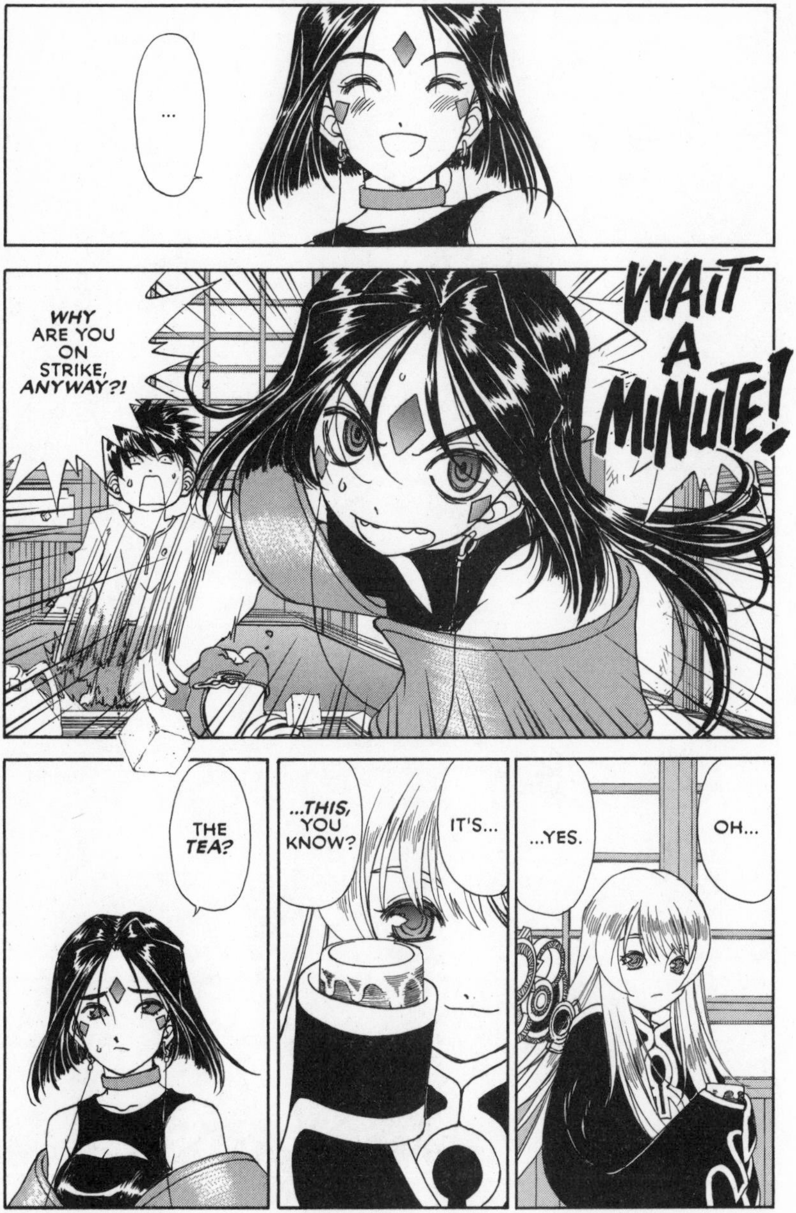
...
WAIT A MINUTE!
WHY ARE YOU ON STRIKE, ANYWAY?!
OH...
...YES.
IT'S...
...THIS, YOU KNOW?
THE TEA?

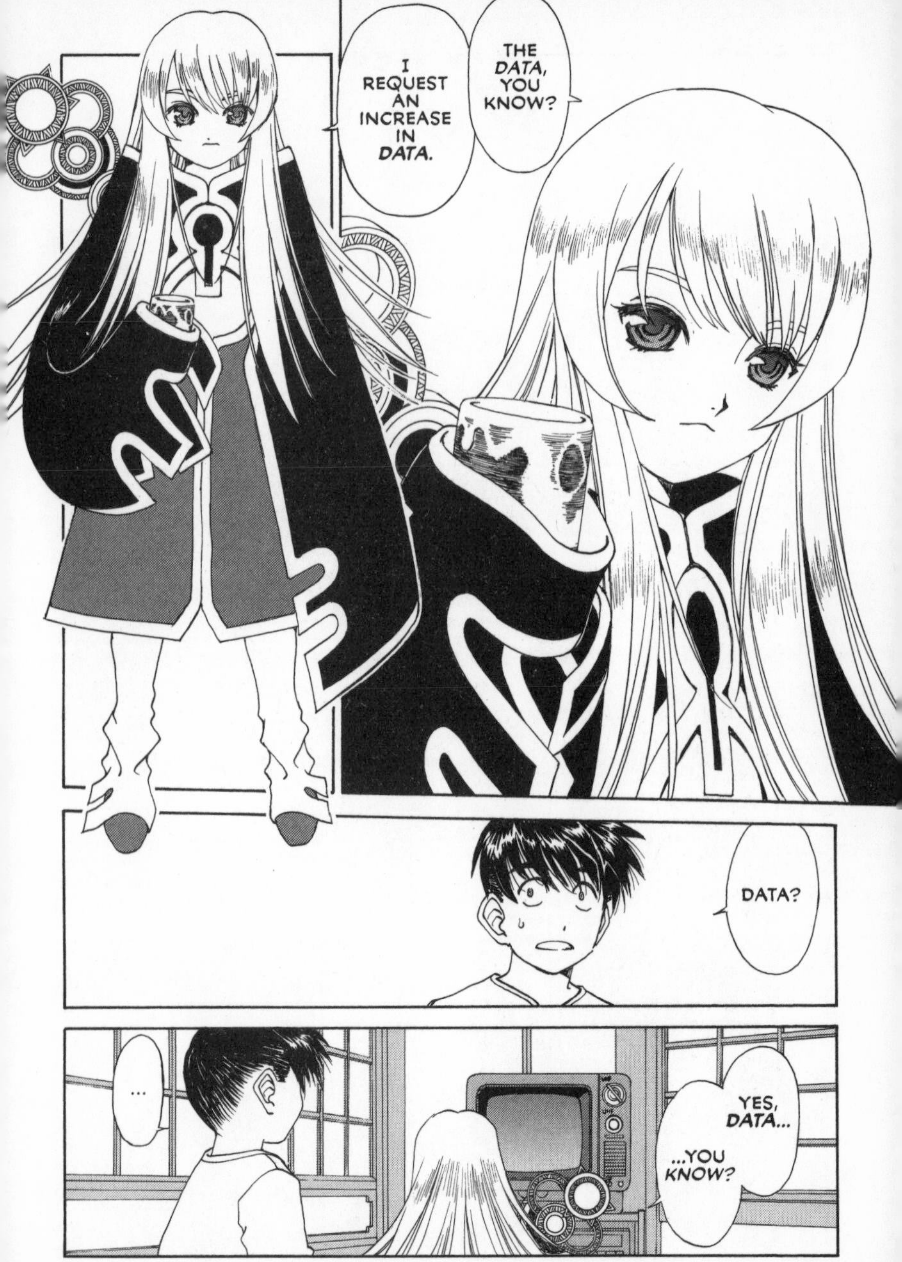
THE DATA, YOU KNOW?
I REQUEST AN INCREASE IN DATA.
DATA?
YES, DATA...
...YOU KNOW?
...

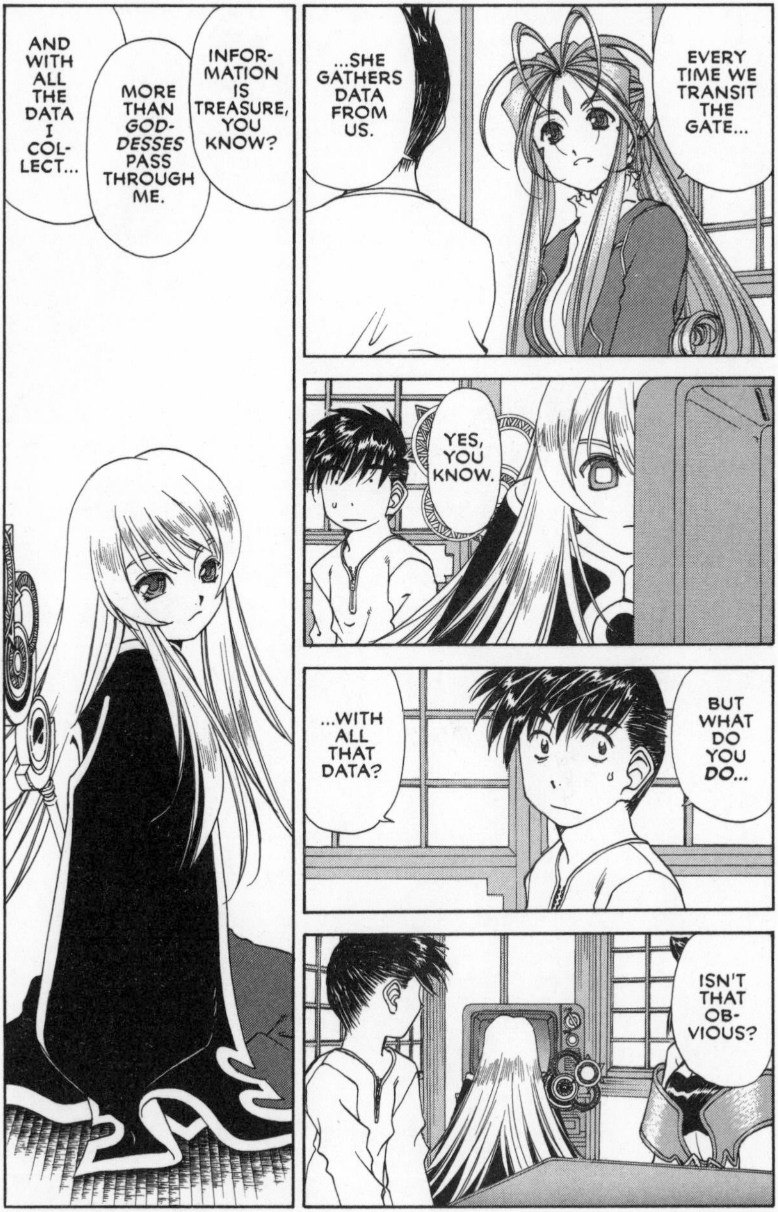
EVERY TIME WE TRANSIT THE GATE...
...SHE GATHERS DATA FROM US.
YES, YOU KNOW.
BUT WHAT DO YOU *DO*...
...WITH ALL THAT DATA?
ISN'T THAT OB-VIOUS?
INFOR-MATION IS TREASURE, YOU KNOW?
MORE THAN *GOD-DESSES* PASS THROUGH ME.
AND WITH ALL THE DATA I COL-LECT...

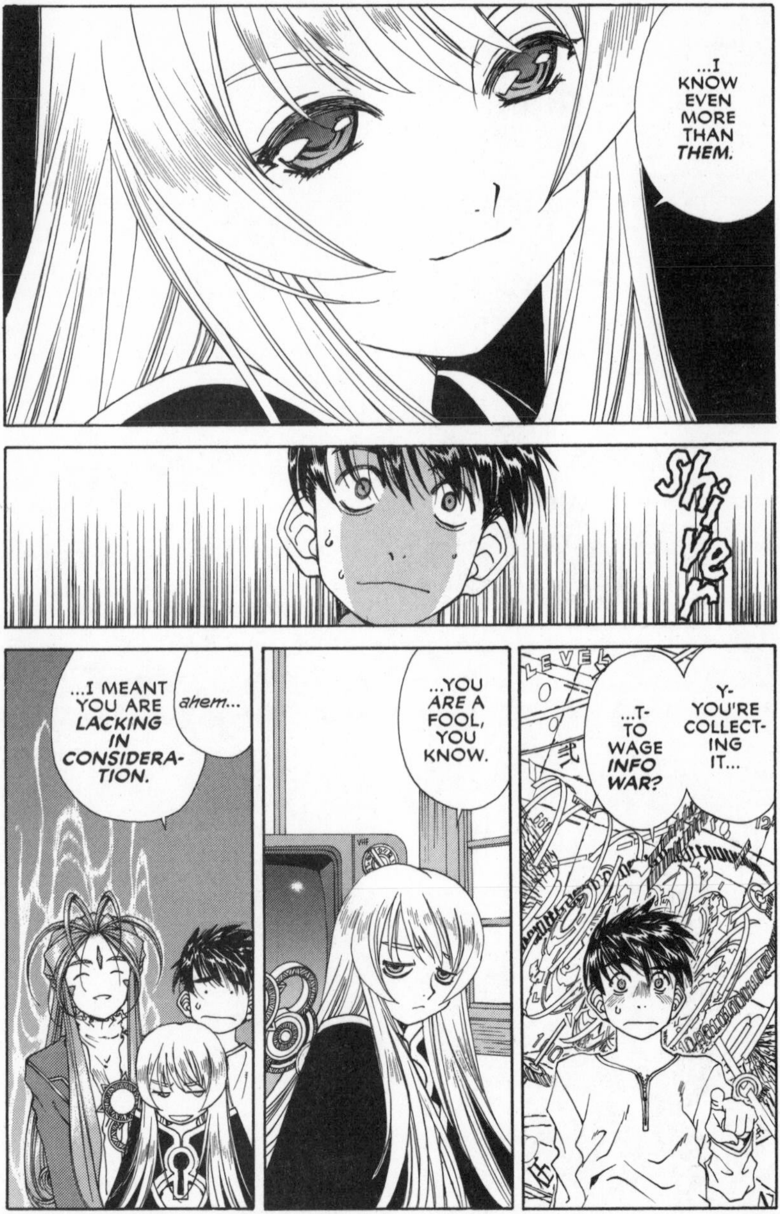
...I KNOW EVEN MORE THAN *THEM.*
Shiver
Y- YOU'RE COLLECTING IT...
...T- TO WAGE *INFO WAR?*
...YOU *ARE* A FOOL, YOU KNOW.
ahem...
...I MEANT YOU ARE *LACKING IN CONSIDERATION.*

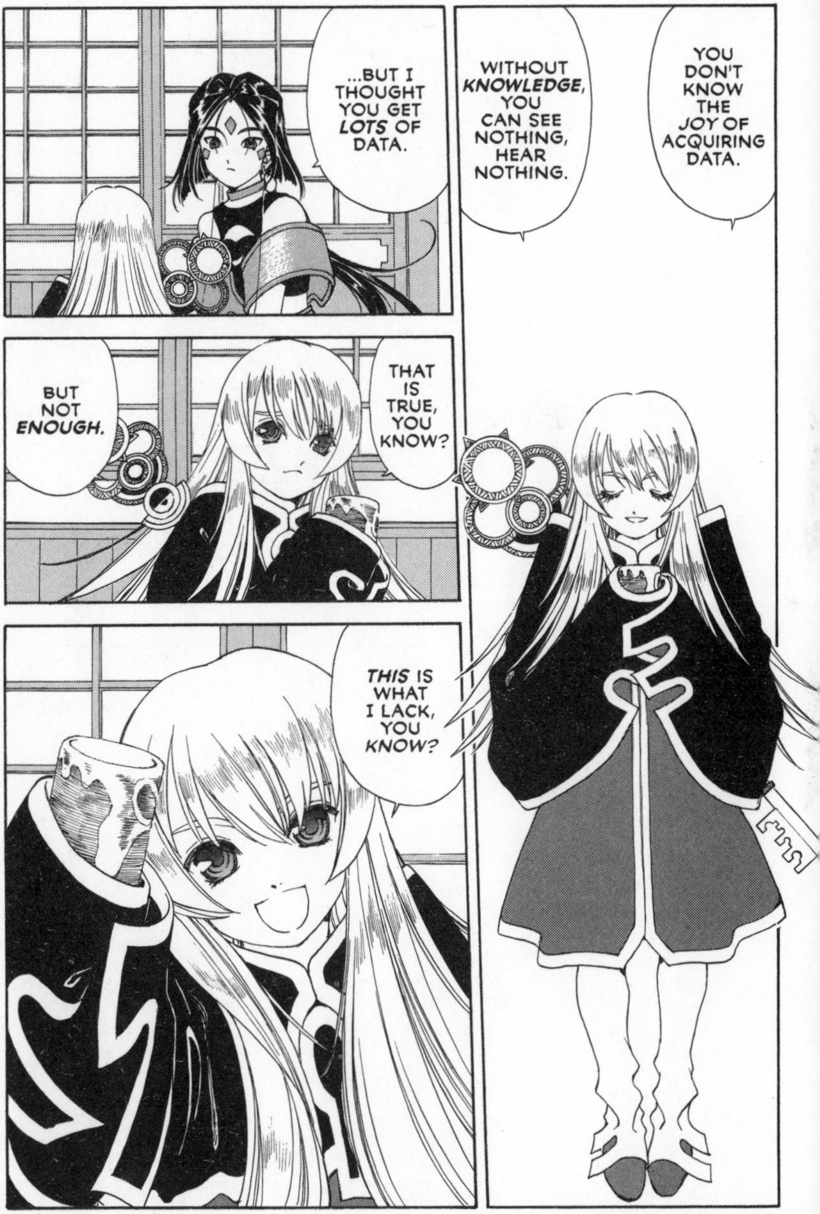
YOU DON'T KNOW THE *JOY* OF ACQUIRING DATA.
WITHOUT *KNOWLEDGE*, YOU CAN SEE NOTHING, HEAR NOTHING.
...BUT I THOUGHT YOU GET *LOTS* OF DATA.
THAT IS TRUE, YOU KNOW?
BUT NOT *ENOUGH*.
THIS IS WHAT I LACK, YOU *KNOW*?

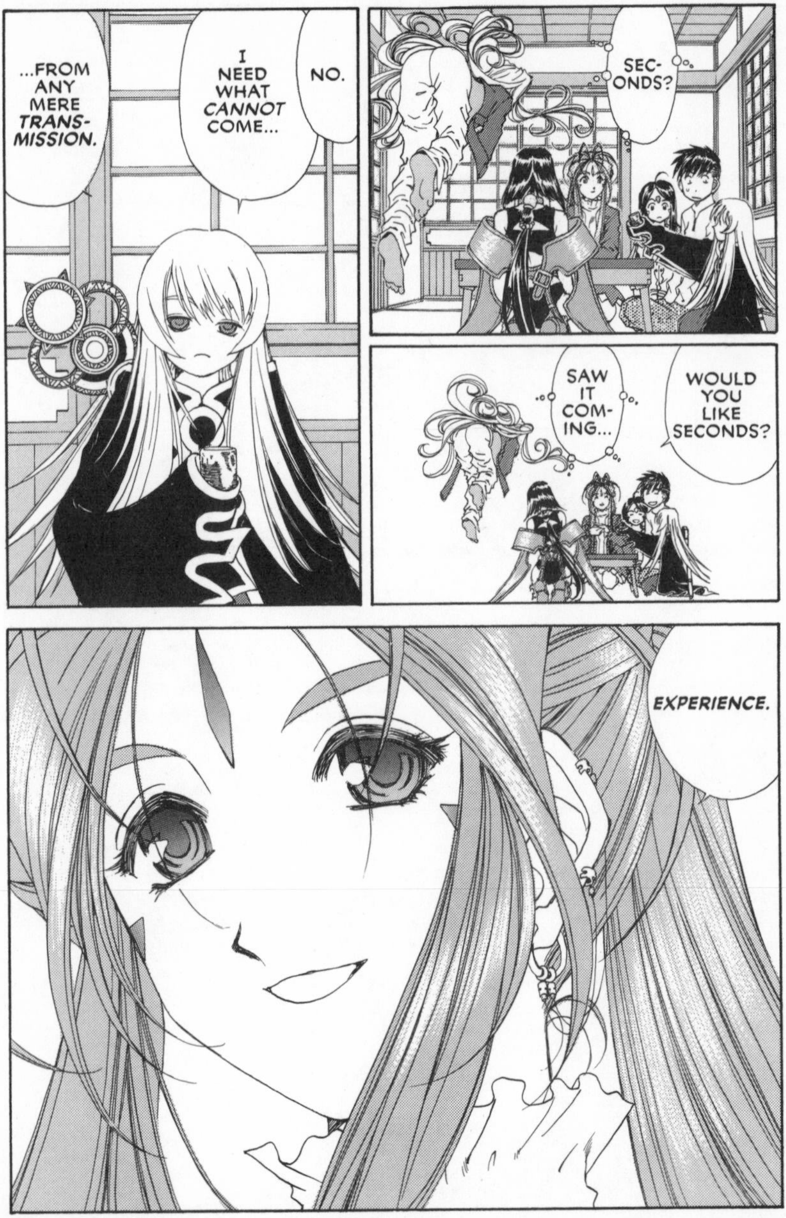
SEC-ONDS?
WOULD YOU LIKE SECONDS?
SAW IT COMING...
NO.
I NEED WHAT *CANNOT* COME...
...FROM ANY MERE *TRANSMISSION.*
EXPERIENCE.

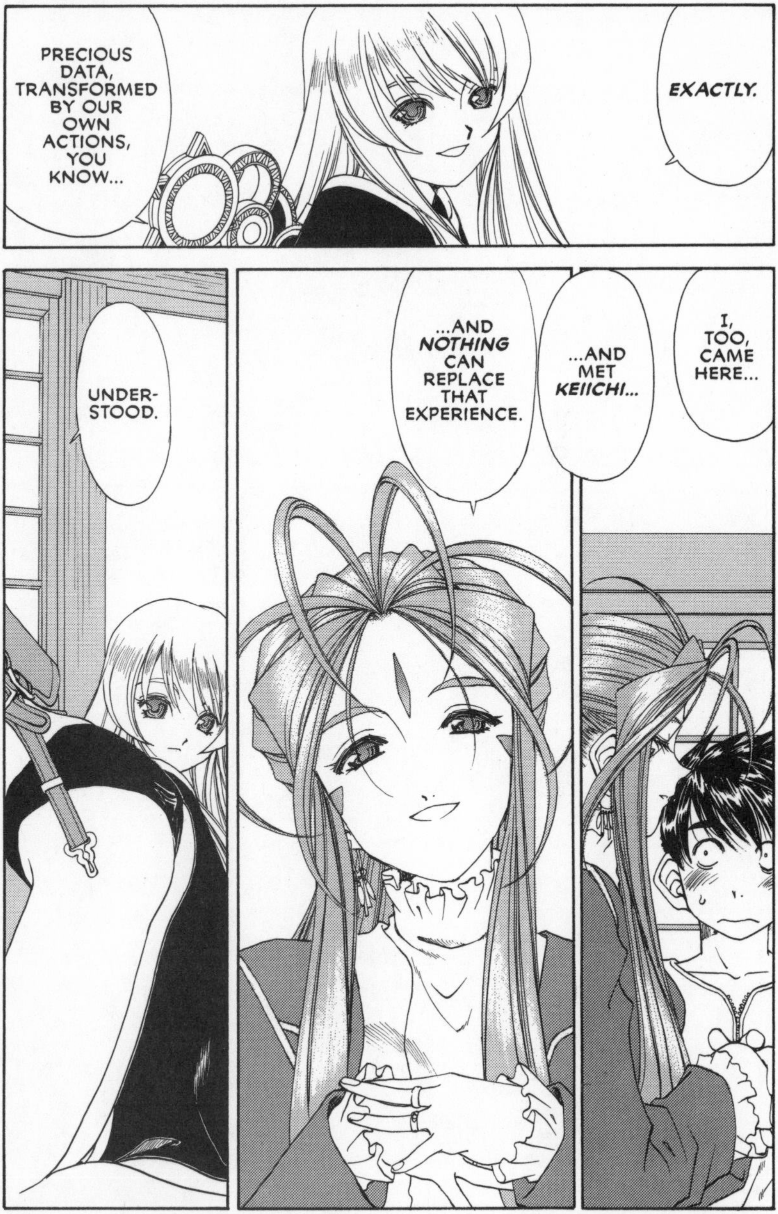
EXACTLY.
PRECIOUS DATA, TRANSFORMED BY OUR OWN ACTIONS, YOU KNOW...
I, TOO, CAME HERE...
...AND MET KEIICHI...
...AND NOTHING CAN REPLACE THAT EXPERIENCE.
UNDER-STOOD.

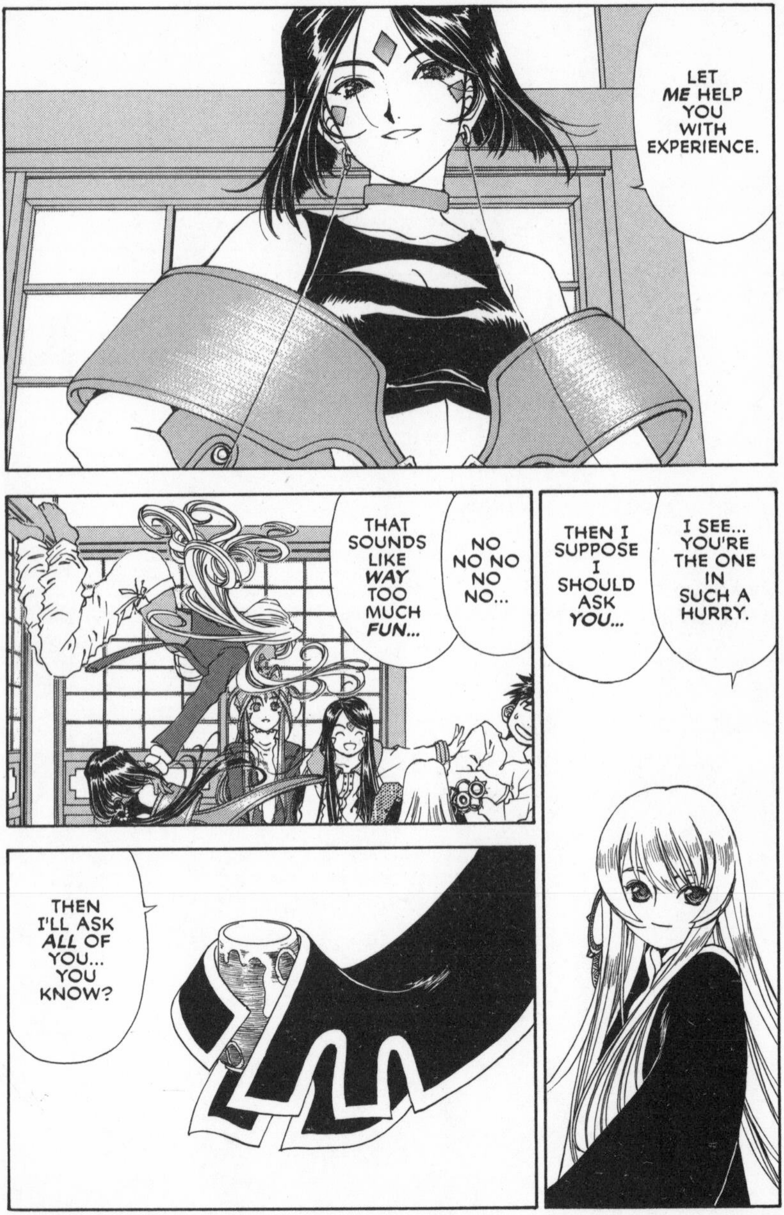
LET *ME* HELP YOU WITH EXPERIENCE.
I SEE... YOU'RE THE ONE IN SUCH A HURRY.
THEN I SUPPOSE I SHOULD ASK *YOU*...
NO NO NO NO NO...
THAT SOUNDS LIKE *WAY* TOO MUCH *FUN*...
THEN I'LL ASK *ALL* OF YOU... YOU KNOW?

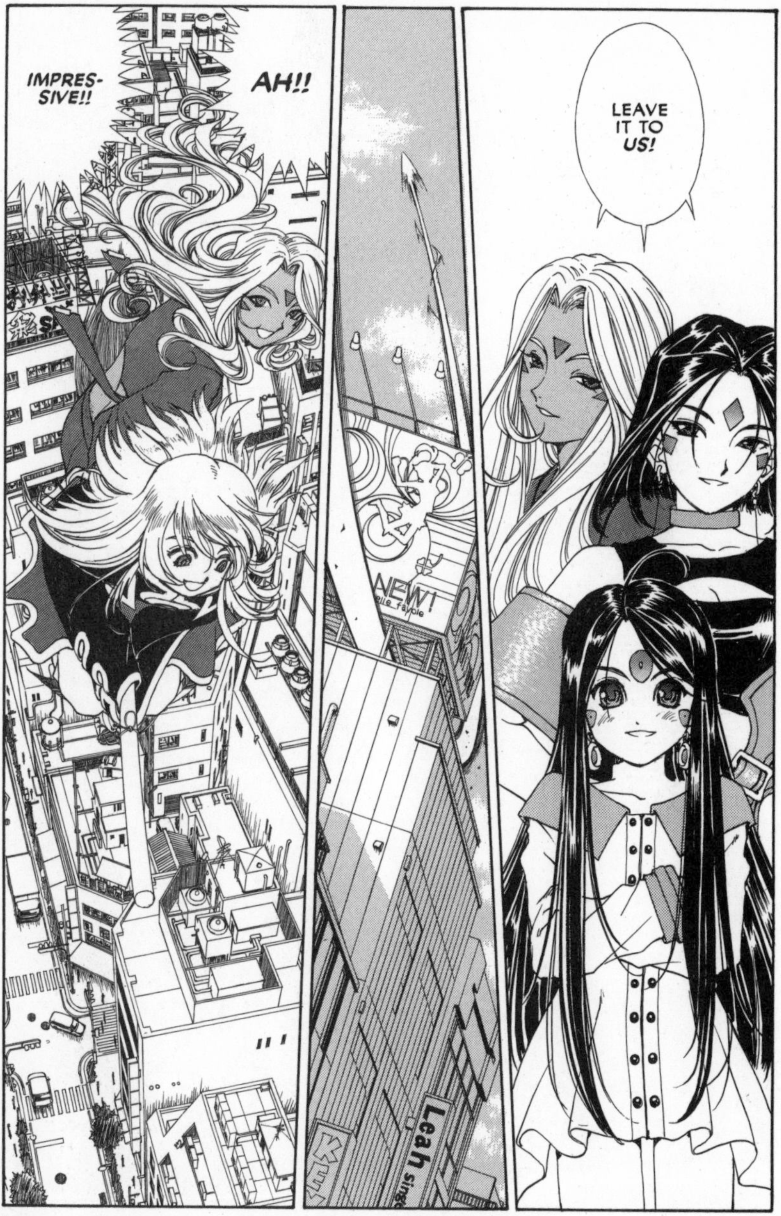
LEAVE IT TO US!
NEW!
Leah
AH!!
IMPRES-SIVE!!

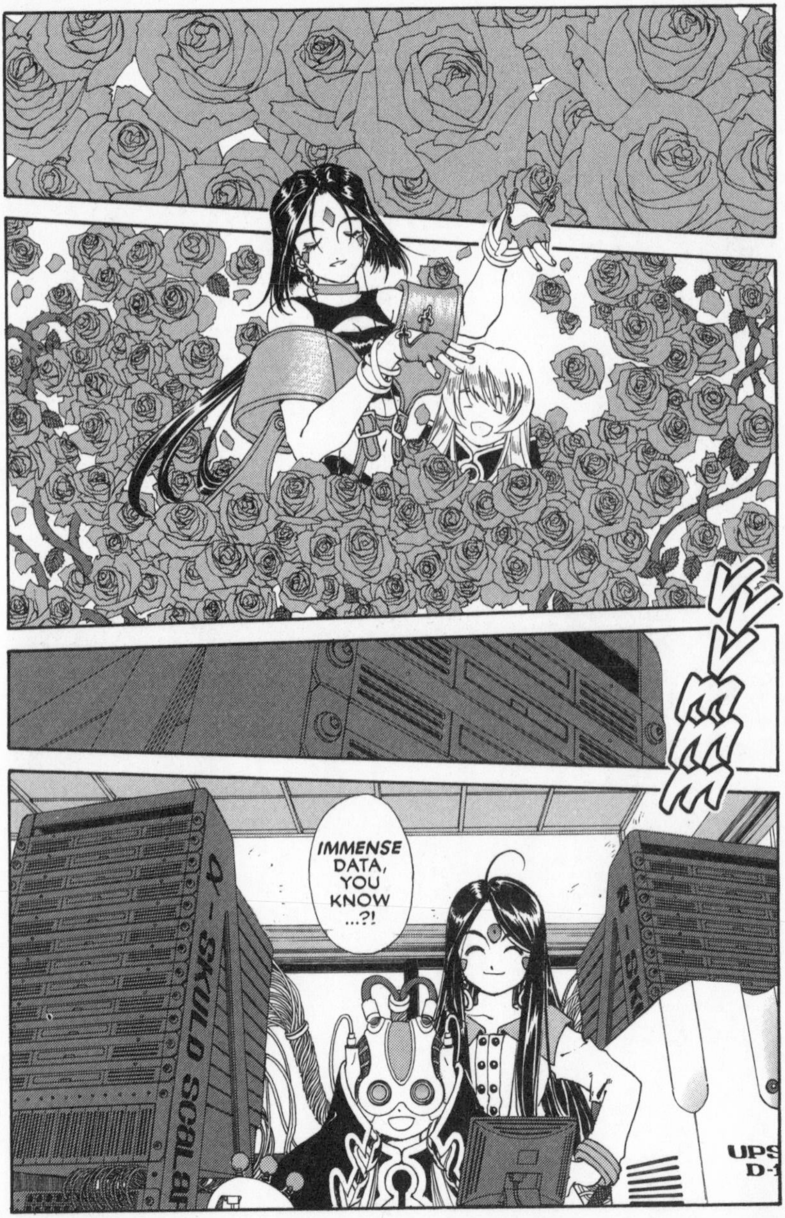
VVVMMM
IMMENSE DATA, YOU KNOW ...?!

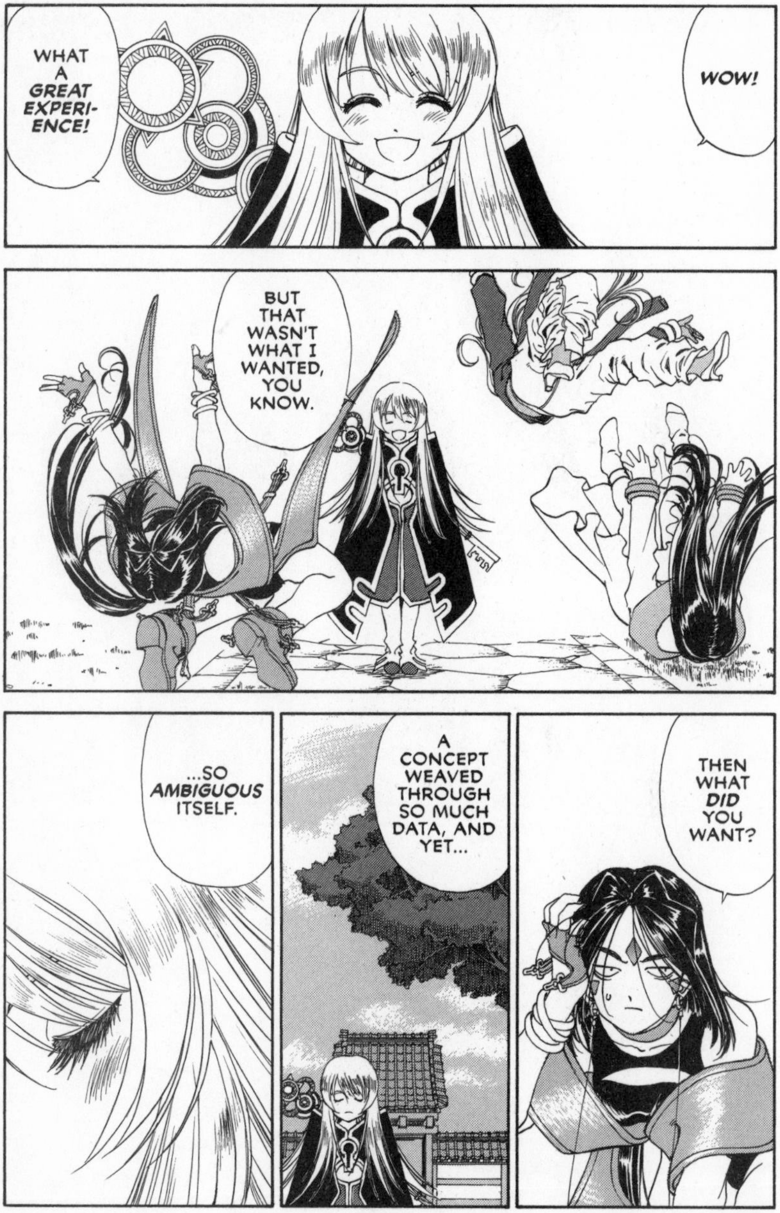
WOW!
WHAT A GREAT EXPERIENCE!
BUT THAT WASN'T WHAT I WANTED, YOU KNOW.
THEN WHAT DID YOU WANT?
A CONCEPT WEAVED THROUGH SO MUCH DATA, AND YET...
...SO AMBIGUOUS ITSELF.

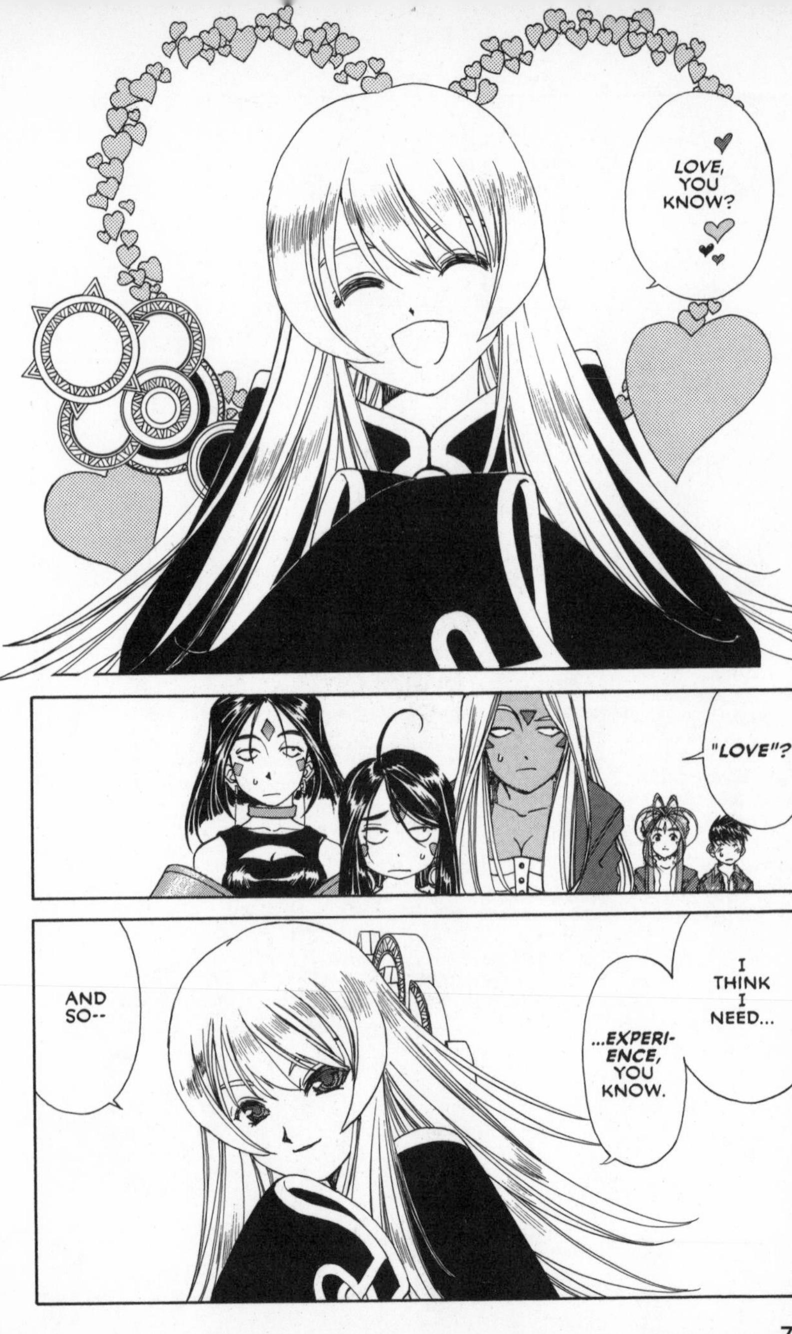
LOVE, YOU KNOW?
"LOVE"?
I THINK I NEED...
...EXPERIENCE, YOU KNOW.
AND SO--

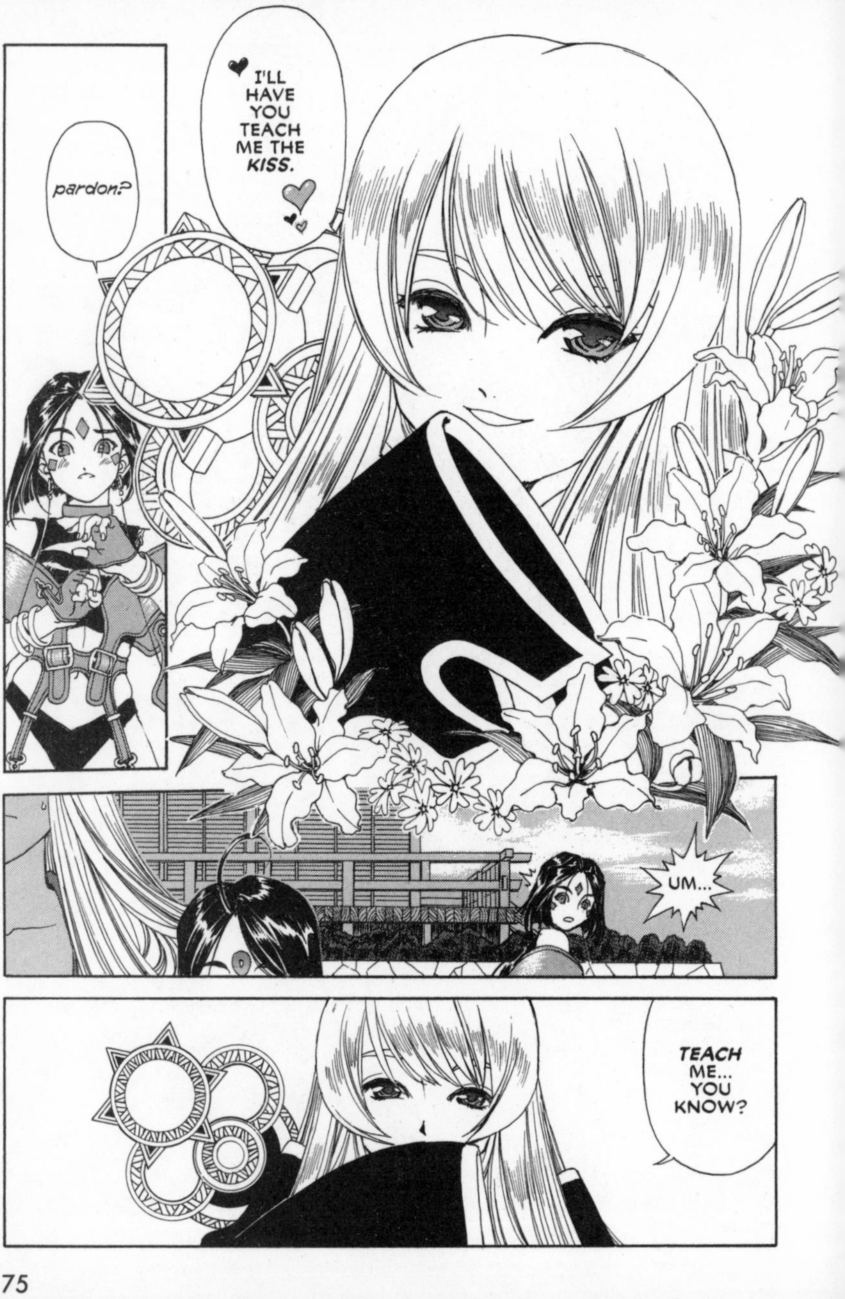
I'LL HAVE YOU TEACH ME THE KISS.
pardon?
UM...
TEACH ME... YOU KNOW?

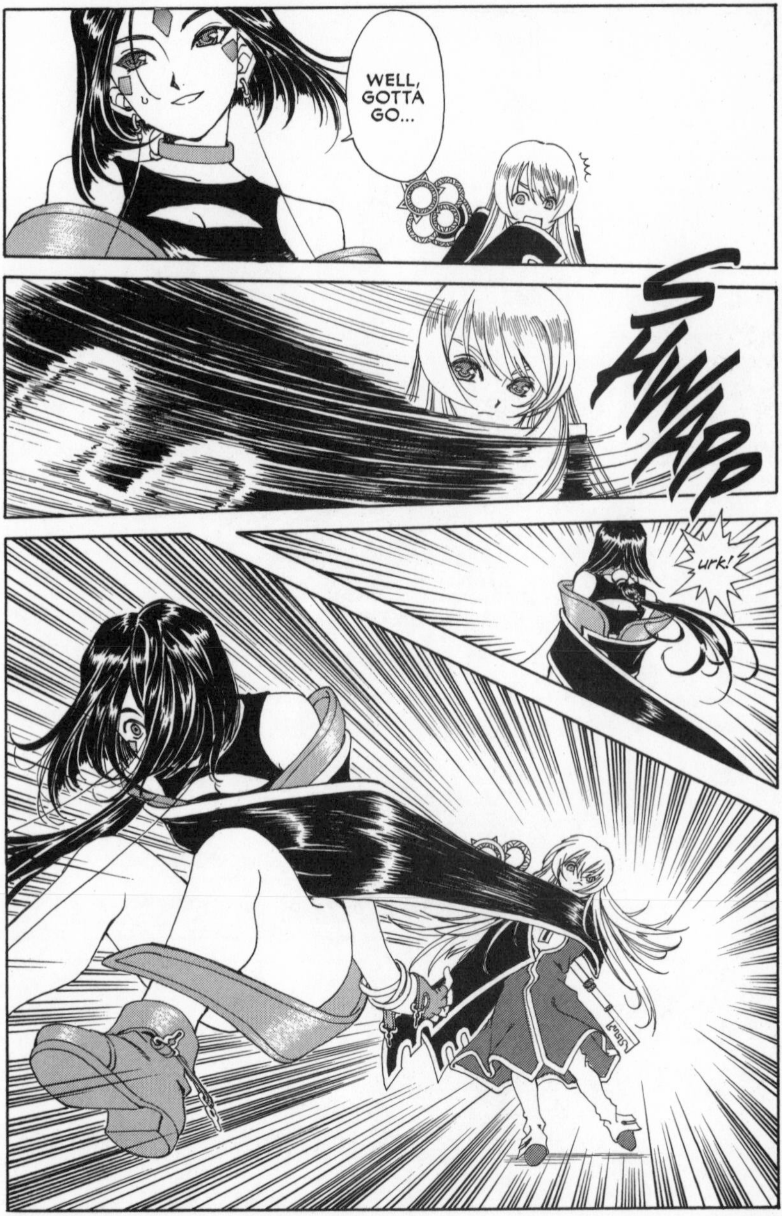
WELL, GOTTA GO...
SHWAPP
urk!

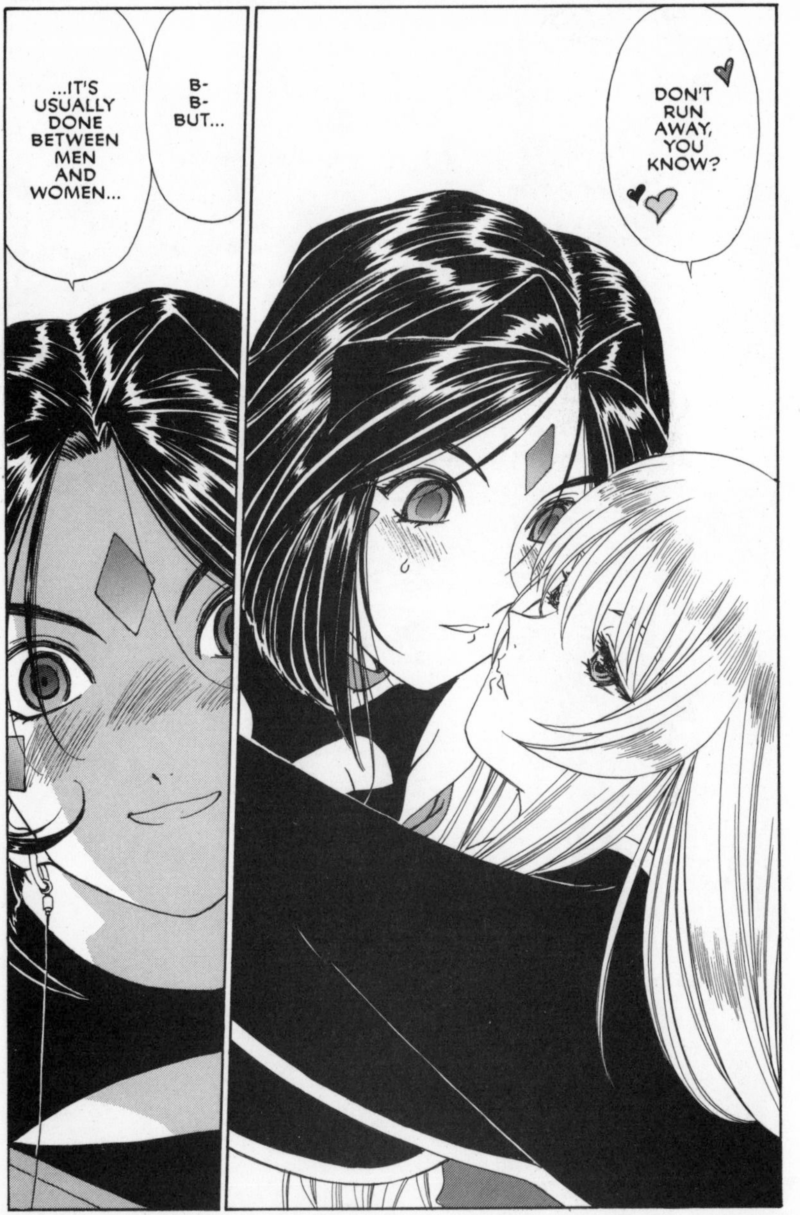
DON'T RUN AWAY, YOU KNOW?
B-B-BUT...
...IT'S USUALLY DONE BETWEEN MEN AND WOMEN...

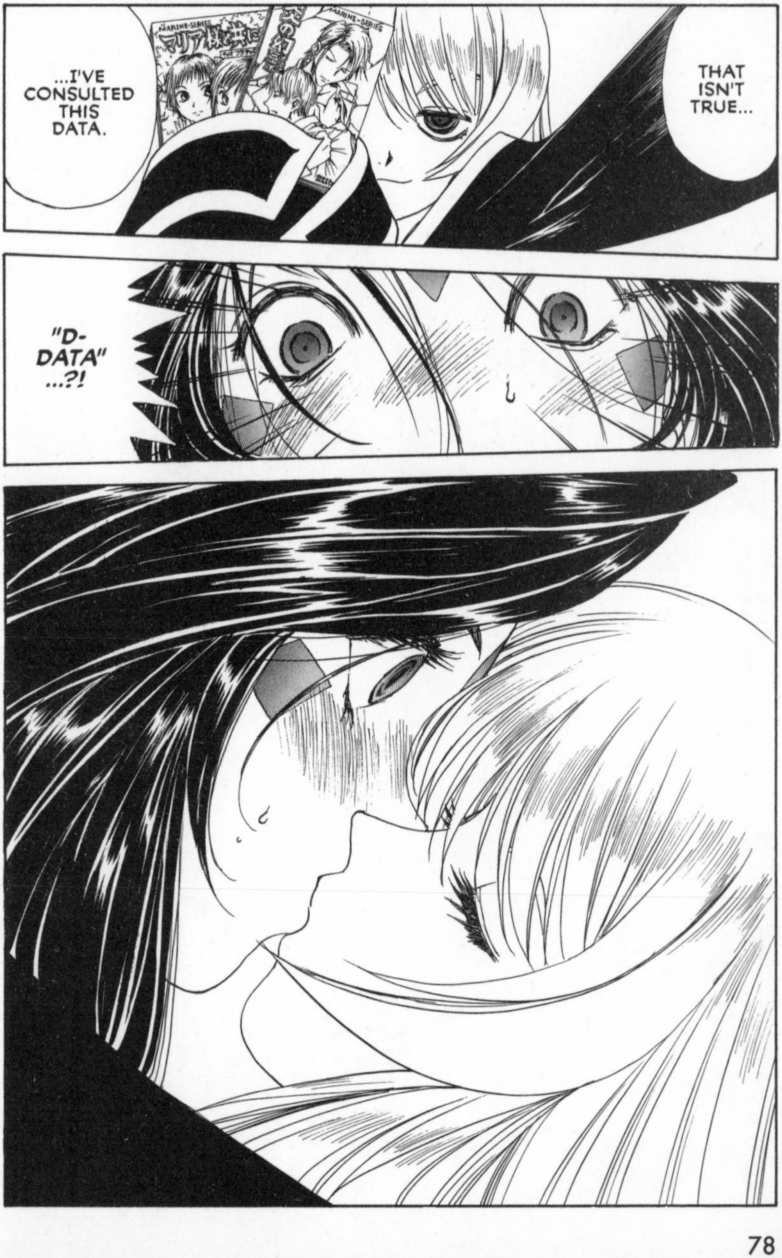
THAT ISN'T TRUE...
...I'VE CONSULTED THIS DATA.
MARINE-SERIES
MARINE-SERIES
"D-DATA" ...?!

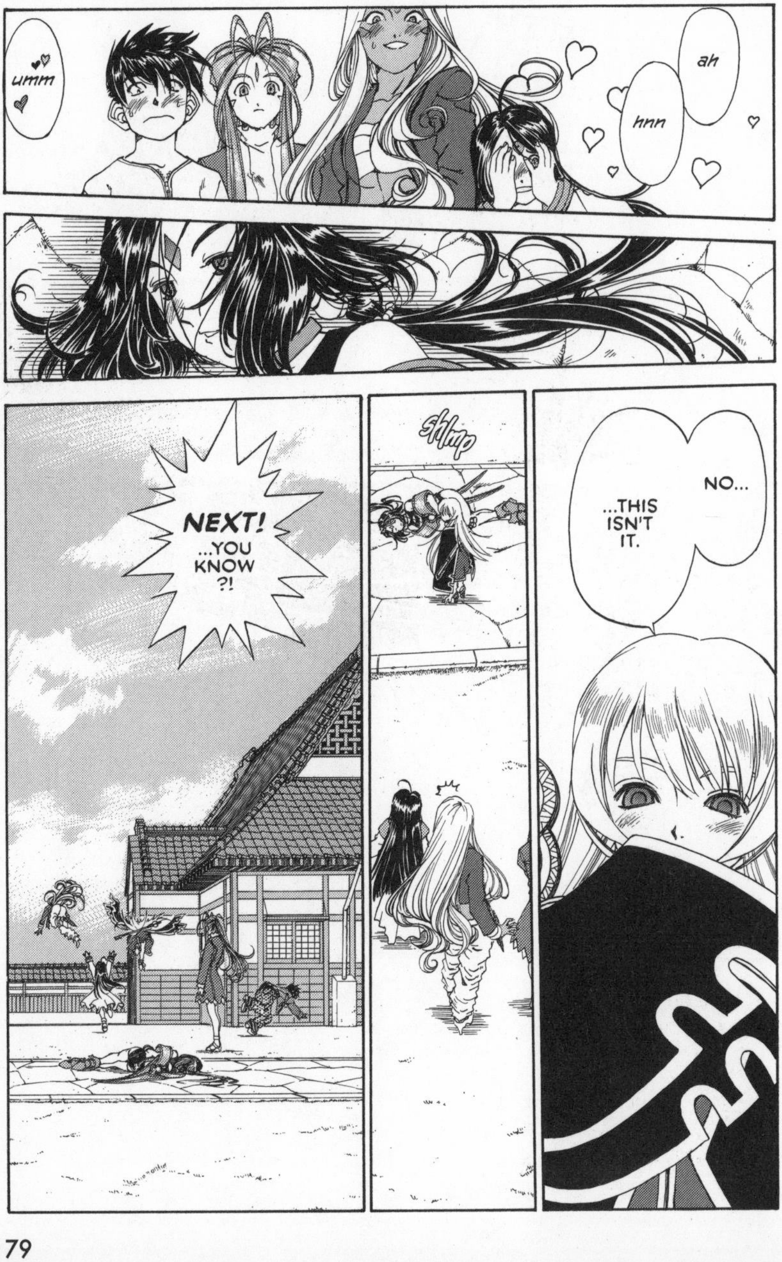
ah
hnn
umm
NO...
...THIS ISN'T IT.
shlmp
NEXT! ...YOU KNOW ?!

OH MY GODDESS!
GATE

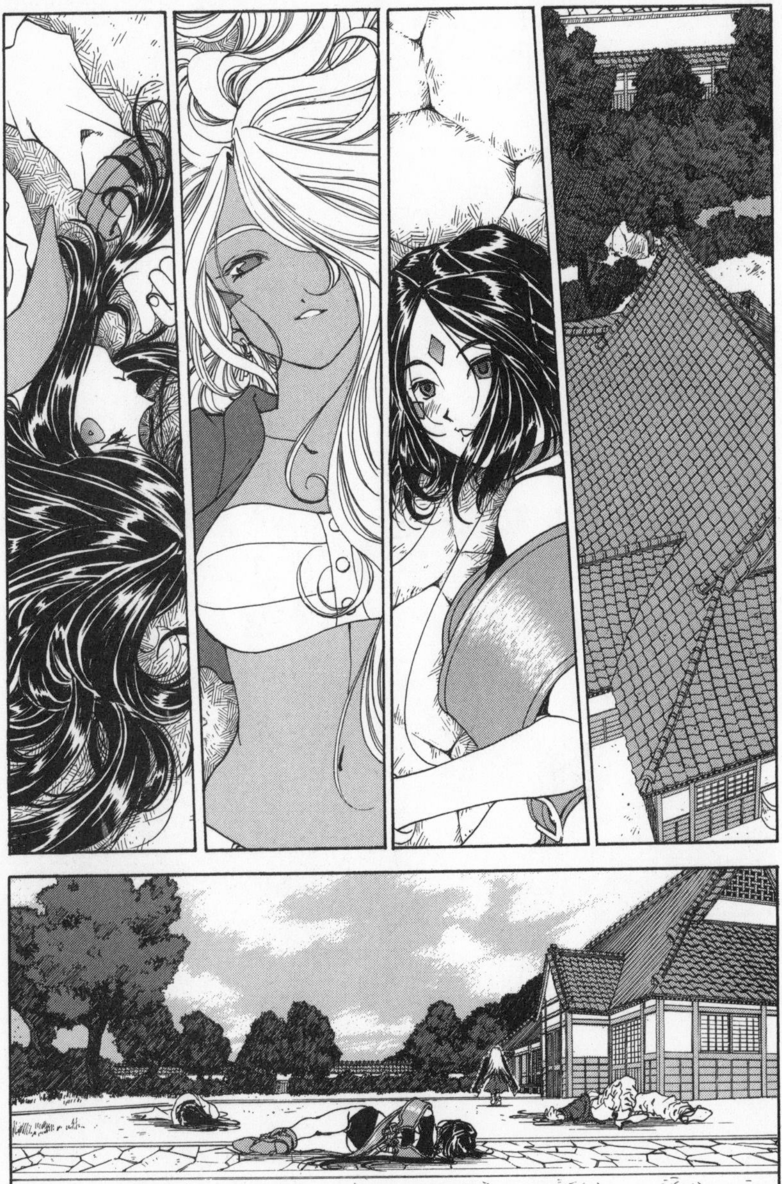

CHAPTER 198
Gotcha? Gotcha!

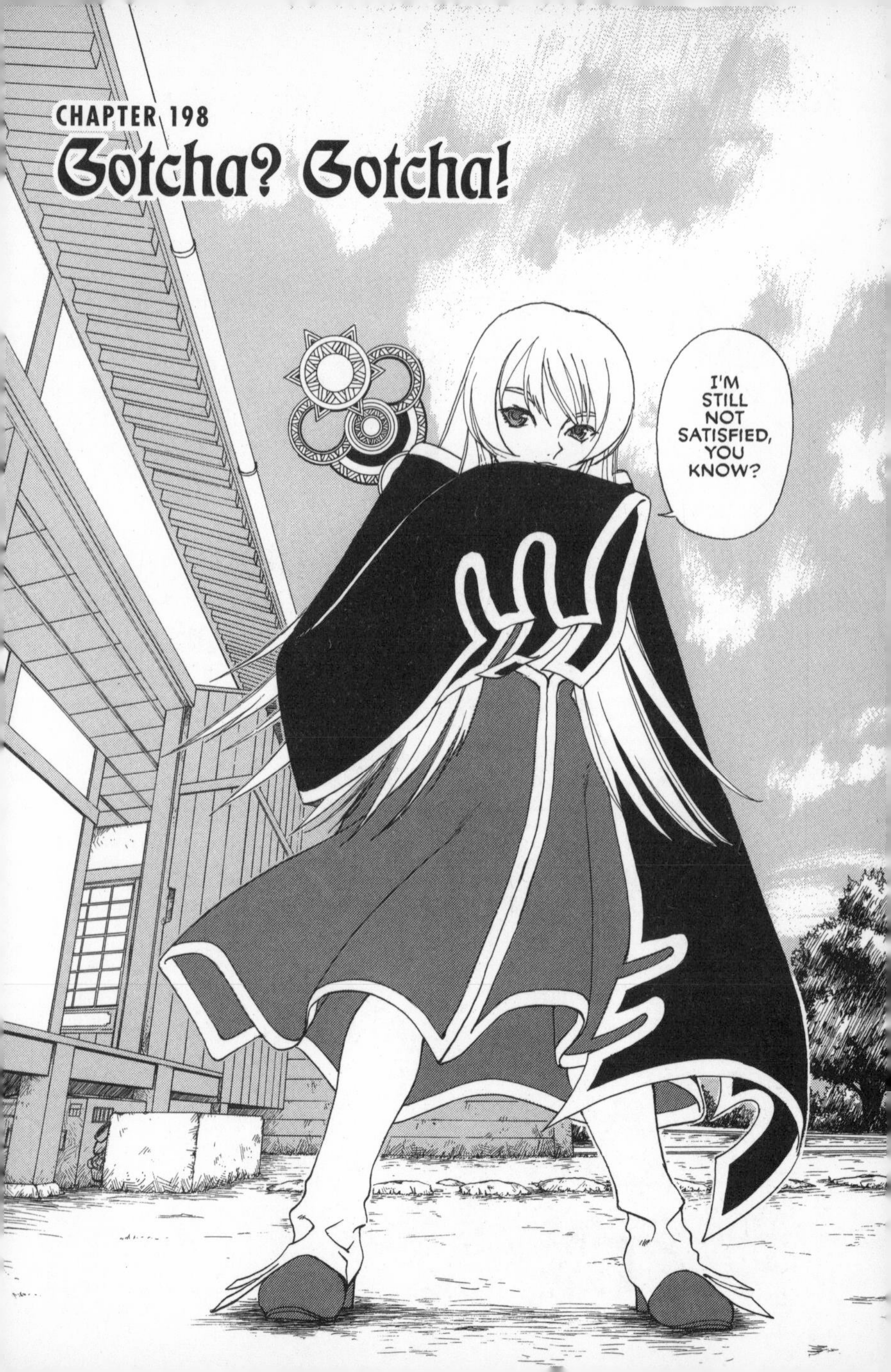
I'M STILL NOT SATISFIED, YOU KNOW?

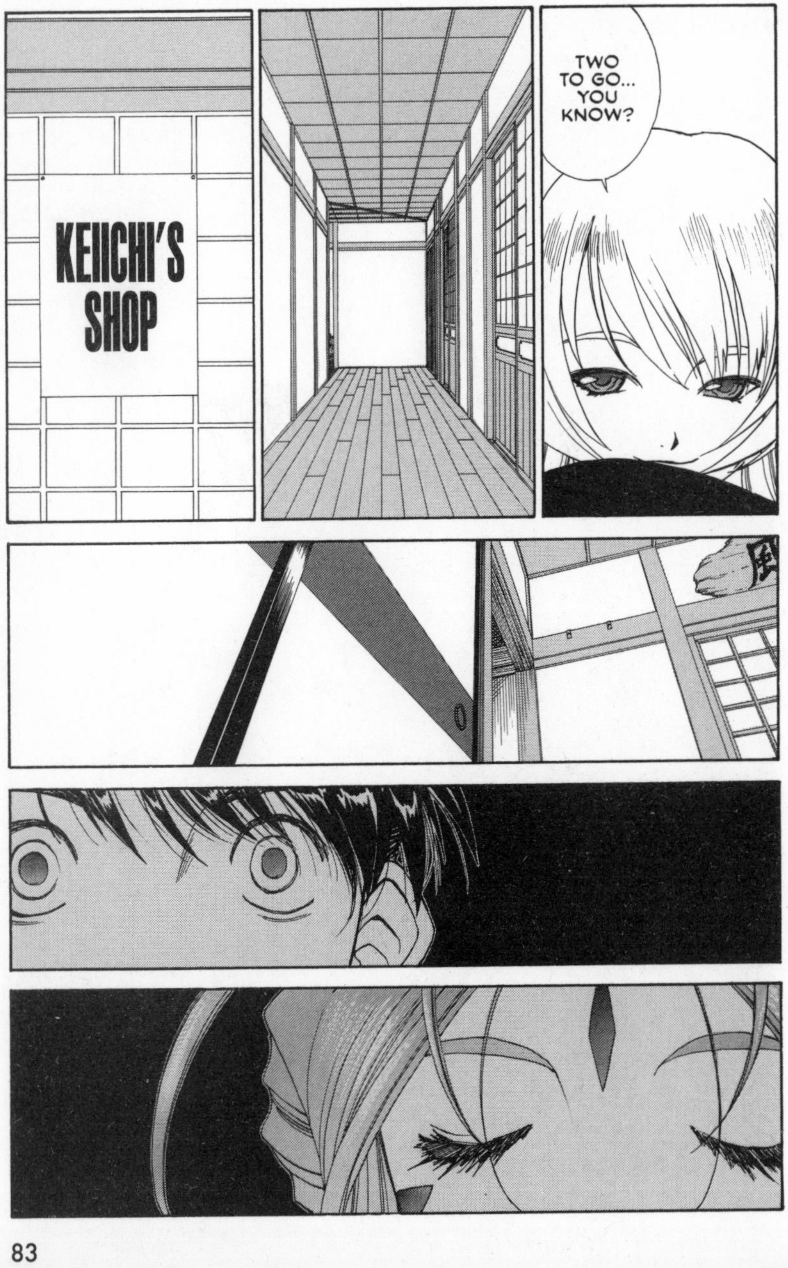
TWO TO GO... YOU KNOW?
KEIICHI'S SHOP

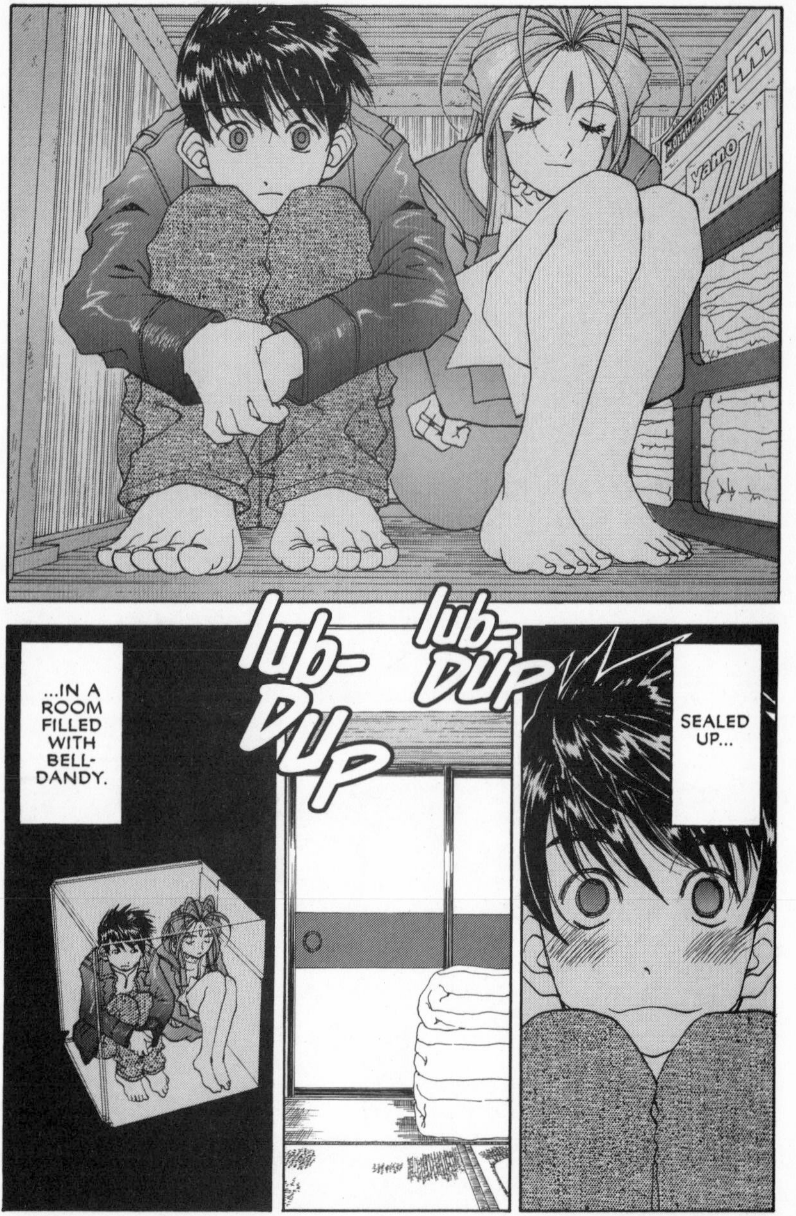
SEALED UP...
lub-DUP
lub-DUP
...IN A ROOM FILLED WITH BELL-DANDY.

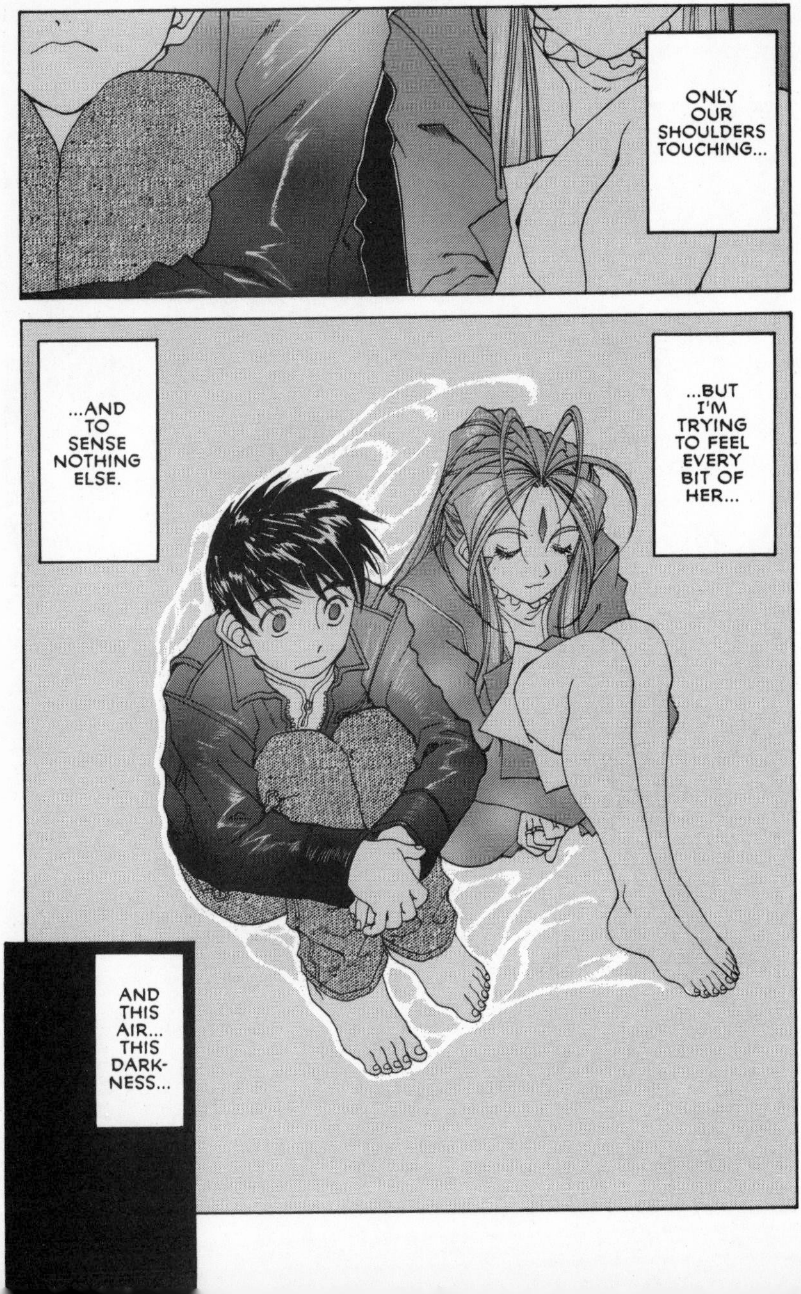
ONLY OUR SHOULDERS TOUCHING...
...BUT I'M TRYING TO FEEL EVERY BIT OF HER...
...AND TO SENSE NOTHING ELSE.
AND THIS AIR... THIS DARK-NESS...

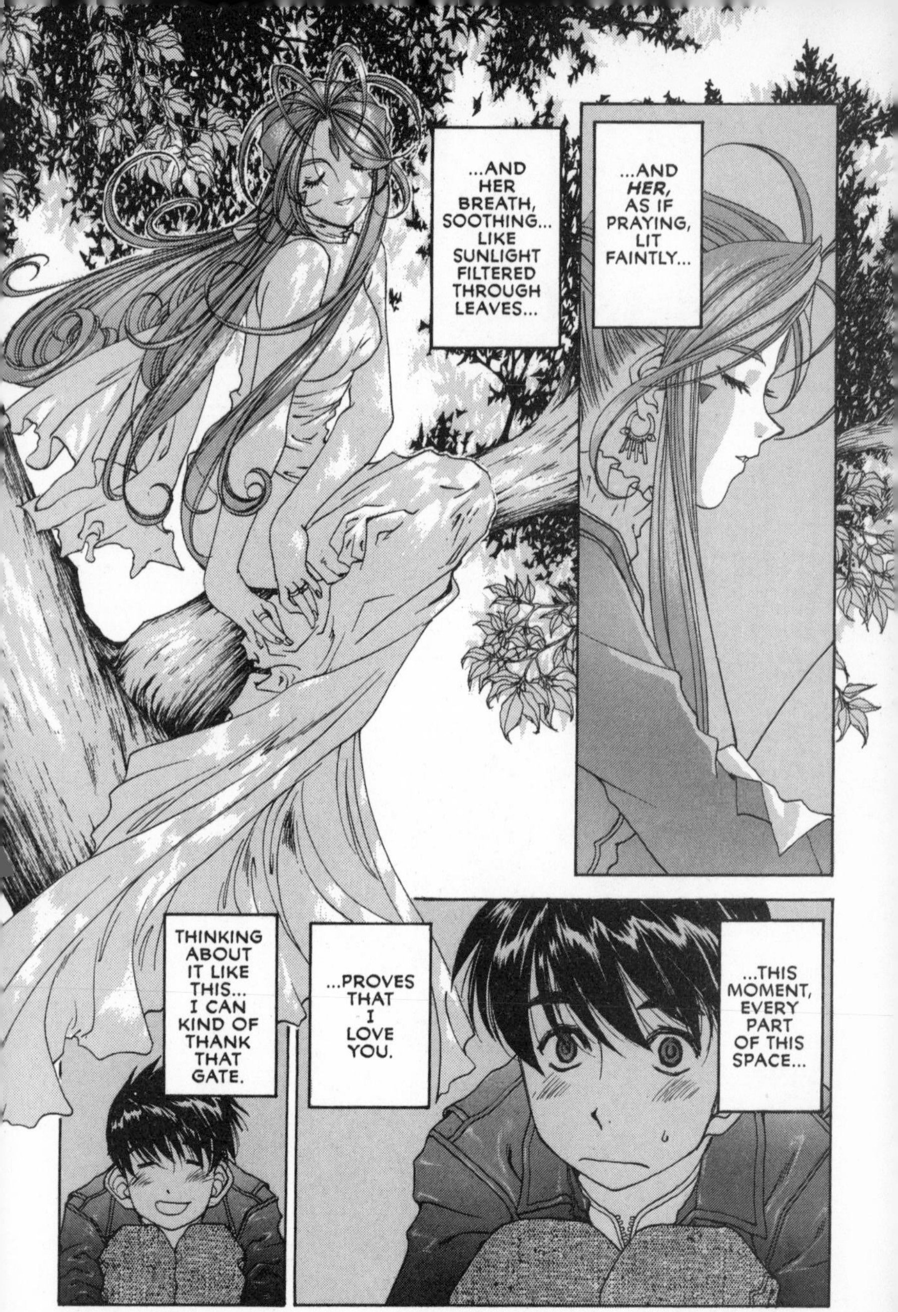
...AND HER, AS IF PRAYING, LIT FAINTLY...
...AND HER BREATH, SOOTHING... LIKE SUNLIGHT FILTERED THROUGH LEAVES...
...THIS MOMENT, EVERY PART OF THIS SPACE...
...PROVES THAT I LOVE YOU.
THINKING ABOUT IT LIKE THIS... I CAN KIND OF THANK THAT GATE.

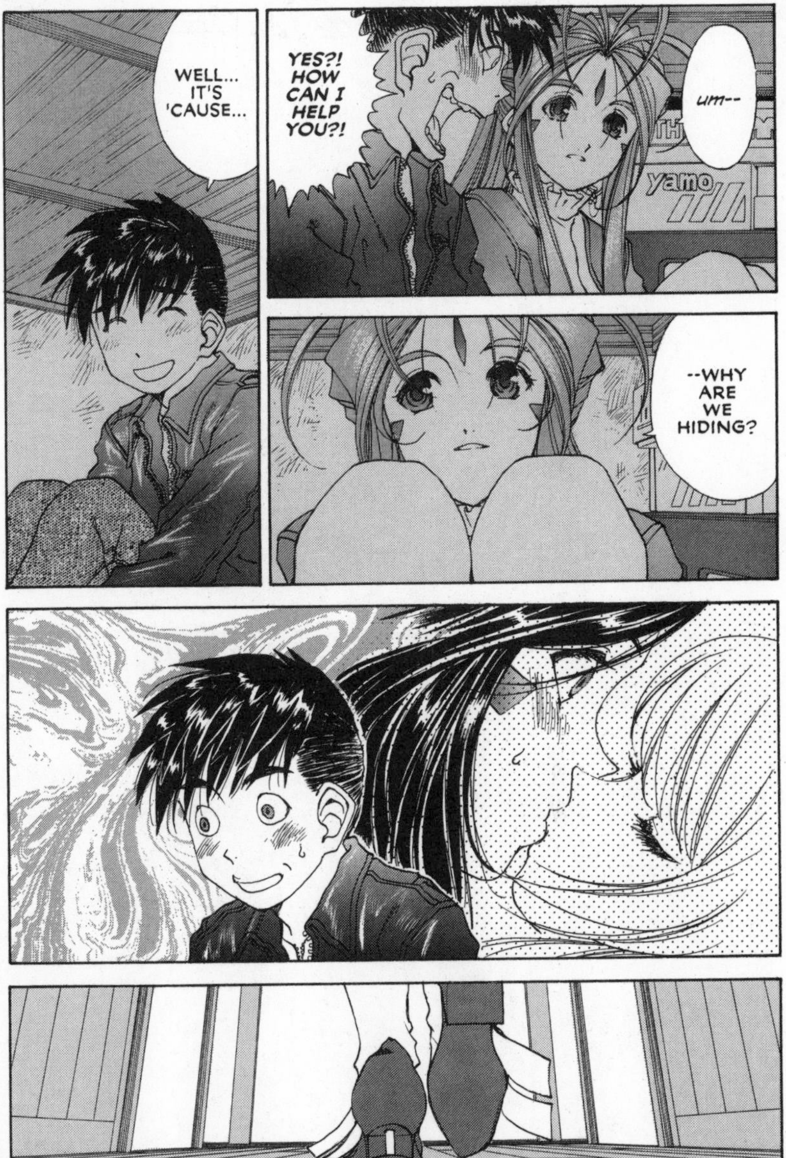
um--
YES?! HOW CAN I HELP YOU?!
--WHY ARE WE HIDING?
WELL... IT'S 'CAUSE...

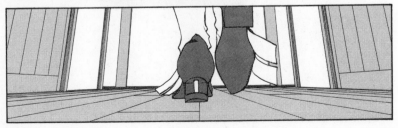

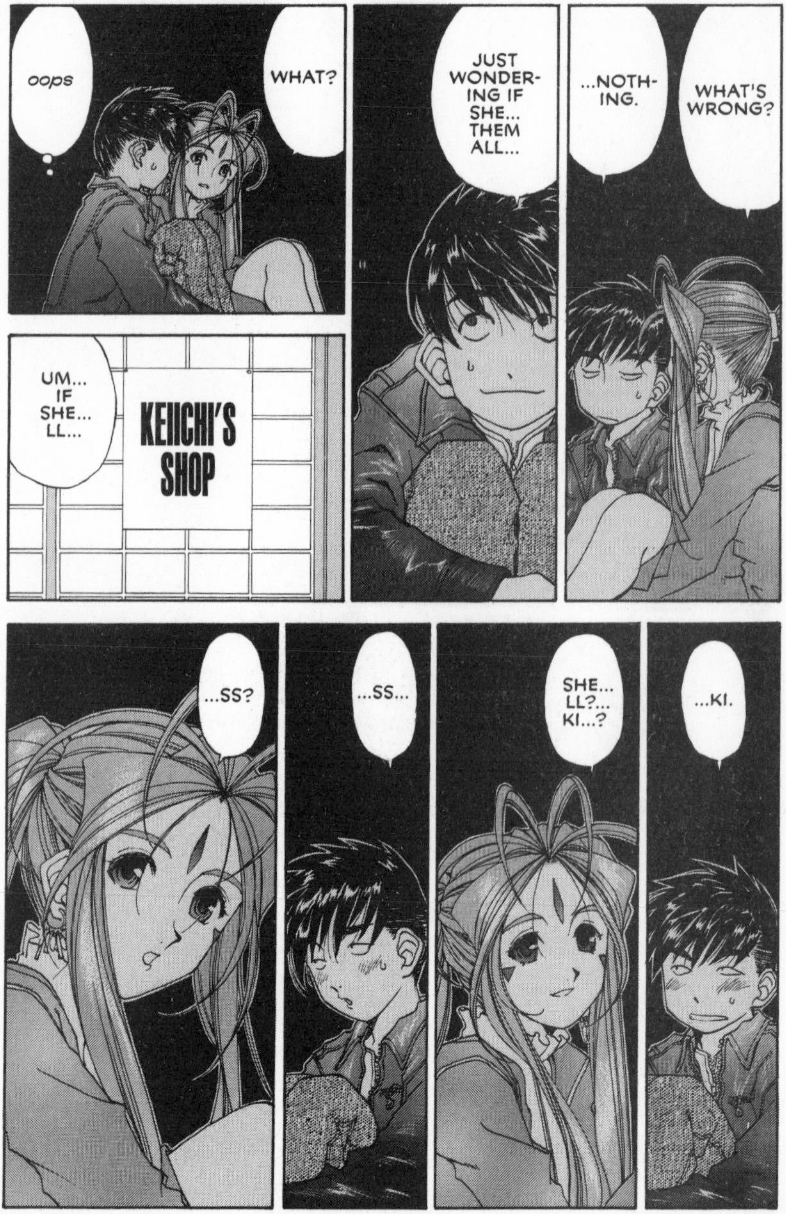
WHAT'S WRONG?
...NOTH-ING.
JUST WONDER-ING IF SHE... THEM ALL...
WHAT?
oops
UM... IF SHE... LL...
KEIICHI'S SHOP
...KI.
SHE... LL?... KI...?
...SS...
...SS?

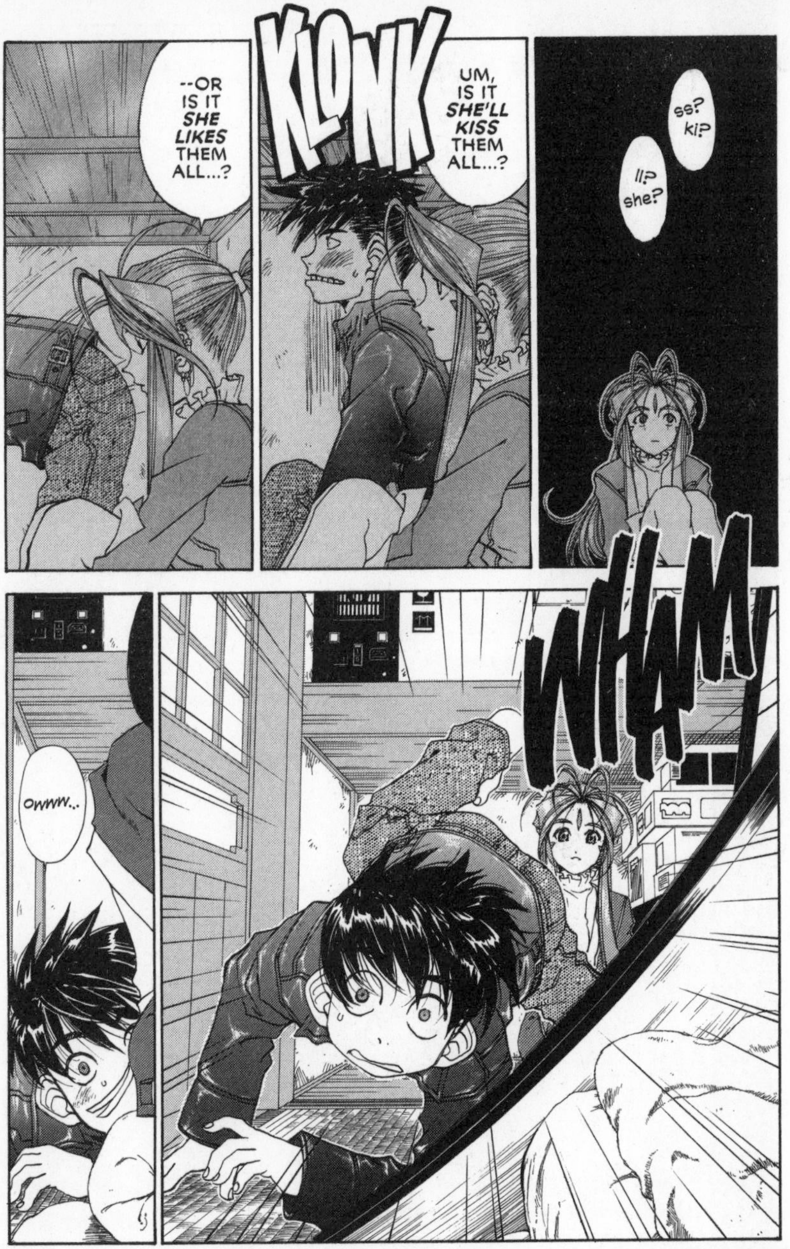
ss? ki?
li? she?
KLONK
UM, IS IT SHE'LL KISS THEM ALL...?
--OR IS IT SHE LIKES THEM ALL...?
WHAM
OWWW...

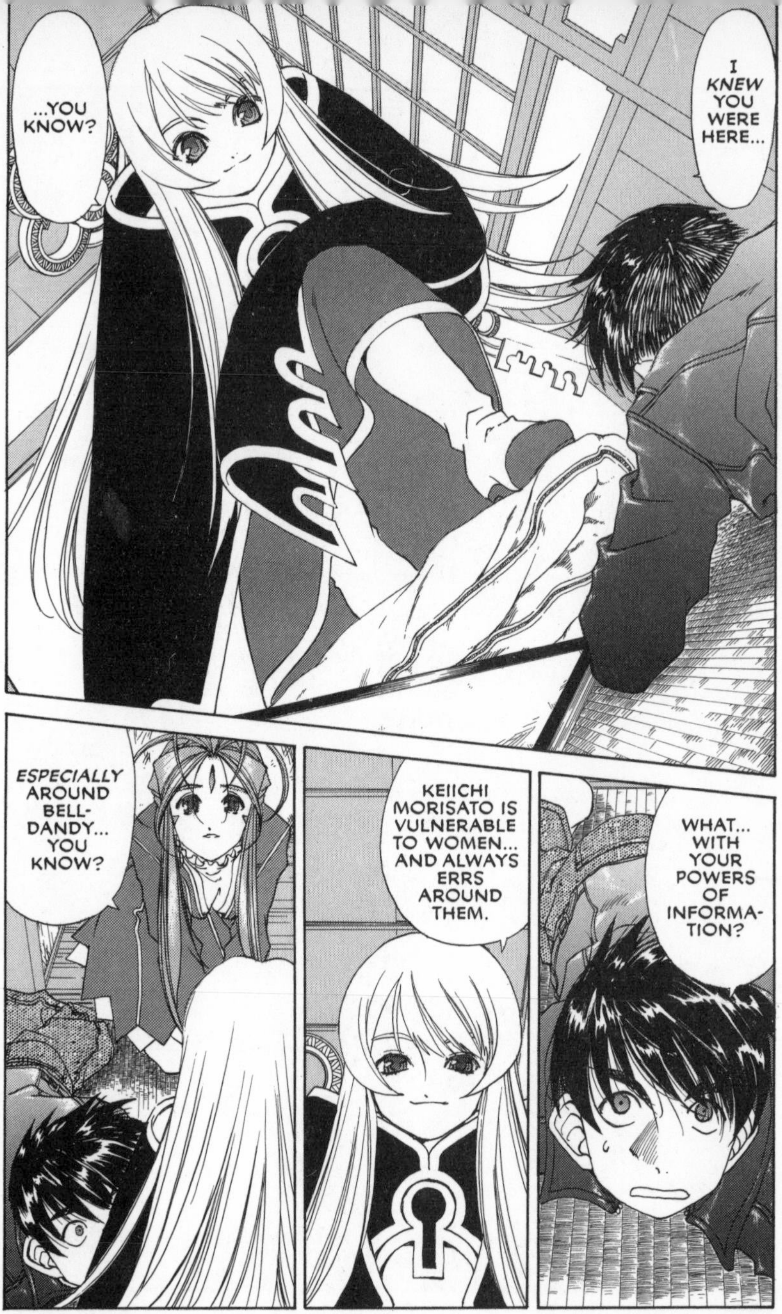
I *KNEW* YOU WERE HERE...
...YOU KNOW?
WHAT... WITH YOUR POWERS OF INFORMA-TION?
KEIICHI MORISATO IS VULNERABLE TO WOMEN... AND ALWAYS ERRS AROUND THEM.
ESPECIALLY AROUND BELL-DANDY... YOU KNOW?

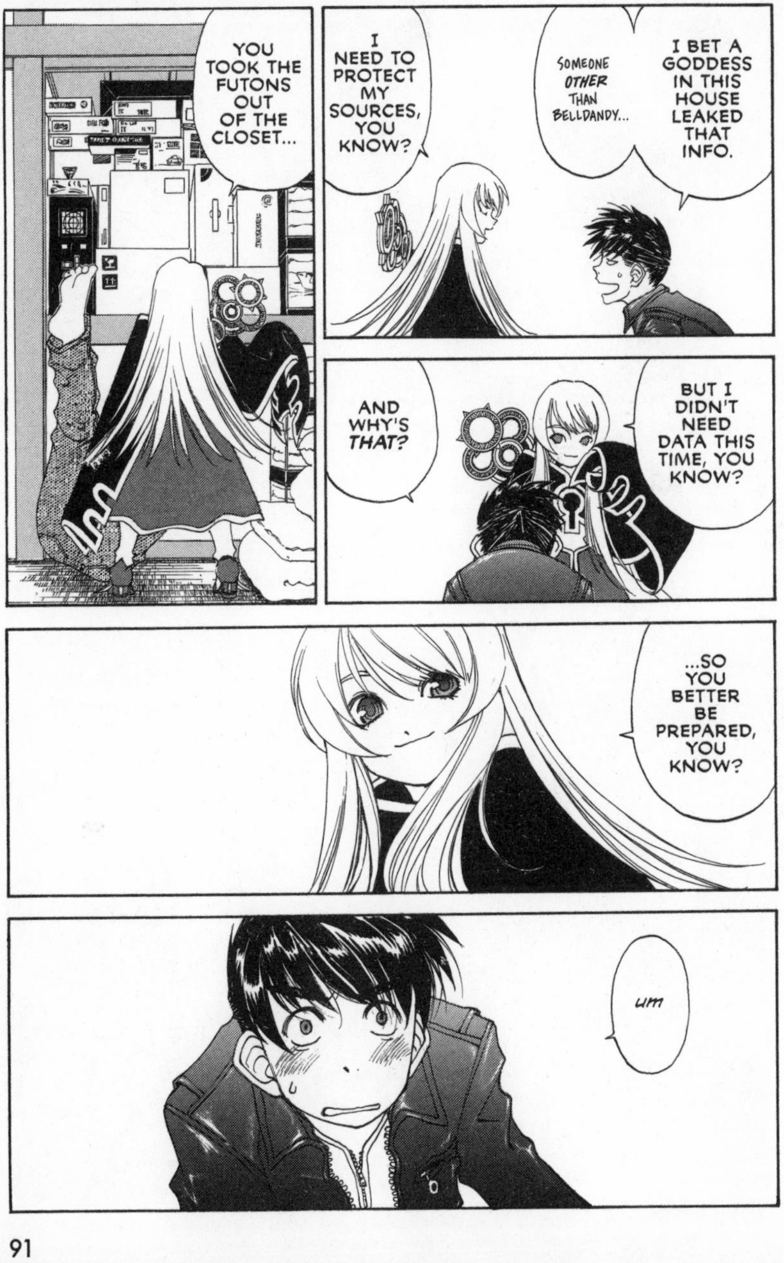
I BET A GODDESS IN THIS HOUSE LEAKED THAT INFO.
SOMEONE *OTHER* THAN BELLDANDY...
I NEED TO PROTECT MY SOURCES, YOU KNOW?
BUT I DIDN'T NEED DATA THIS TIME, YOU KNOW?
AND WHY'S *THAT*?
YOU TOOK THE FUTONS OUT OF THE CLOSET...
...SO YOU BETTER BE PREPARED, YOU KNOW?
um

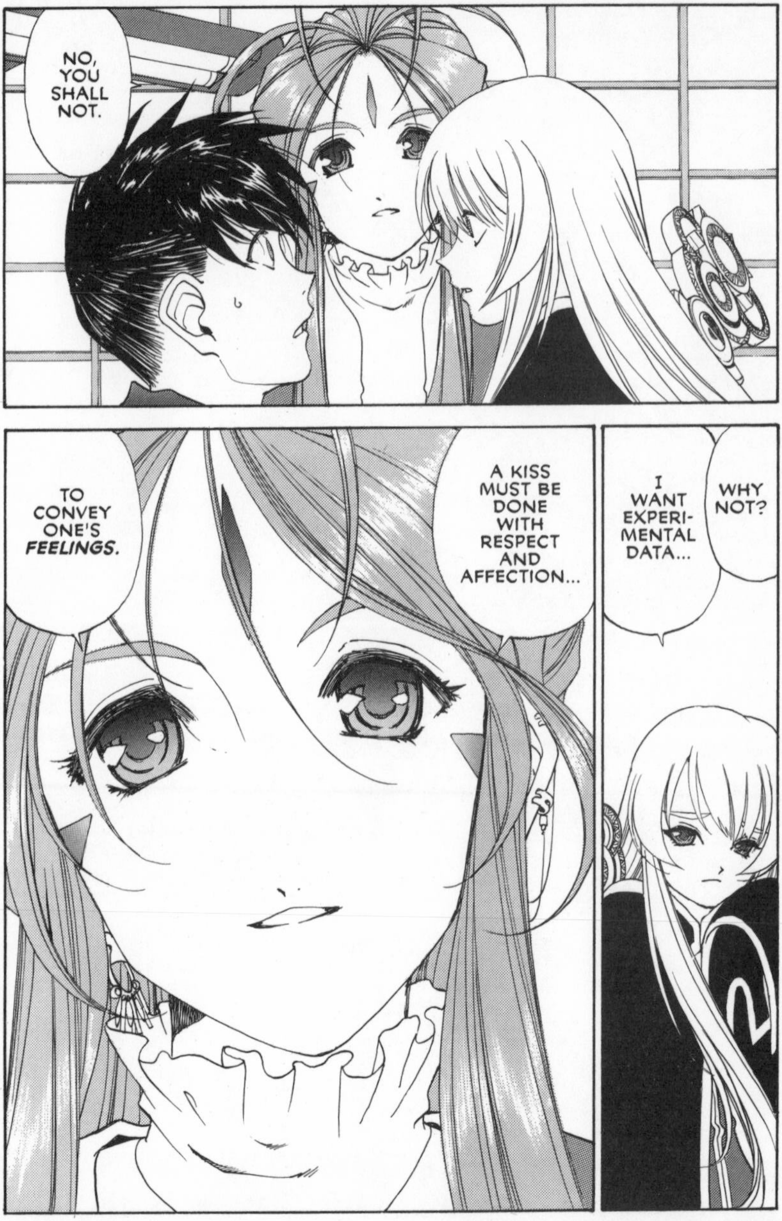
NO, YOU SHALL NOT.
WHY NOT?
I WANT EXPERIMENTAL DATA...
A KISS MUST BE DONE WITH RESPECT AND AFFECTION...
TO CONVEY ONE'S *FEELINGS.*

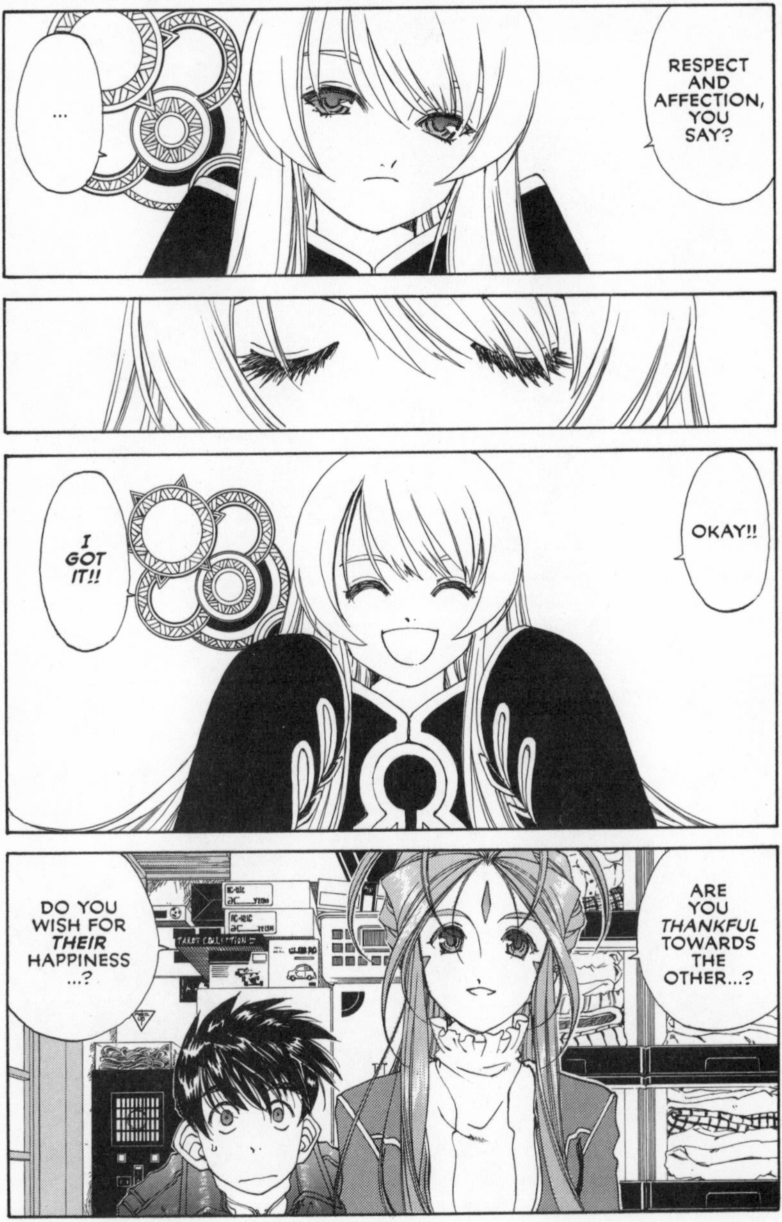
RESPECT AND AFFECTION, YOU SAY?
...
OKAY!!
I GOT IT!!
ARE YOU *THANKFUL* TOWARDS THE OTHER...?
DO YOU WISH FOR ***THEIR*** HAPPINESS ...?

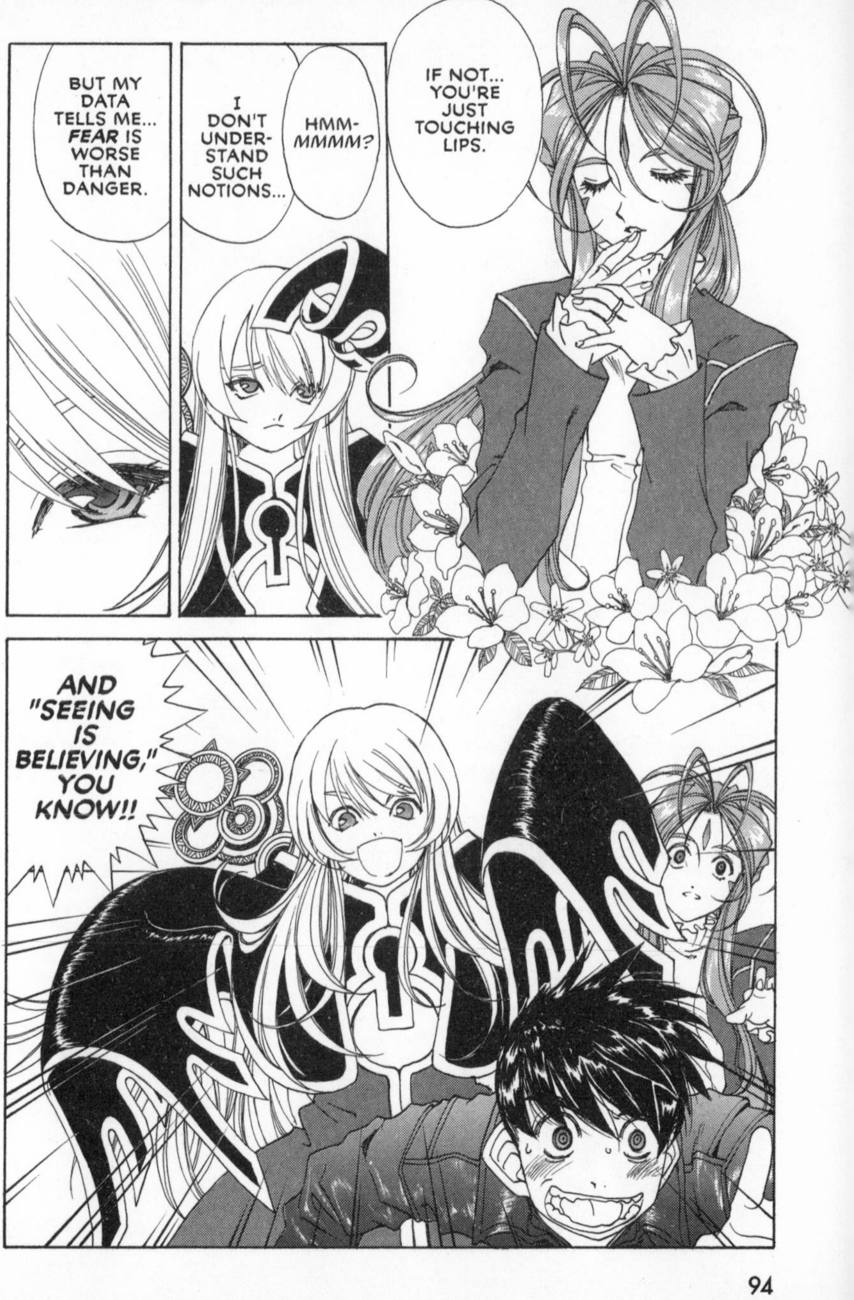
IF NOT... YOU'RE JUST TOUCHING LIPS.
HMM-MMMM?
I DON'T UNDER-STAND SUCH NOTIONS...
BUT MY DATA TELLS ME... *FEAR* IS WORSE THAN DANGER.
AND "SEEING IS BELIEVING," YOU KNOW!!

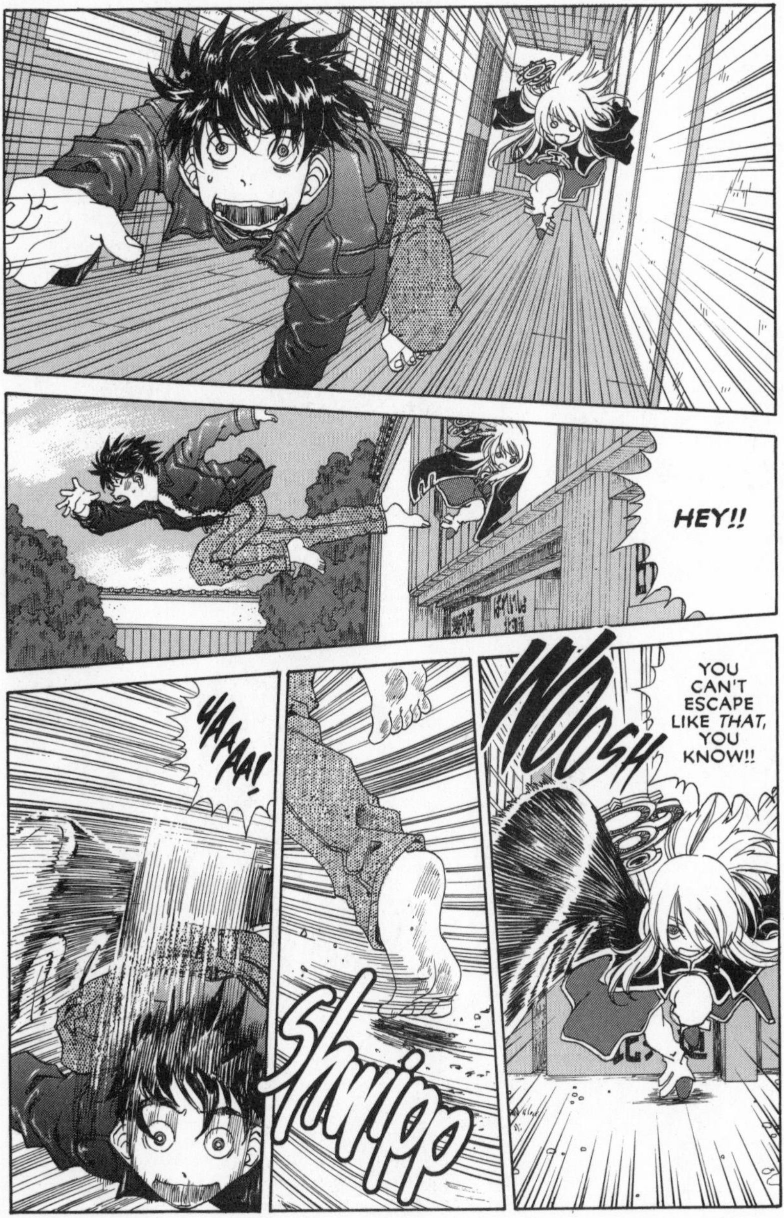
HEY!!
WOOSH
YOU CAN'T ESCAPE LIKE *THAT*, YOU KNOW!!
Shwipp
UAAAAA!

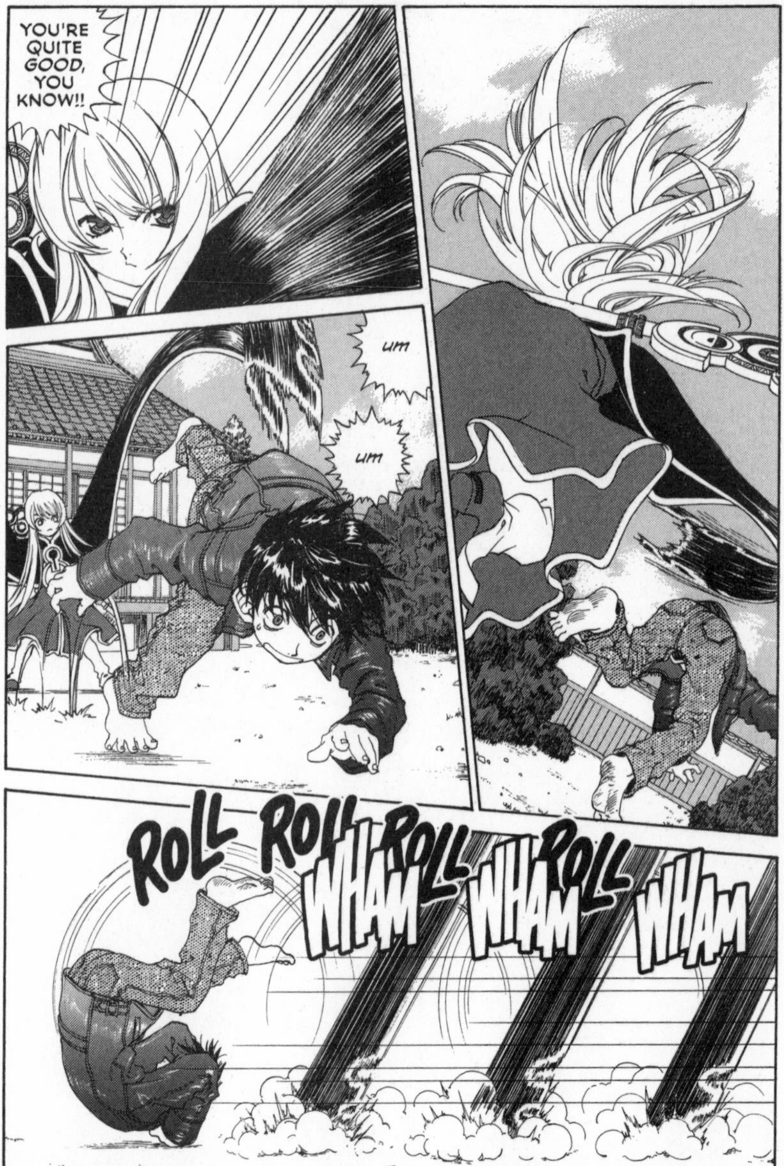
YOU'RE QUITE GOOD, YOU KNOW!!
um
um
ROLL ROLL ROLL ROLL
WHAM WHAM WHAM

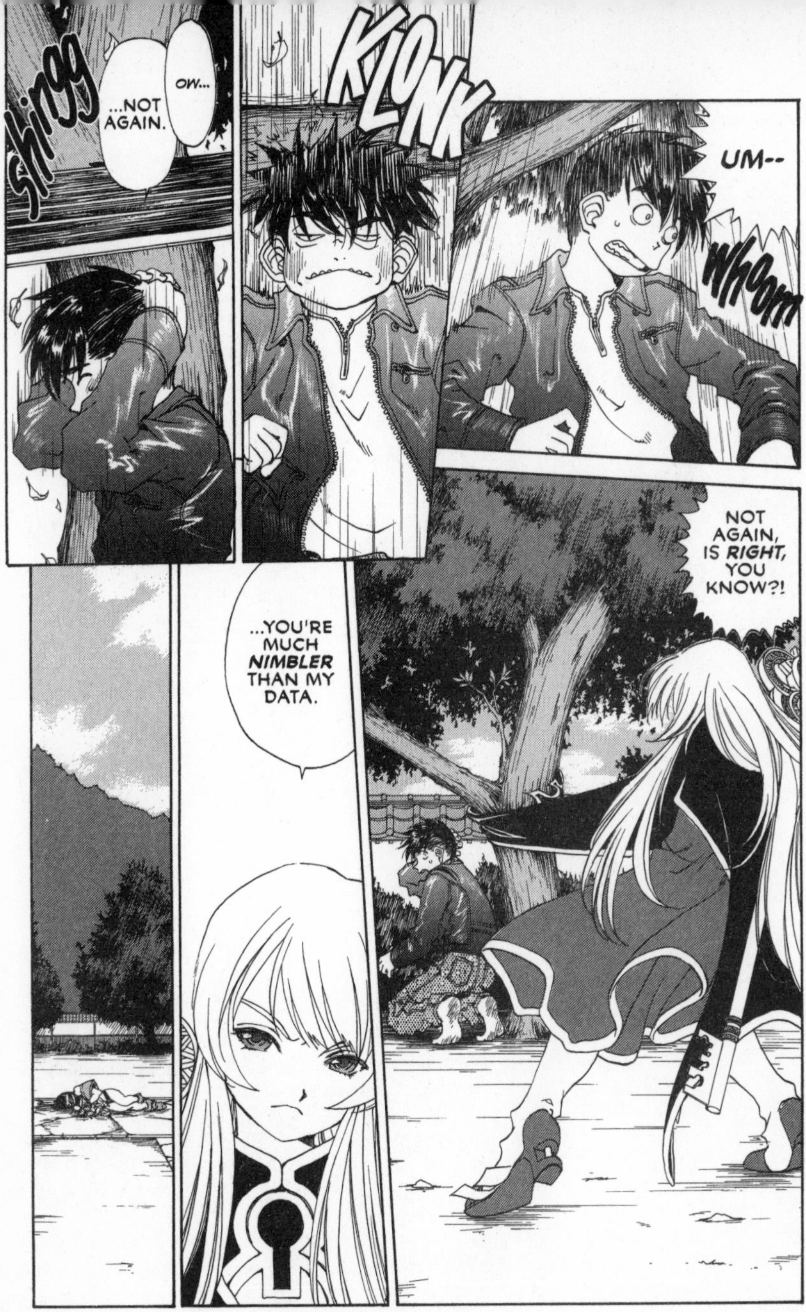
UM--
whoom
KLONK
Shingg
OW...
...NOT AGAIN.
NOT AGAIN, IS RIGHT, YOU KNOW?!
...YOU'RE MUCH NIMBLER THAN MY DATA.

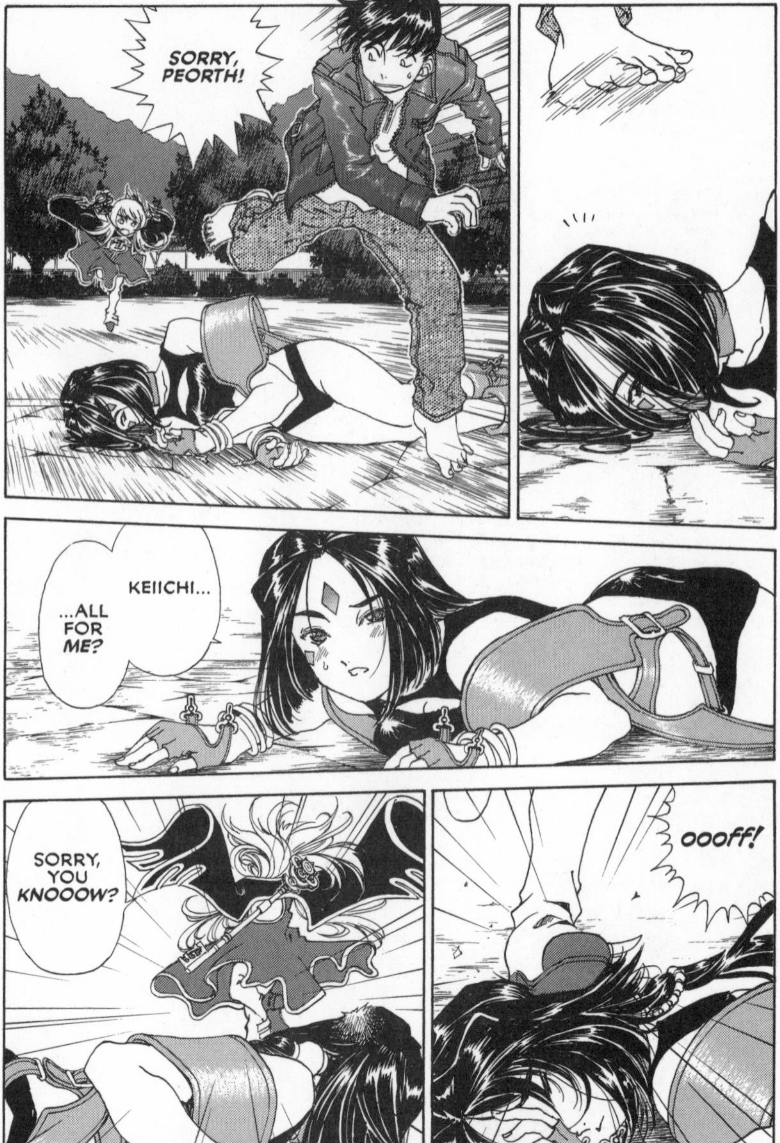
SORRY, PEORTH!
KEIICHI...
...ALL FOR ME?
oooff!
SORRY, YOU KNOOOW?

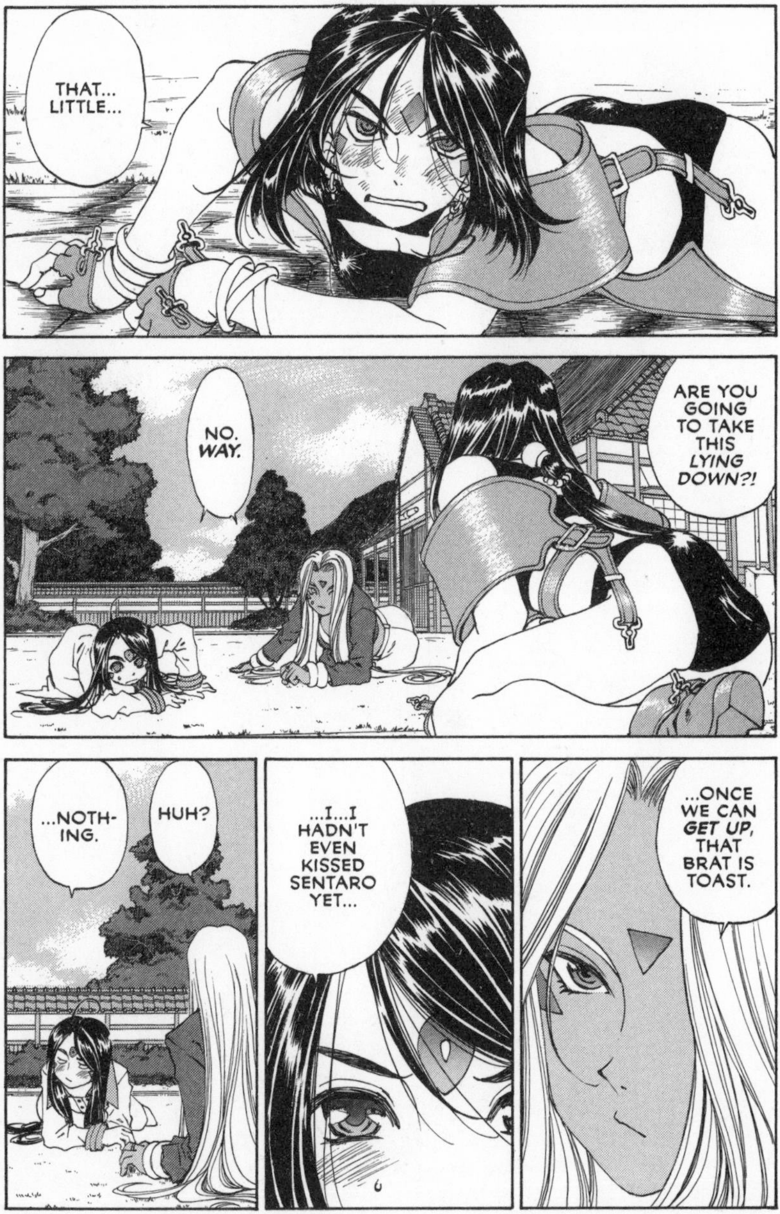
THAT... LITTLE...
ARE YOU GOING TO TAKE THIS *LYING DOWN?!*
NO. *WAY.*
...ONCE WE CAN *GET UP,* THAT BRAT IS TOAST.
...I...I HADN'T EVEN KISSED SENTARO YET...
HUH?
...NOTH-ING.

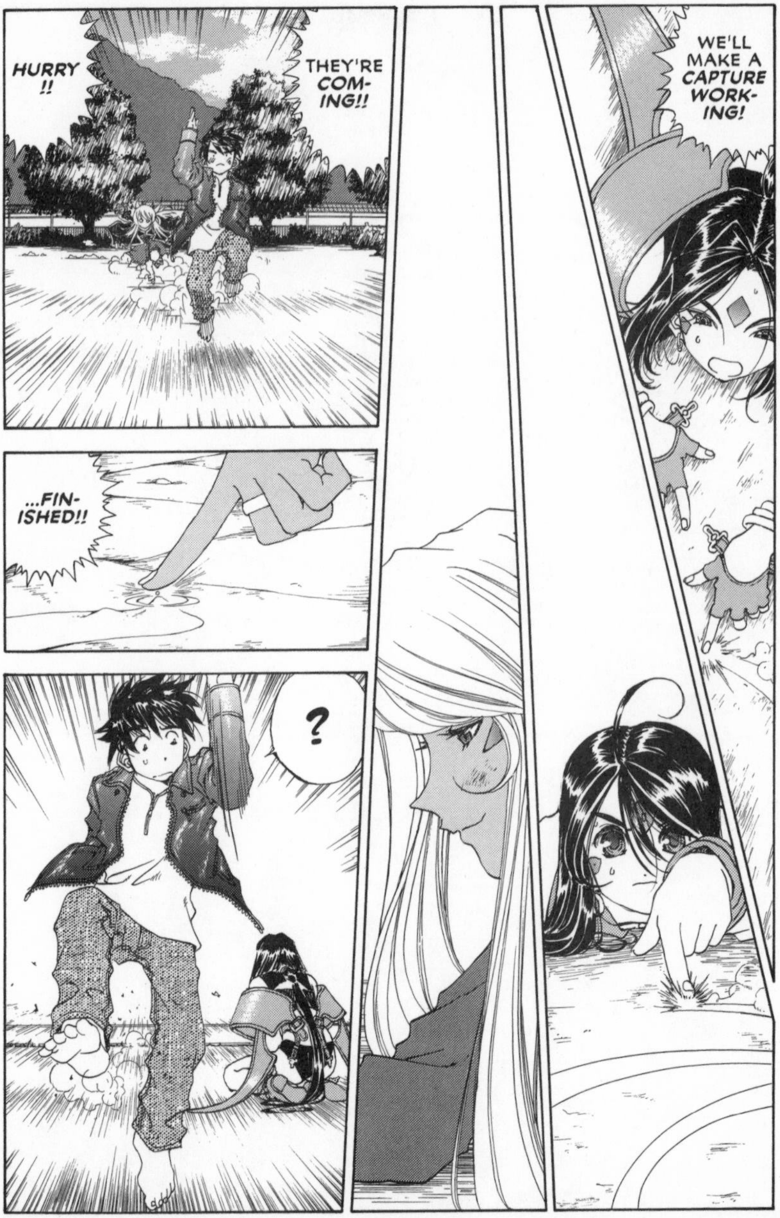
WE'LL MAKE A CAPTURE WORKING!
THEY'RE COMING!!
HURRY!!
...FINISHED!!
?

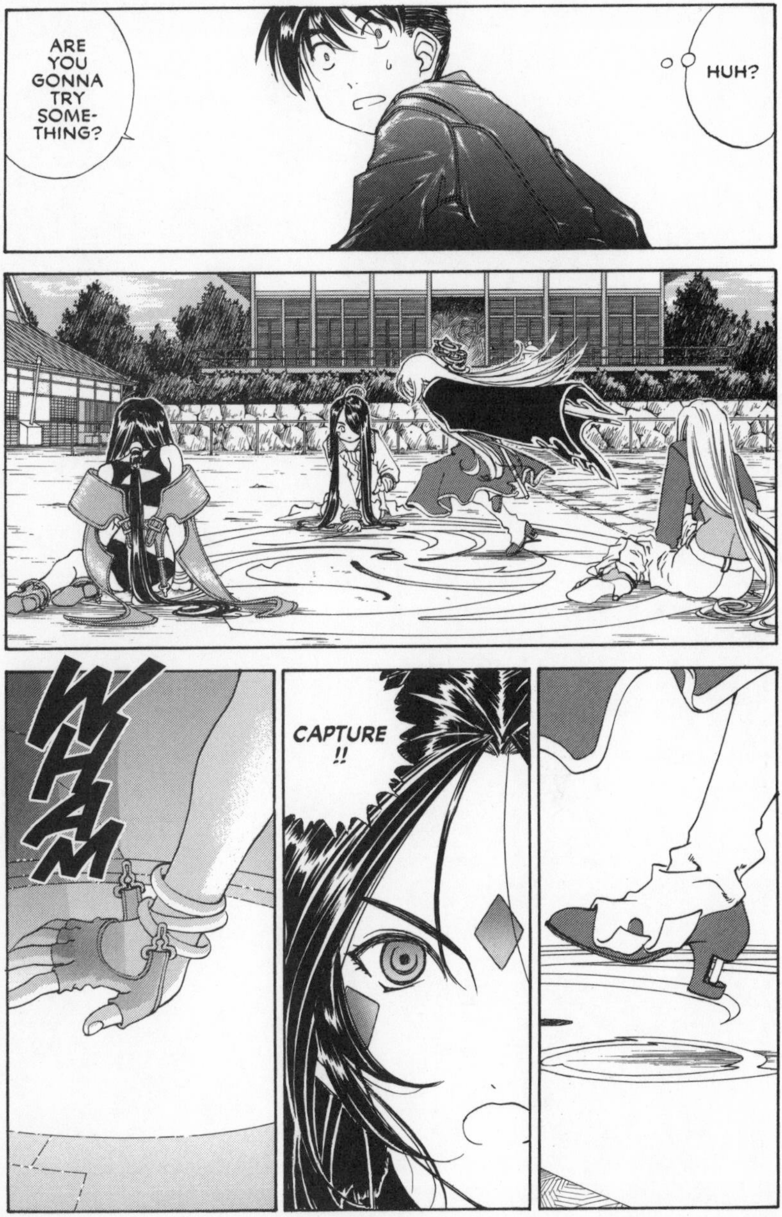
HUH?
ARE YOU GONNA TRY SOME-THING?
CAPTURE !!
WHAM

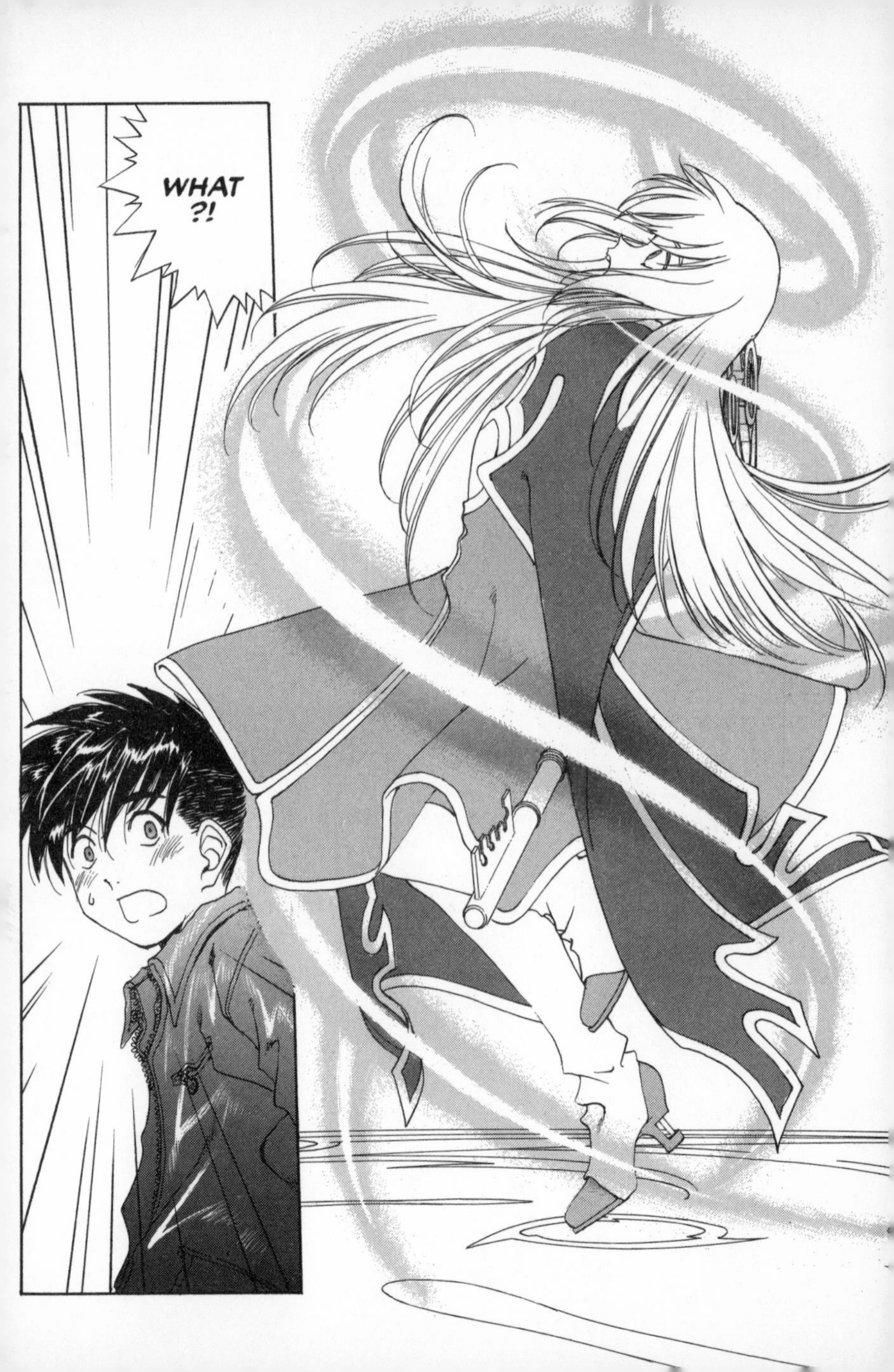
WHAT ?!

CHAPTER 199

A Goddess's Duty

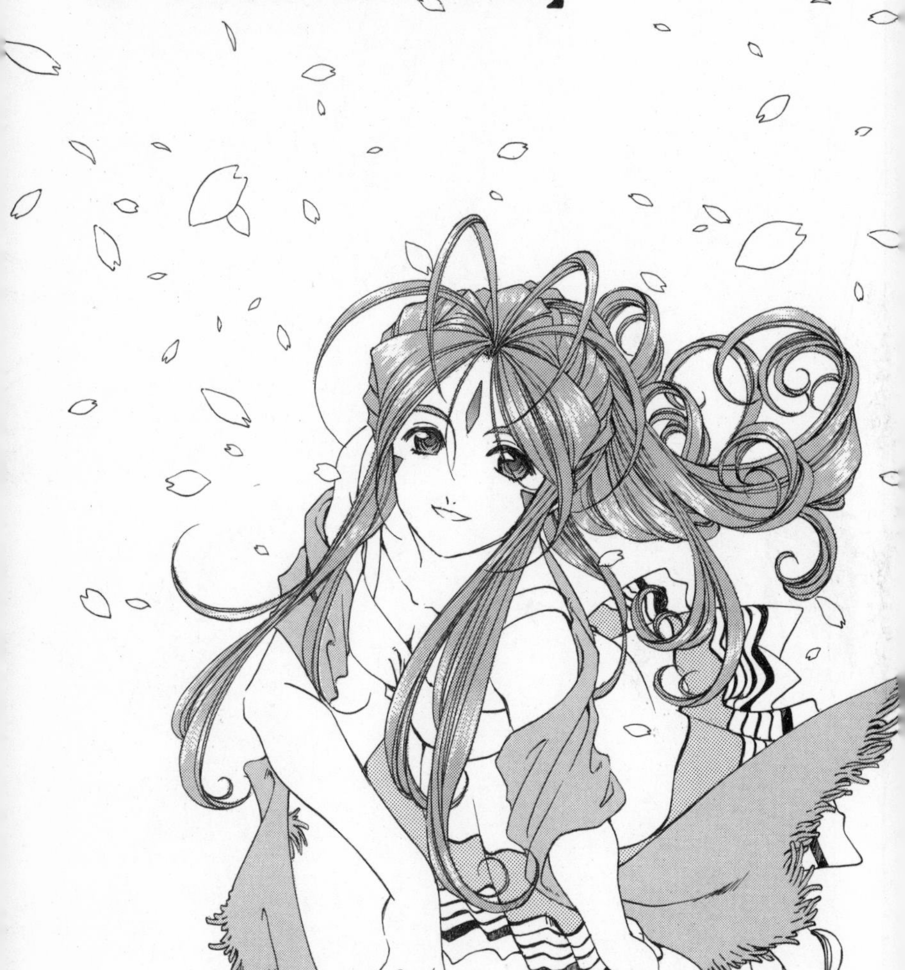

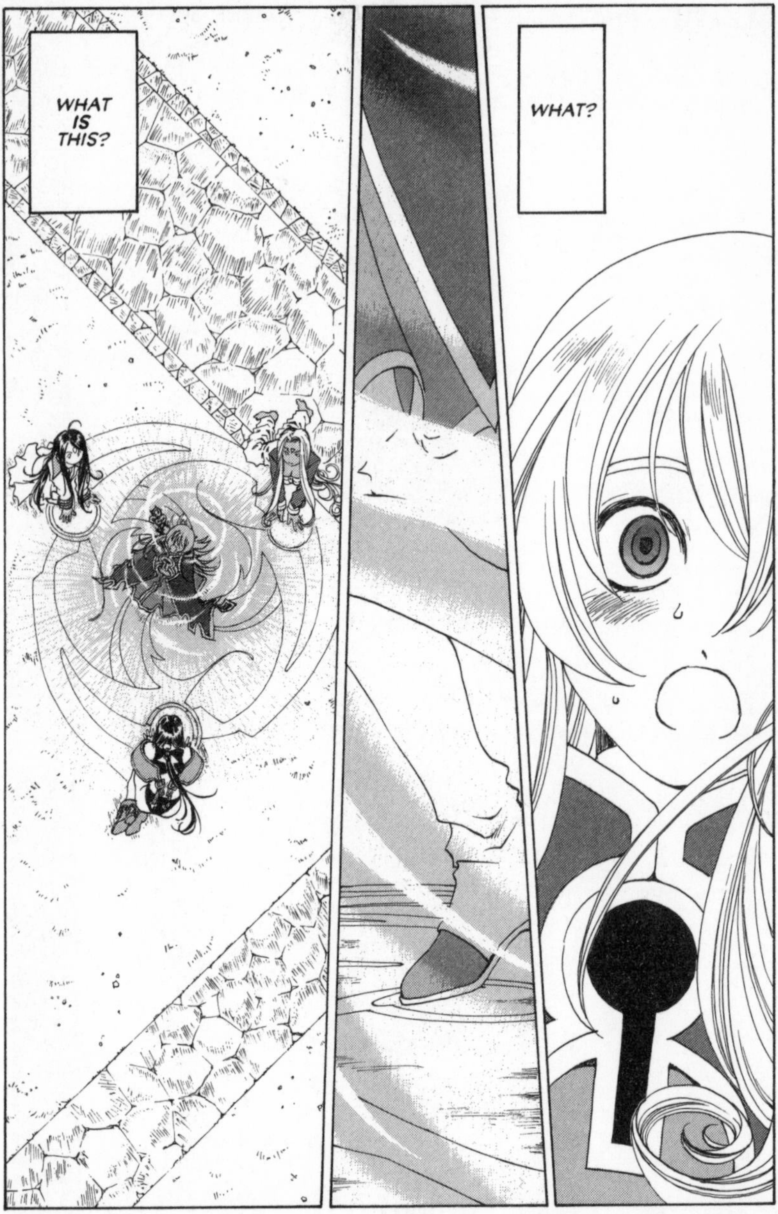
WHAT?
WHAT IS THIS?

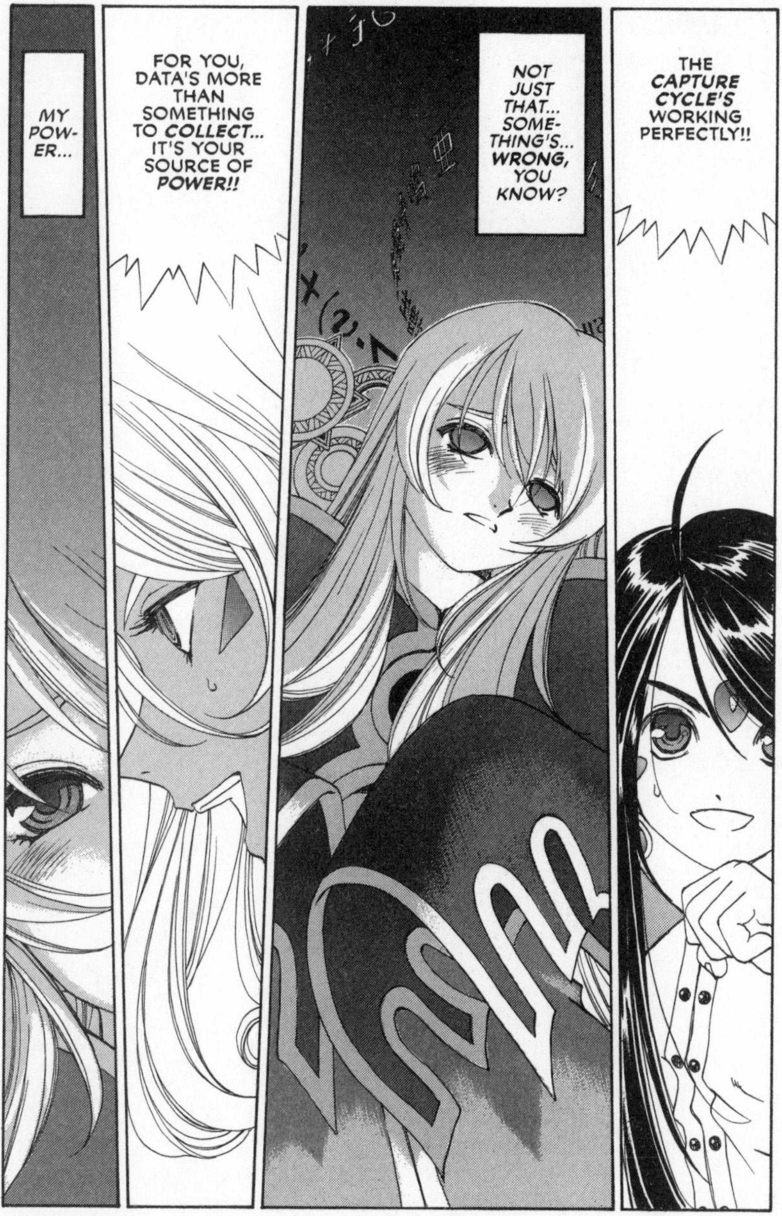
THE CAPTURE CYCLE'S WORKING PERFECTLY!!
NOT JUST THAT... SOMETHING'S... WRONG, YOU KNOW?
FOR YOU, DATA'S MORE THAN SOMETHING TO COLLECT... IT'S YOUR SOURCE OF POWER!!
MY POWER...

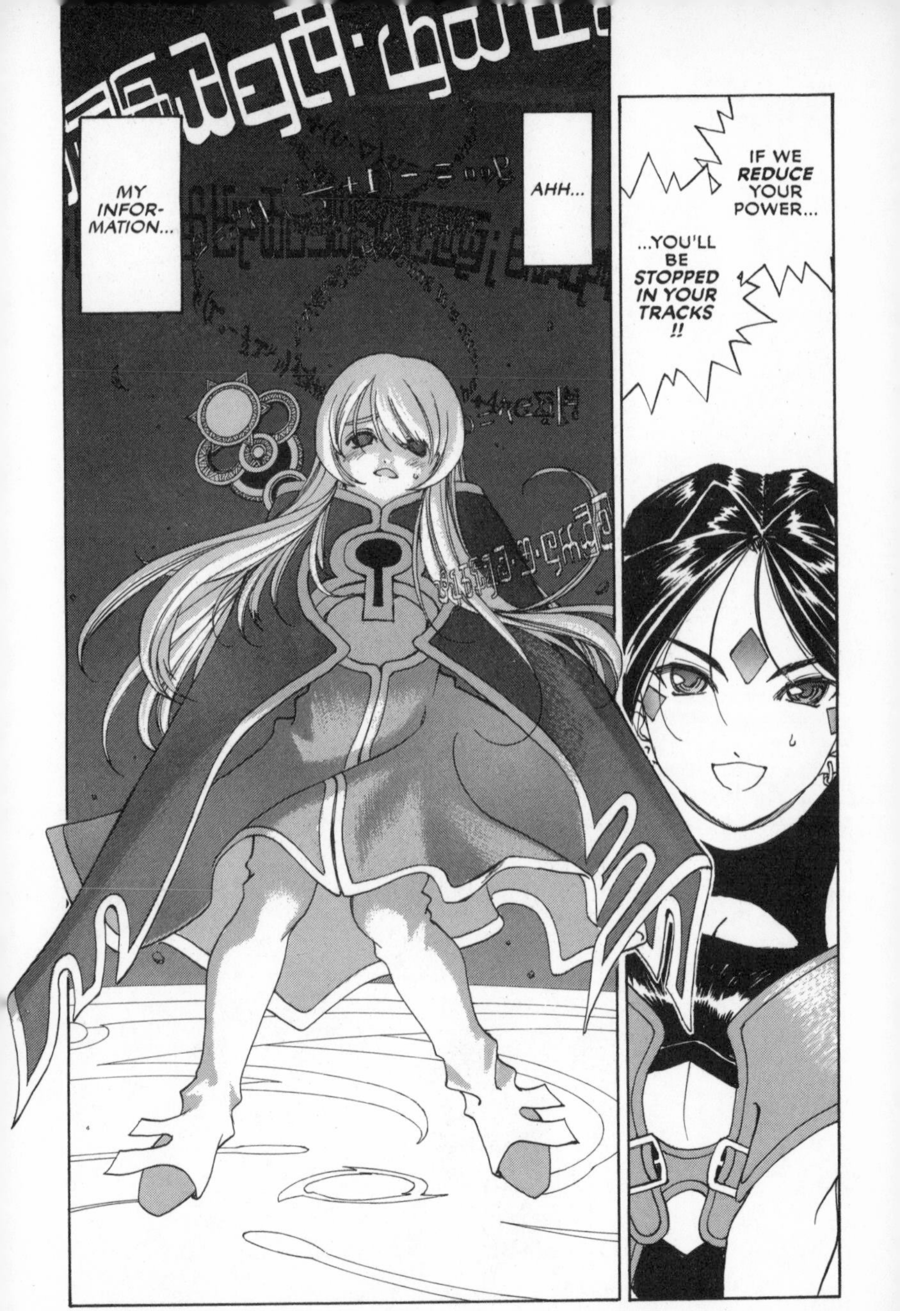
IF WE REDUCE YOUR POWER...
...YOU'LL BE STOPPED IN YOUR TRACKS !!
AHH...
MY INFORMATION...

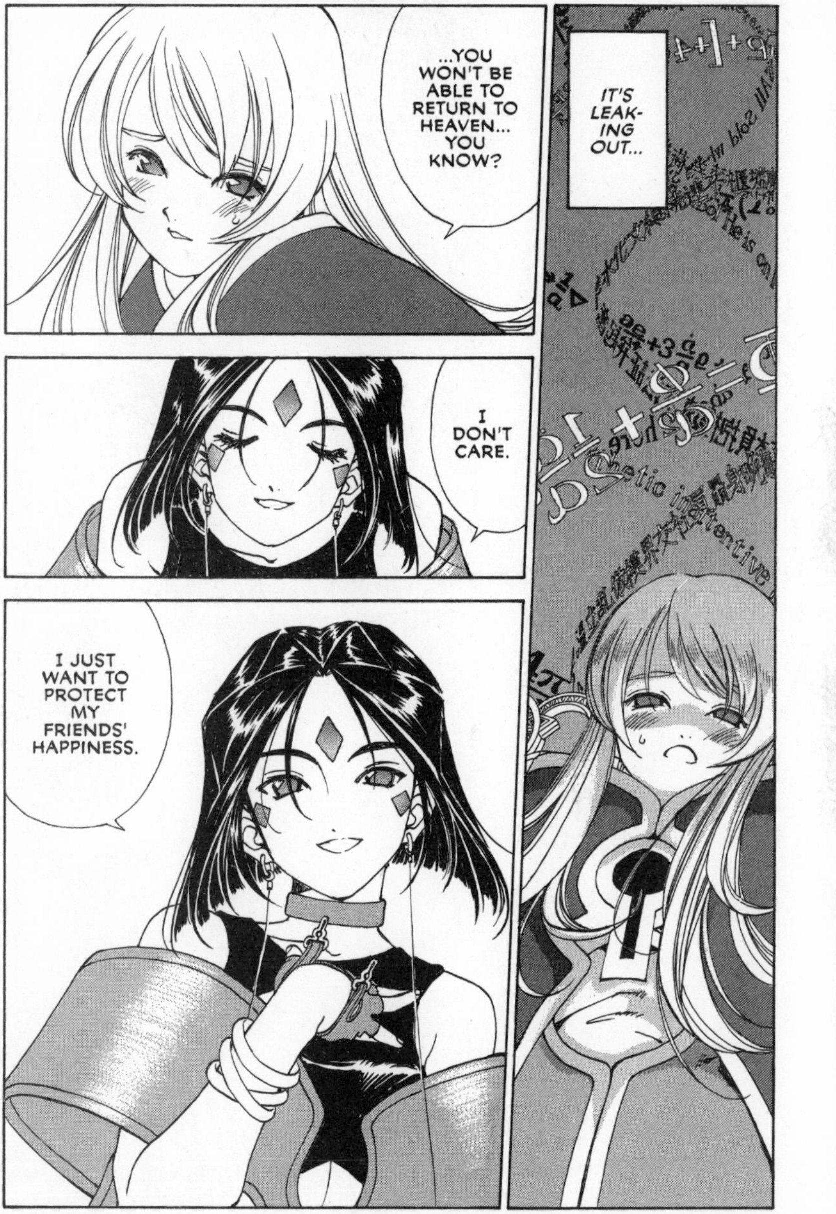
IT'S LEAK-ING OUT...
...YOU WON'T BE ABLE TO RETURN TO HEAVEN... YOU KNOW?
I DON'T CARE.
I JUST WANT TO PROTECT MY FRIENDS' HAPPINESS.

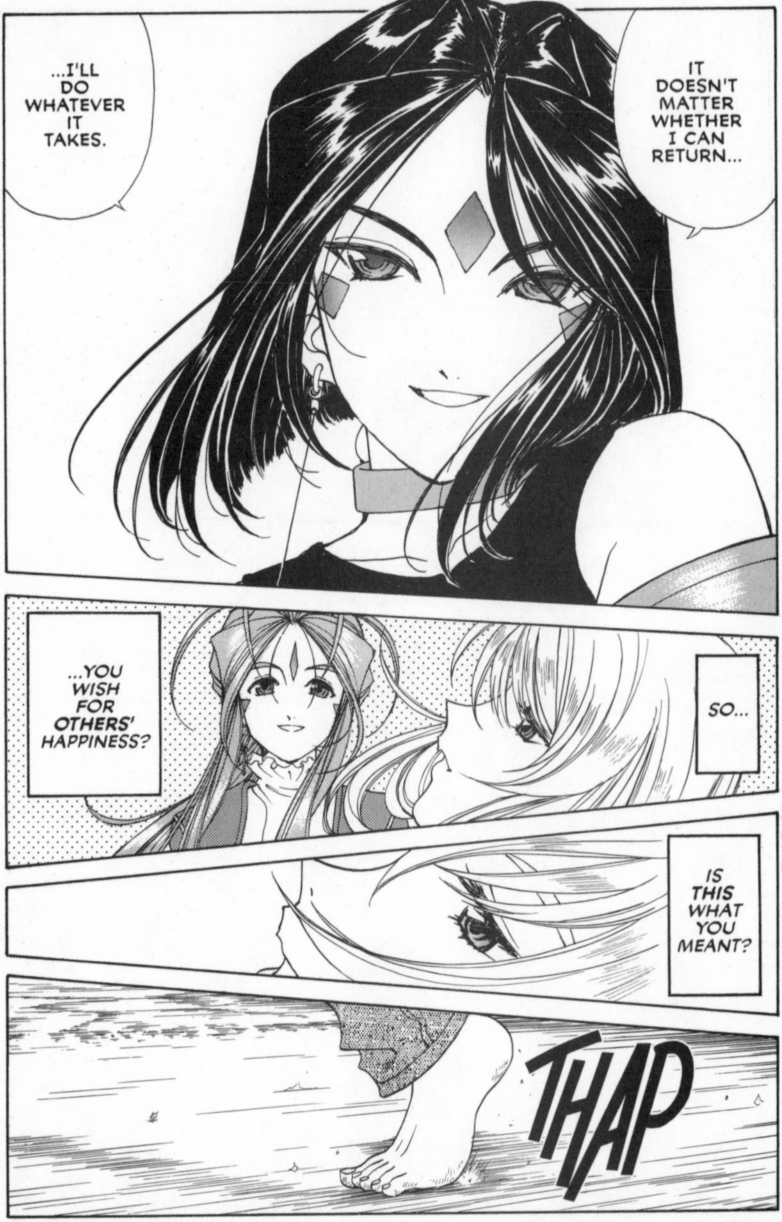
IT DOESN'T MATTER WHETHER I CAN RETURN...
...I'LL DO WHATEVER IT TAKES.
SO...
...YOU WISH FOR OTHERS' HAPPINESS?
IS THIS WHAT YOU MEANT?
THAP

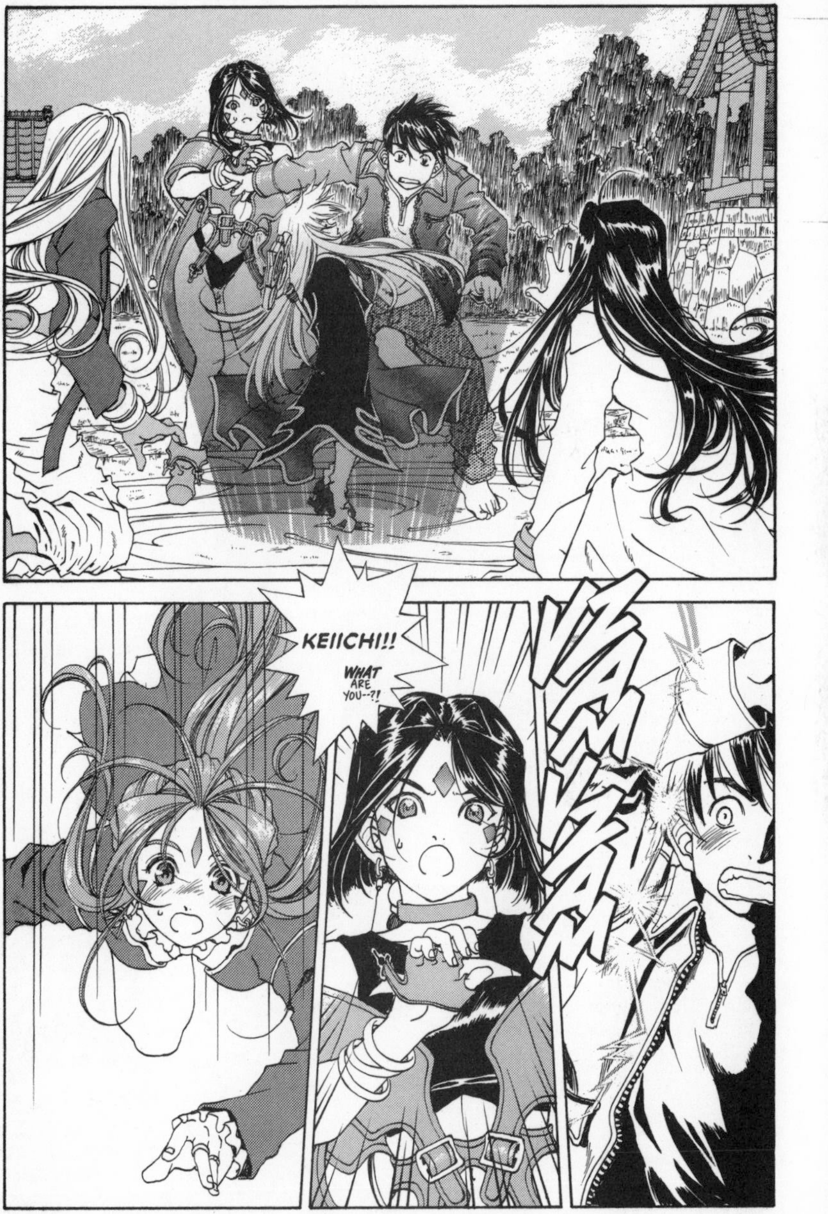
KEIICHI!!
WHAT ARE YOU--?!
WAMWAMWAM

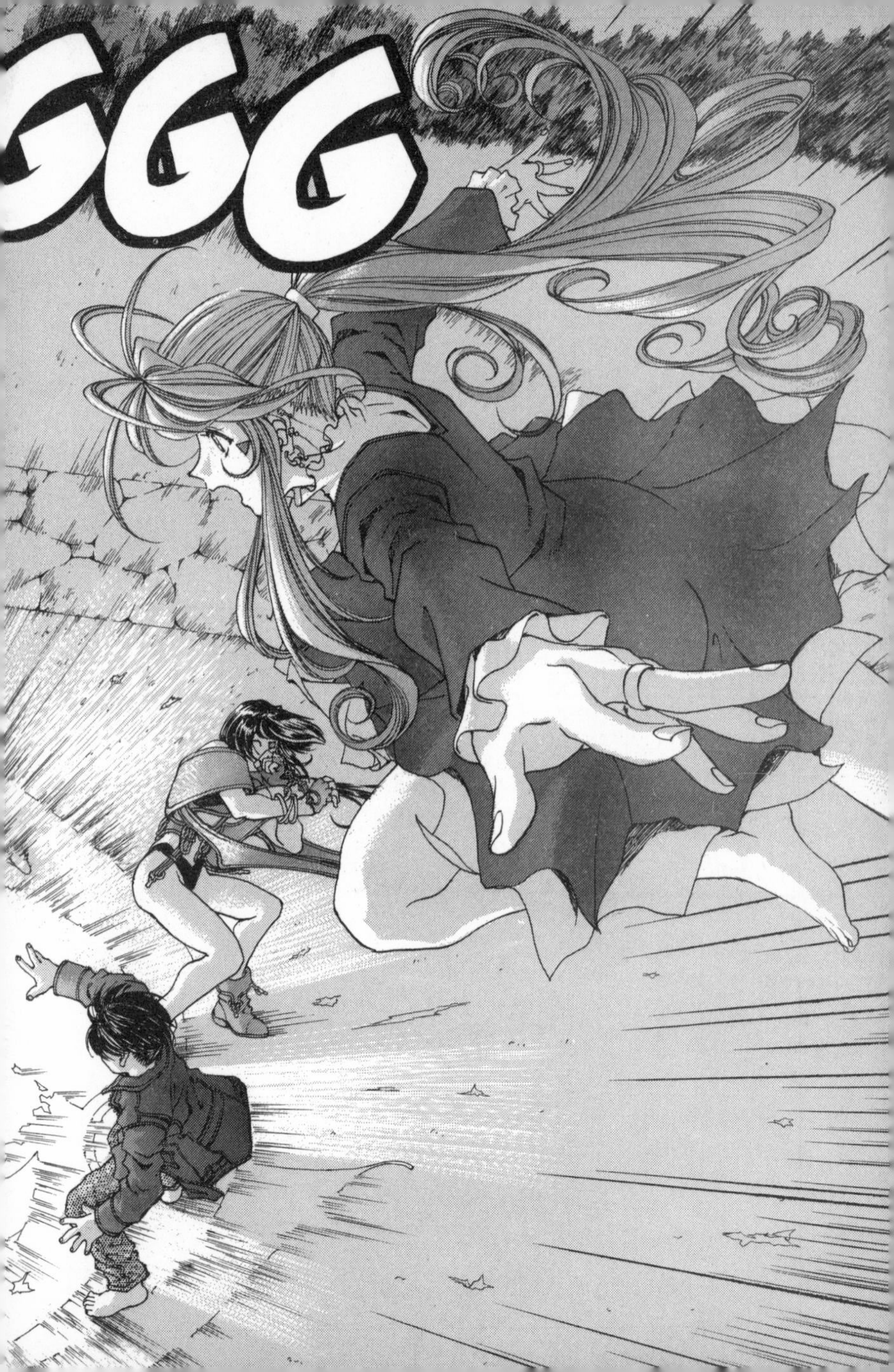
GGG

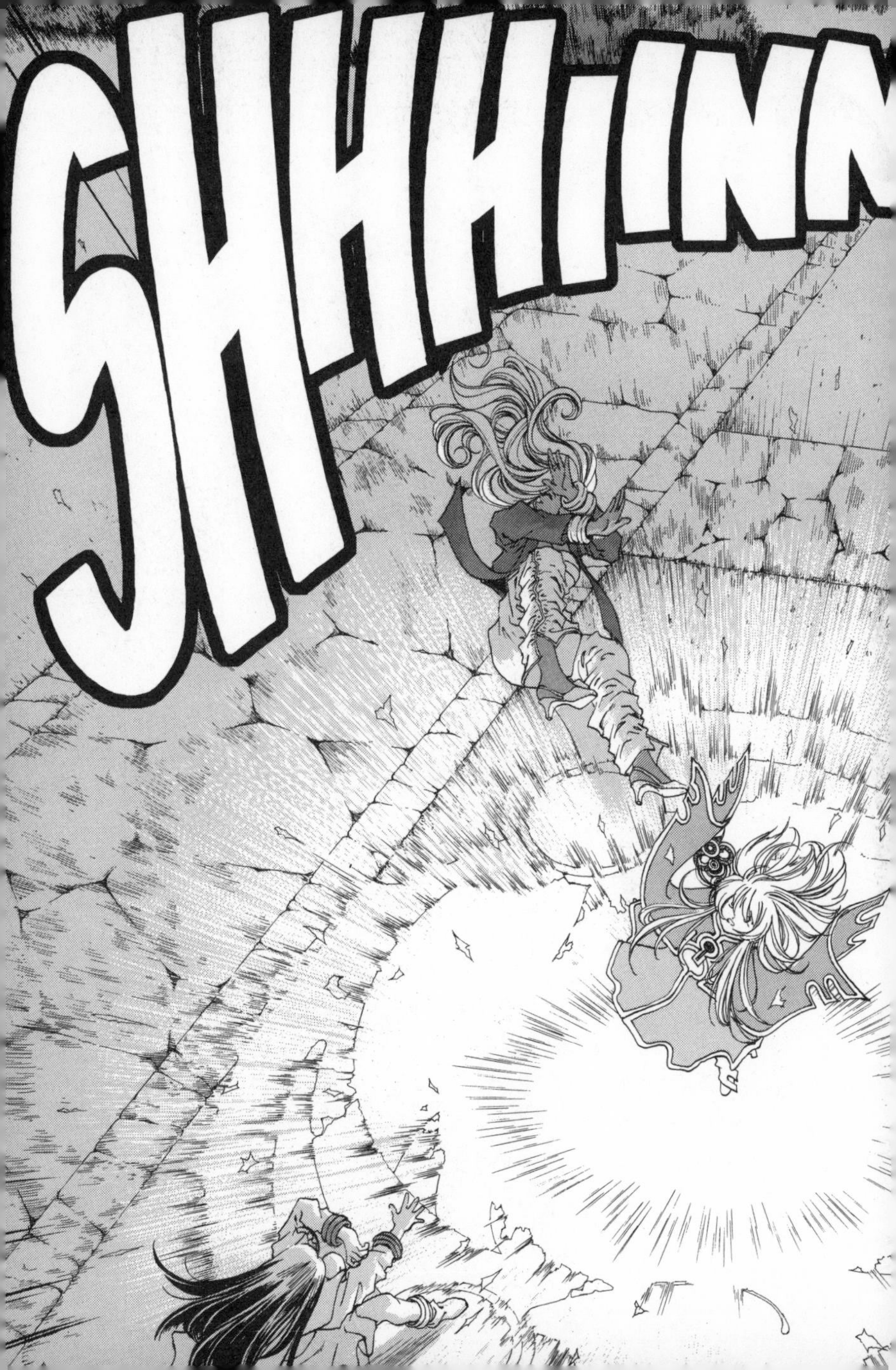
SHHHIINN

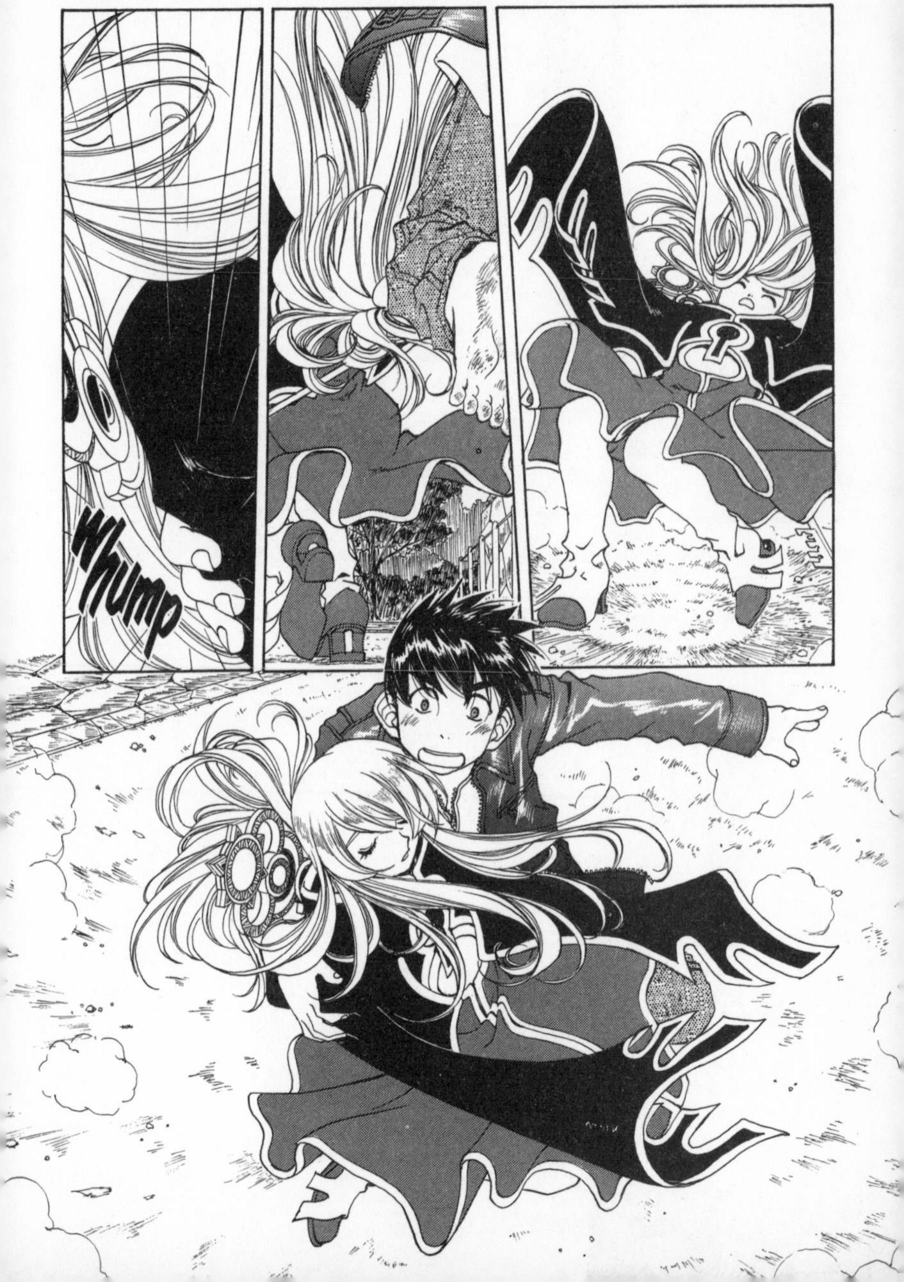
Whump

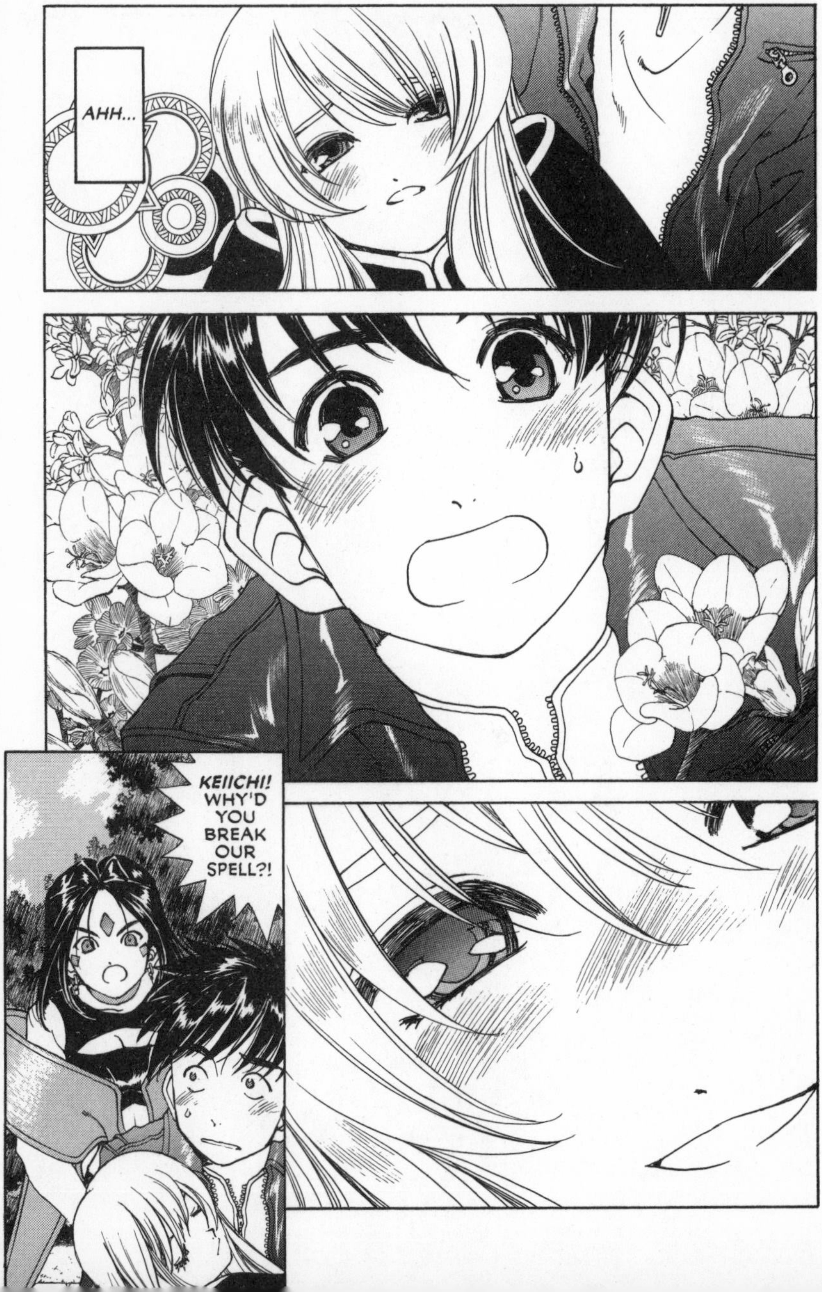
AHH...
KEIICHI! WHY'D YOU BREAK OUR SPELL?!

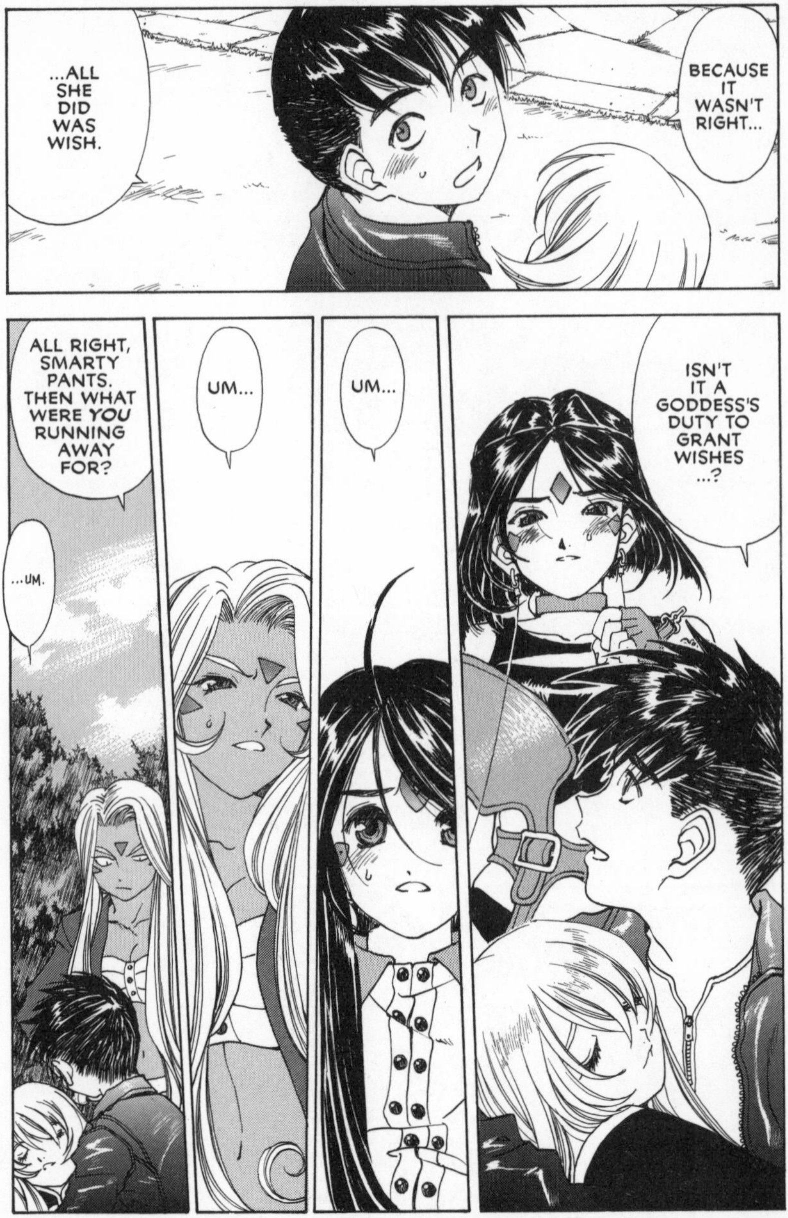
BECAUSE IT WASN'T RIGHT...
...ALL SHE DID WAS WISH.
ISN'T IT A GODDESS'S DUTY TO GRANT WISHES ...?
UM...
UM...
ALL RIGHT, SMARTY PANTS. THEN WHAT WERE *YOU* RUNNING AWAY FOR?
...UM.

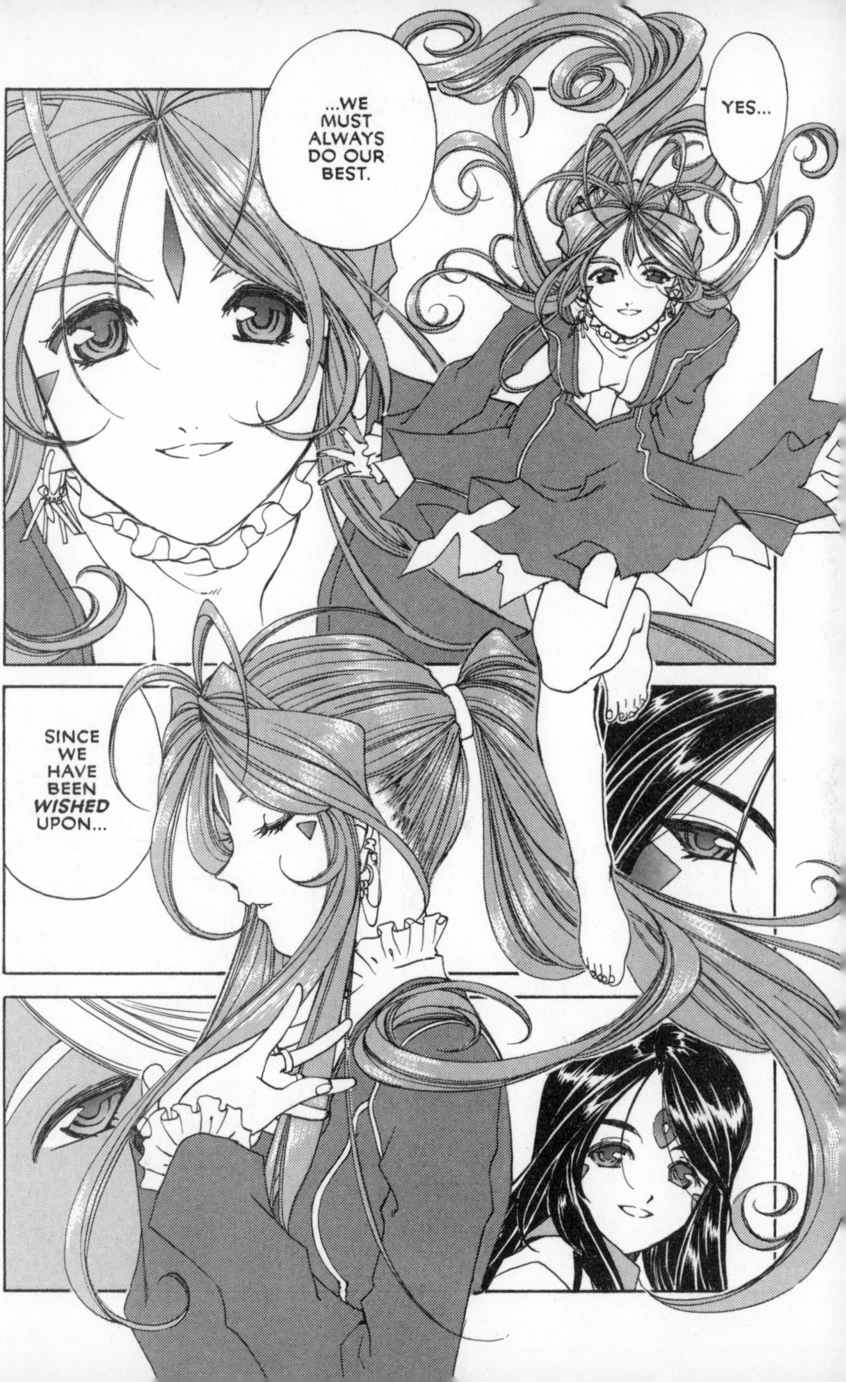
YES...
...WE MUST ALWAYS DO OUR BEST.
SINCE WE HAVE BEEN *WISHED* UPON...

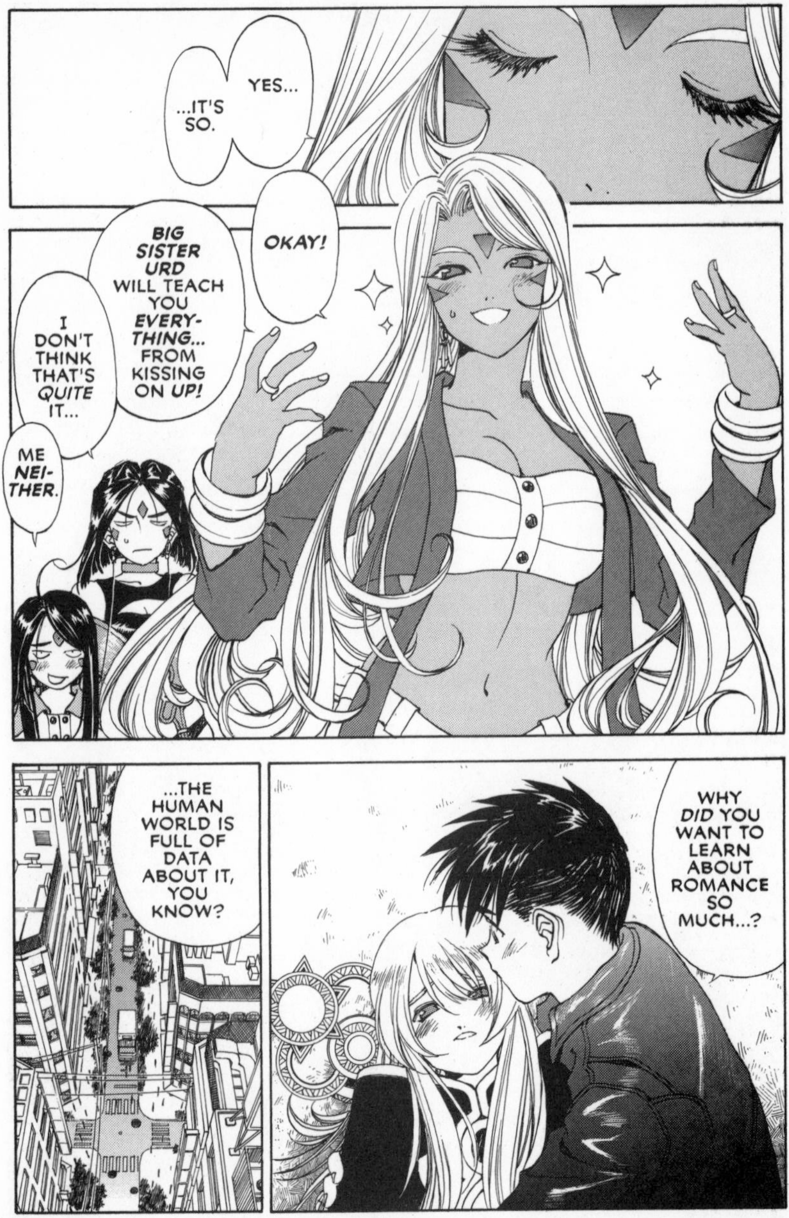
YES...
...IT'S SO.
OKAY!
BIG SISTER URD WILL TEACH YOU EVERYTHING... FROM KISSING ON UP!
I DON'T THINK THAT'S QUITE IT...
ME NEITHER.
WHY DID YOU WANT TO LEARN ABOUT ROMANCE SO MUCH...?
...THE HUMAN WORLD IS FULL OF DATA ABOUT IT, YOU KNOW?

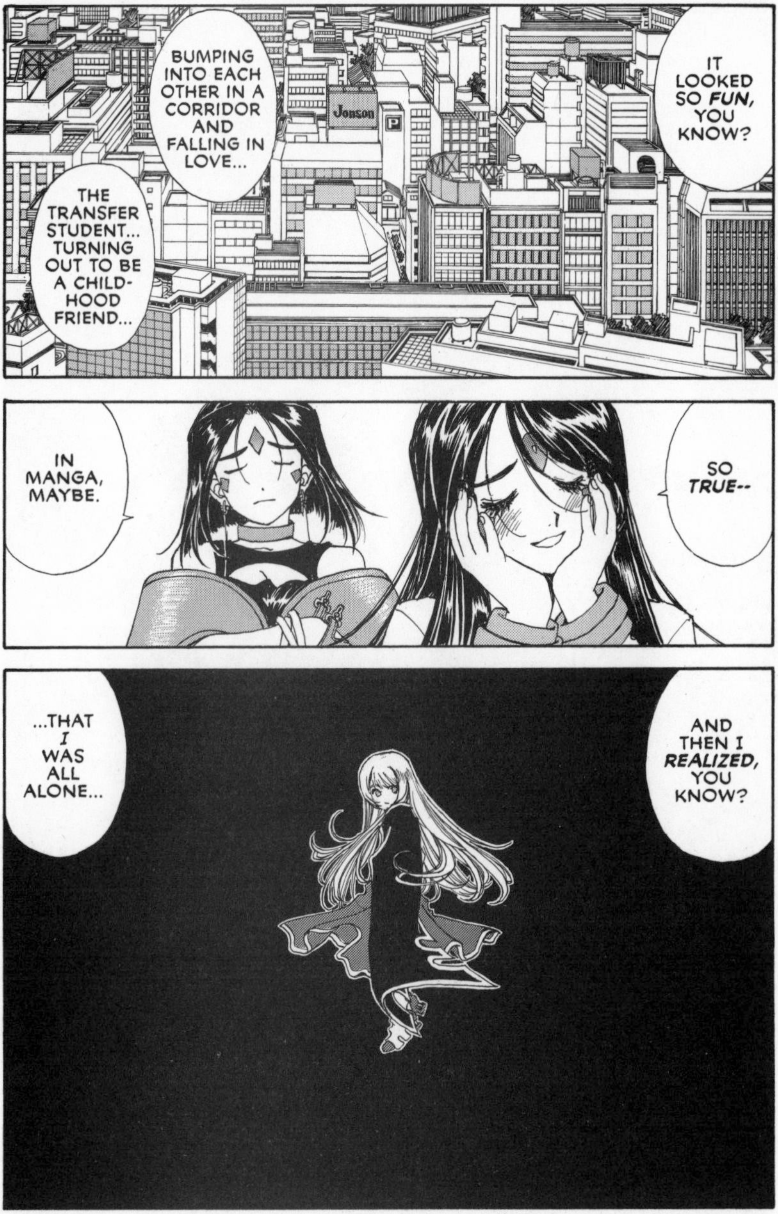
IT LOOKED SO *FUN,* YOU KNOW?
BUMPING INTO EACH OTHER IN A CORRIDOR AND FALLING IN LOVE...
Jonson
P
THE TRANSFER STUDENT... TURNING OUT TO BE A CHILD-HOOD FRIEND...
SO *TRUE--*
IN MANGA, MAYBE.
AND THEN I *REALIZED,* YOU KNOW?
...THAT *I* WAS ALL ALONE...

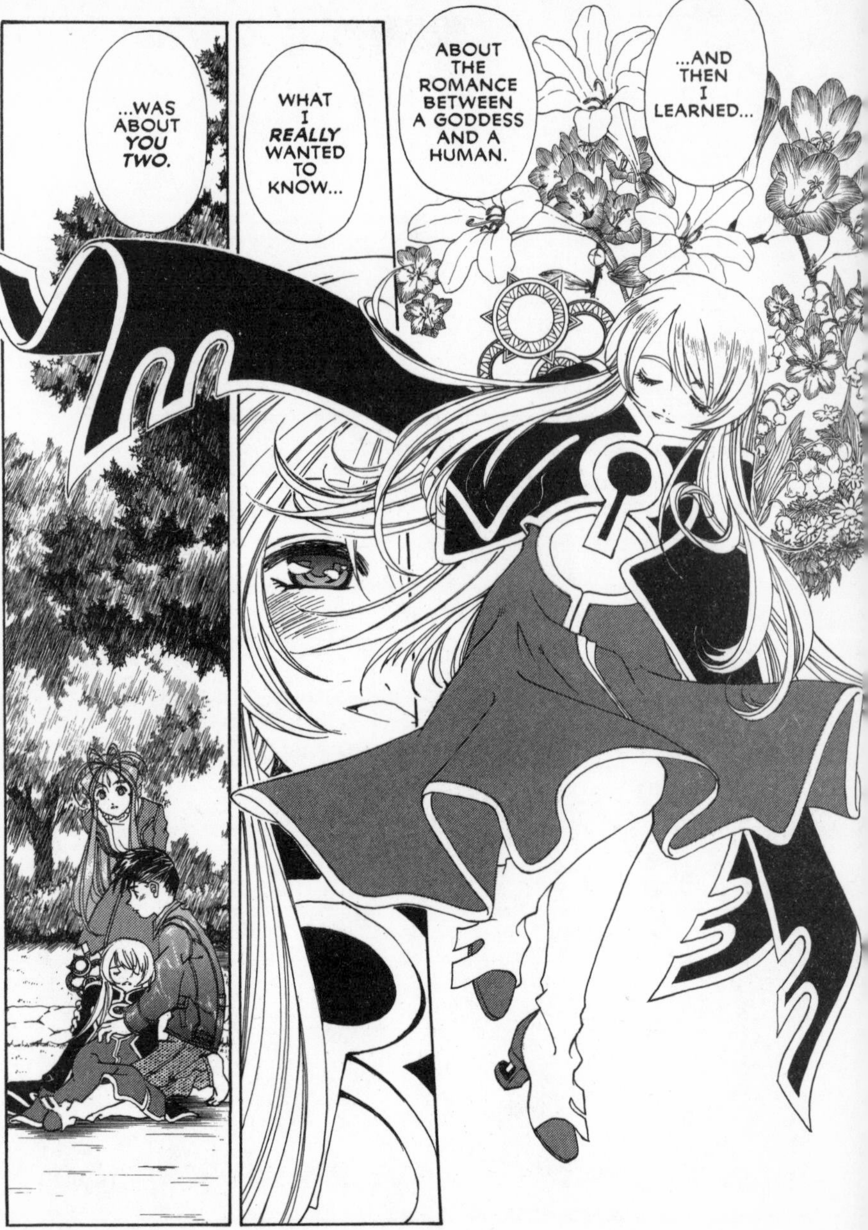
...AND THEN I LEARNED...
ABOUT THE ROMANCE BETWEEN A GODDESS AND A HUMAN.
WHAT I *REALLY* WANTED TO KNOW...
...WAS ABOUT *YOU TWO.*

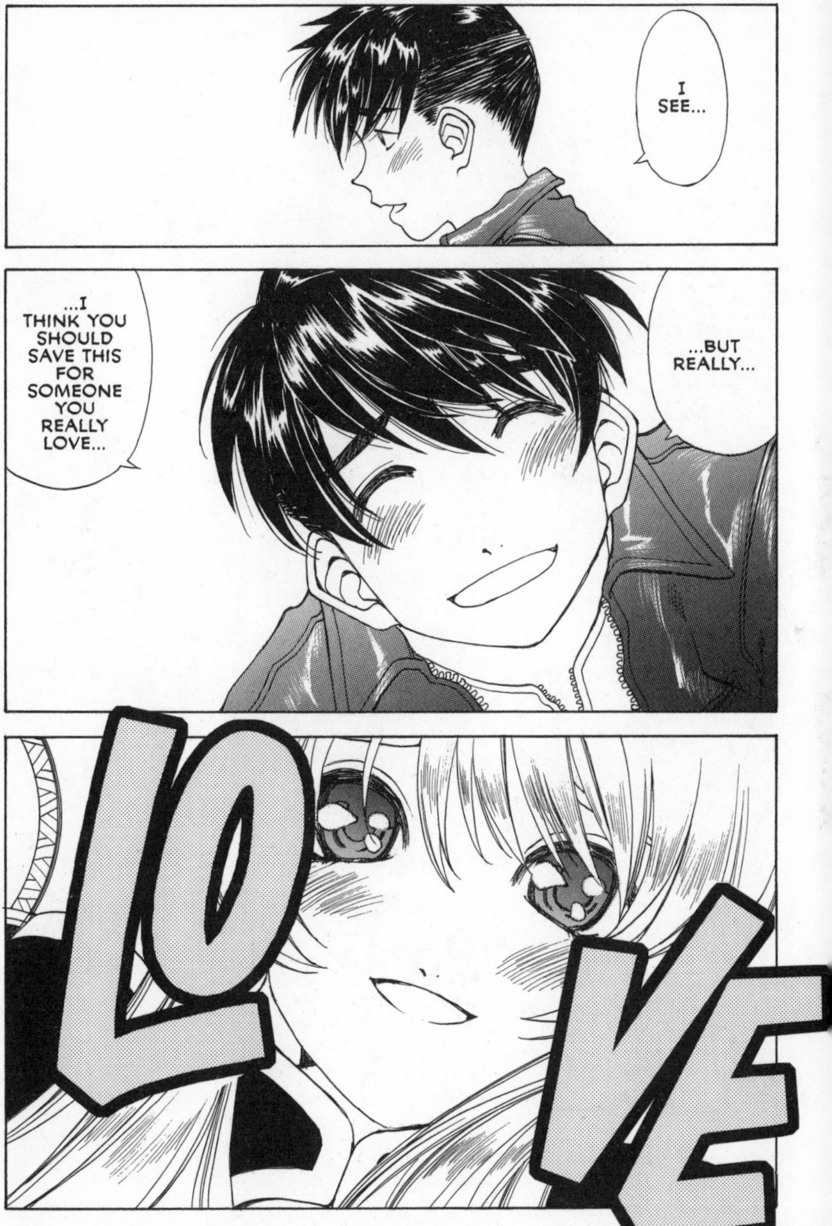
I SEE...
...BUT REALLY...
...I THINK YOU SHOULD SAVE THIS FOR SOMEONE YOU REALLY LOVE...
LOVE

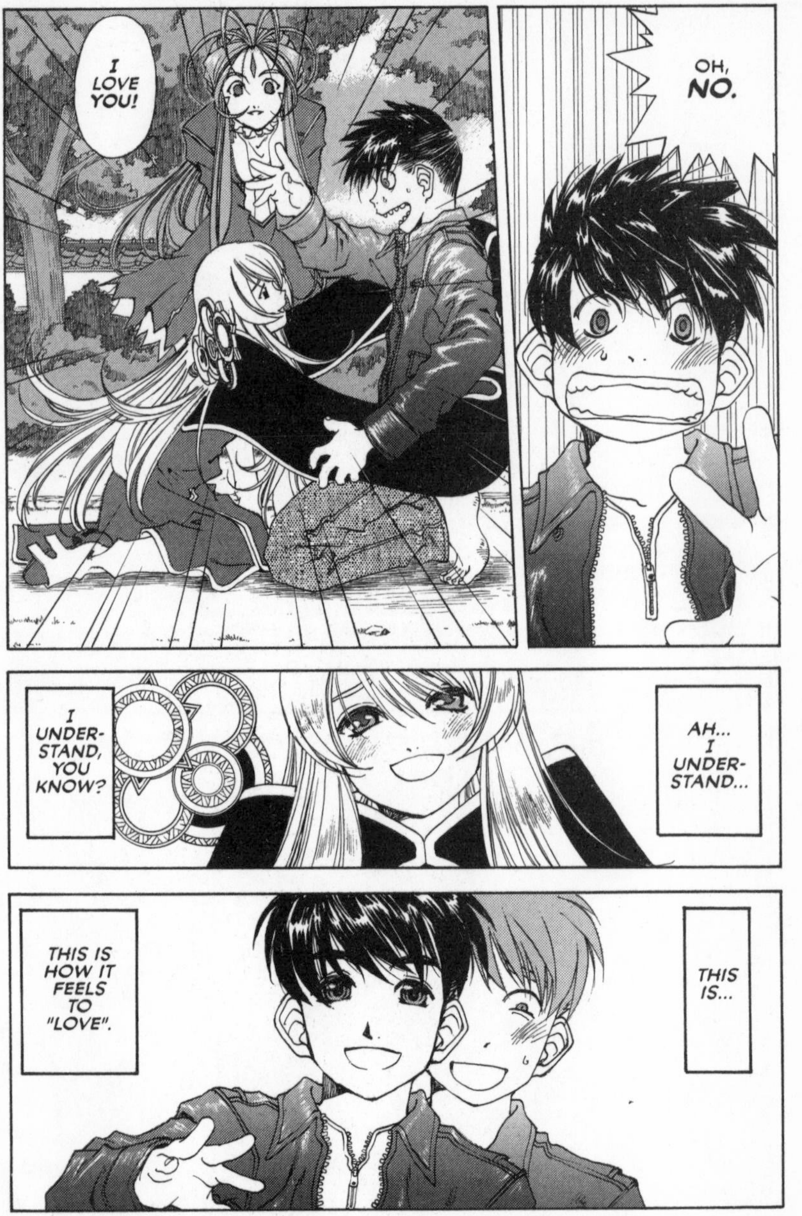
OH, NO.
I LOVE YOU!
AH... I UNDER-STAND...
I UNDER-STAND, YOU KNOW?
THIS IS...
THIS IS HOW IT FEELS TO "LOVE".

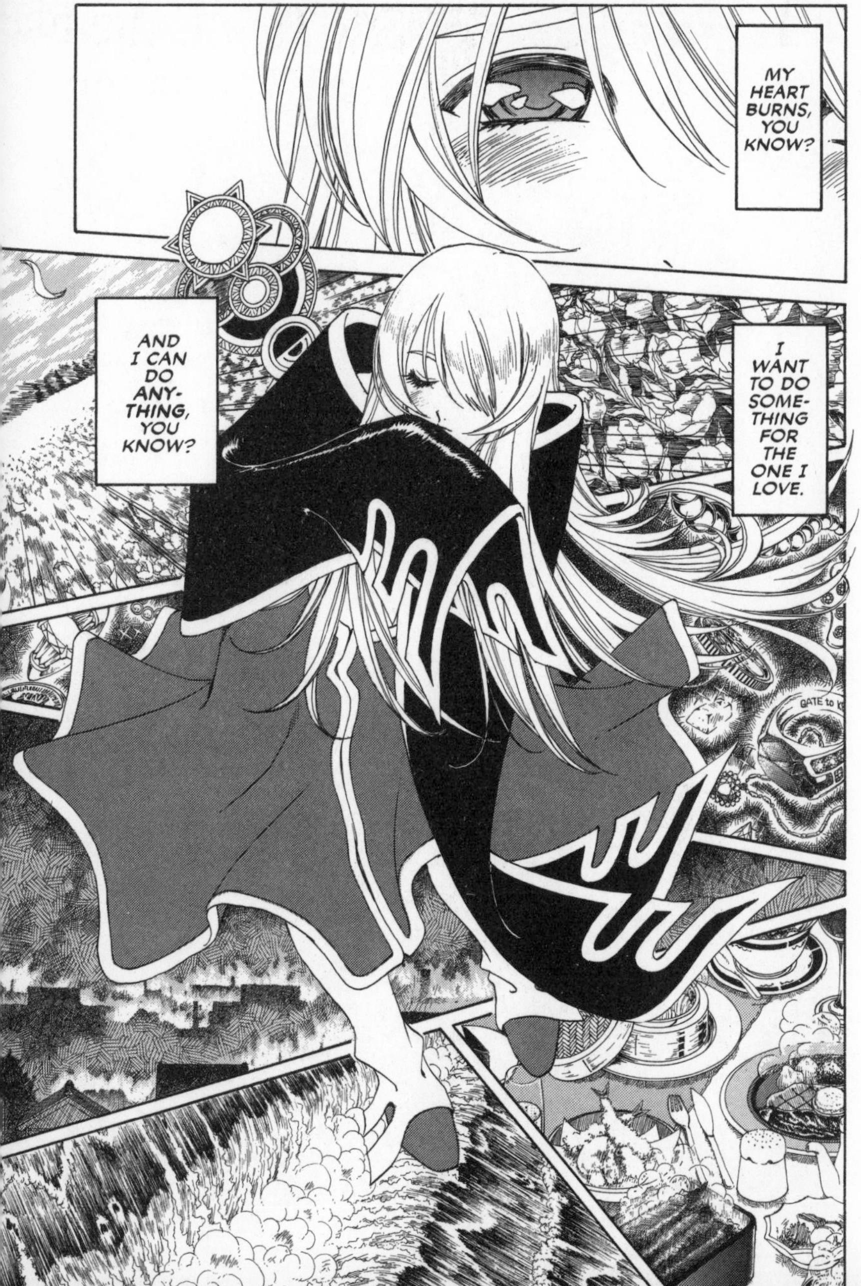
MY HEART BURNS, YOU KNOW?
I WANT TO DO SOMETHING FOR THE ONE I LOVE.
AND I CAN DO ANYTHING, YOU KNOW?

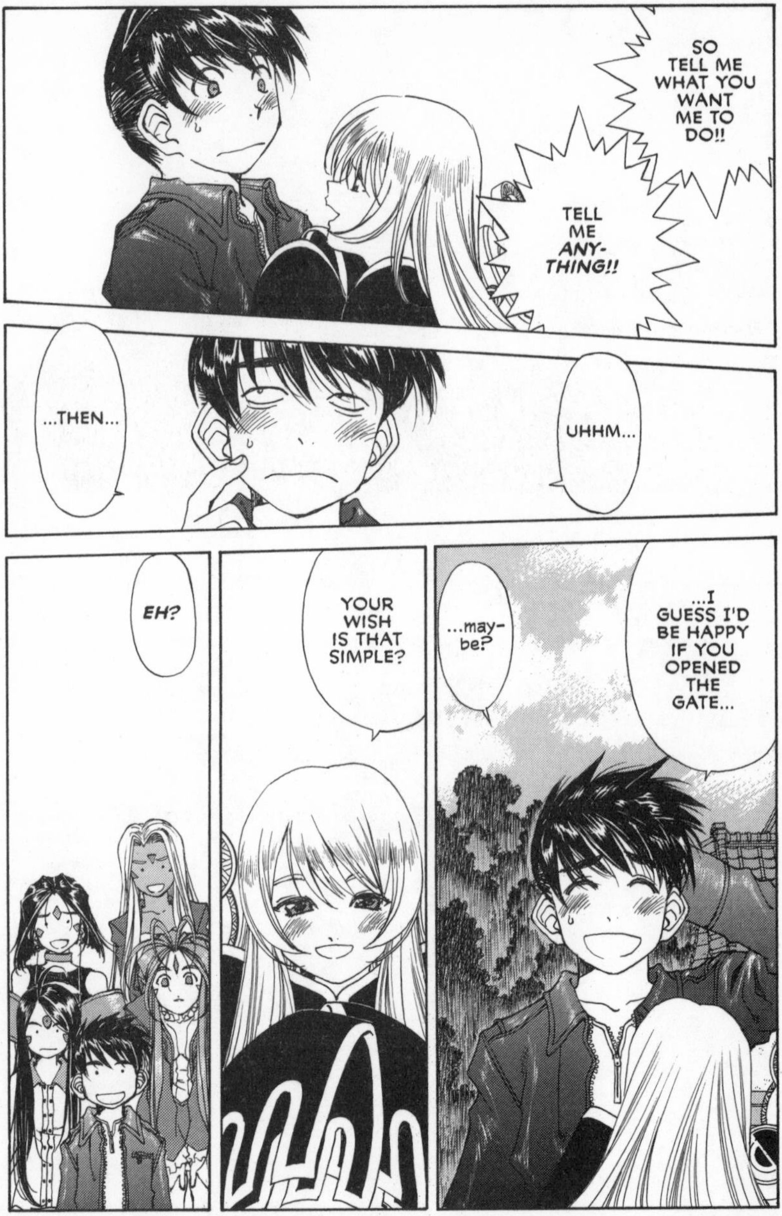
SO TELL ME WHAT YOU WANT ME TO DO!!
TELL ME *ANYTHING!!*
UHHM...
...THEN...
...I GUESS I'D BE HAPPY IF YOU OPENED THE GATE...
...may-be?
YOUR WISH IS THAT SIMPLE?
EH?

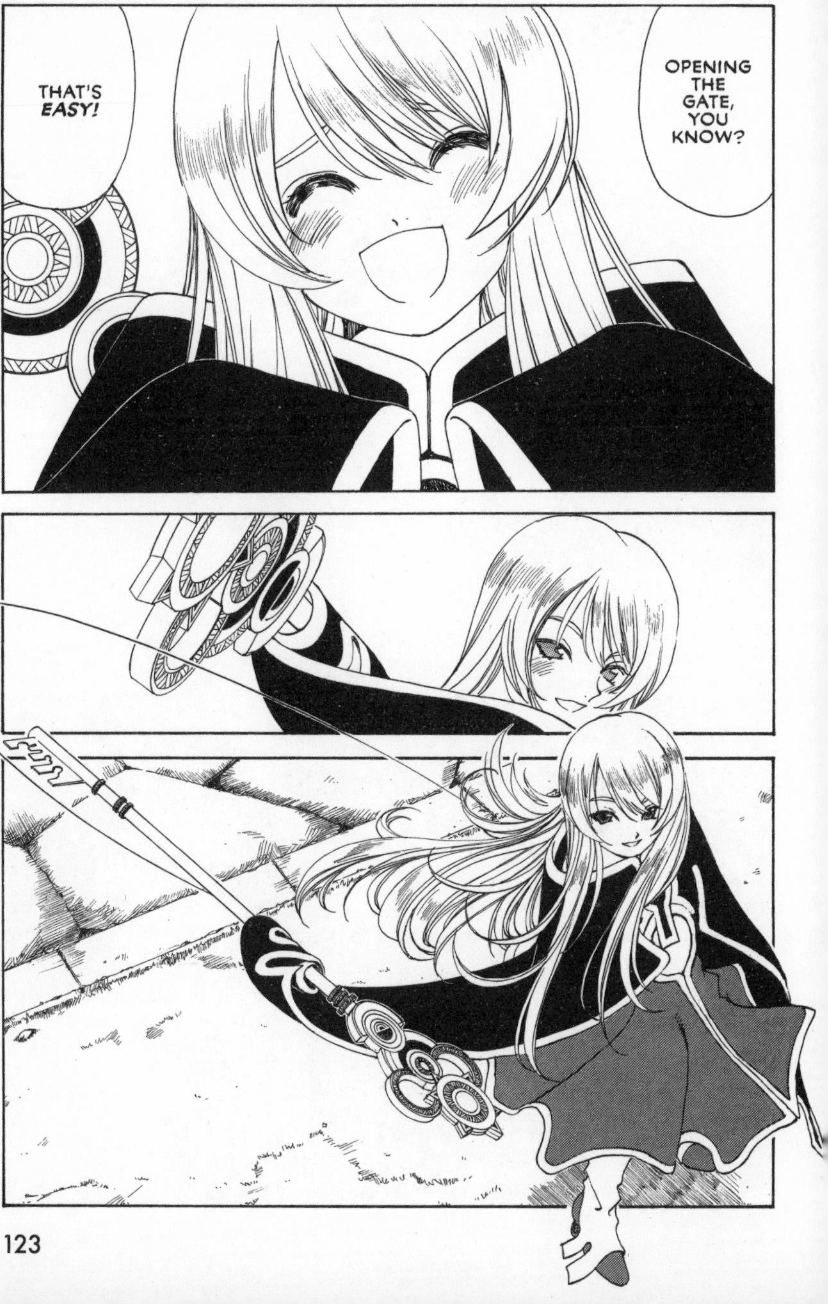
OPENING THE GATE, YOU KNOW?
THAT'S *EASY!*

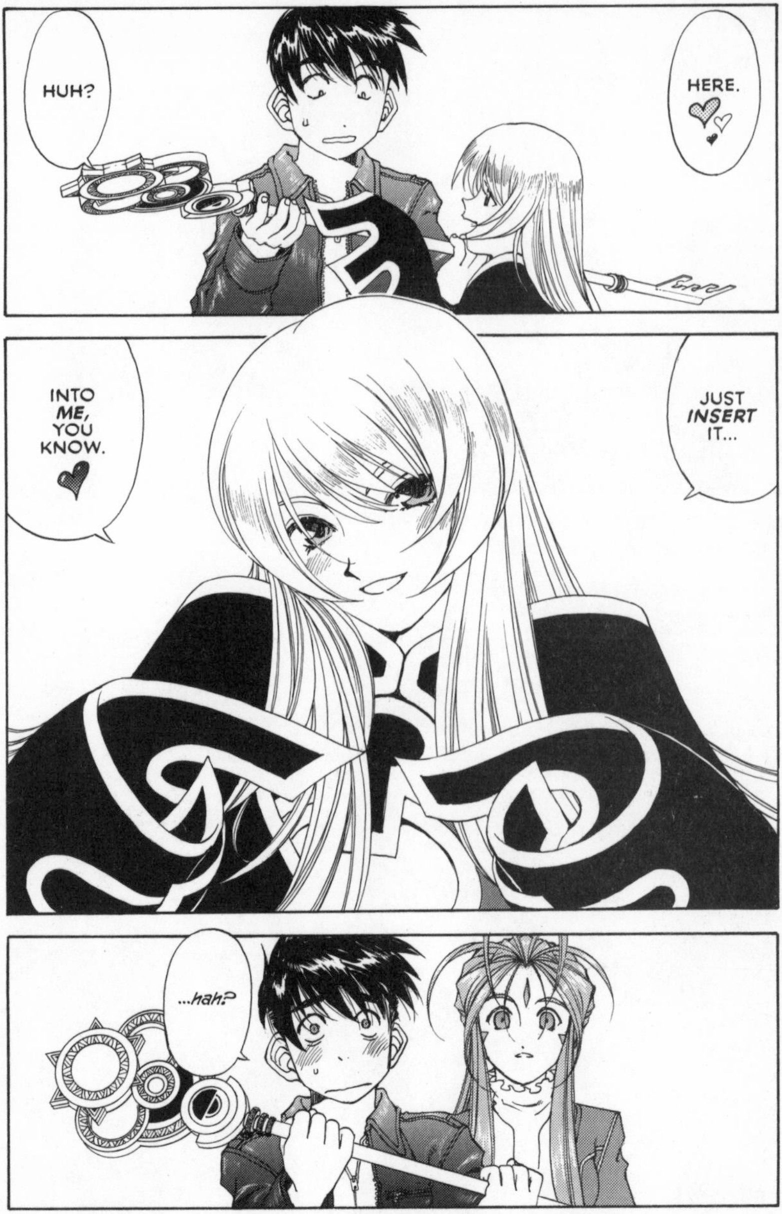
HERE.
HUH?
JUST *INSERT* IT...
INTO *ME*, YOU KNOW.
...hah?

CHAPTER 200

I Open Just for You

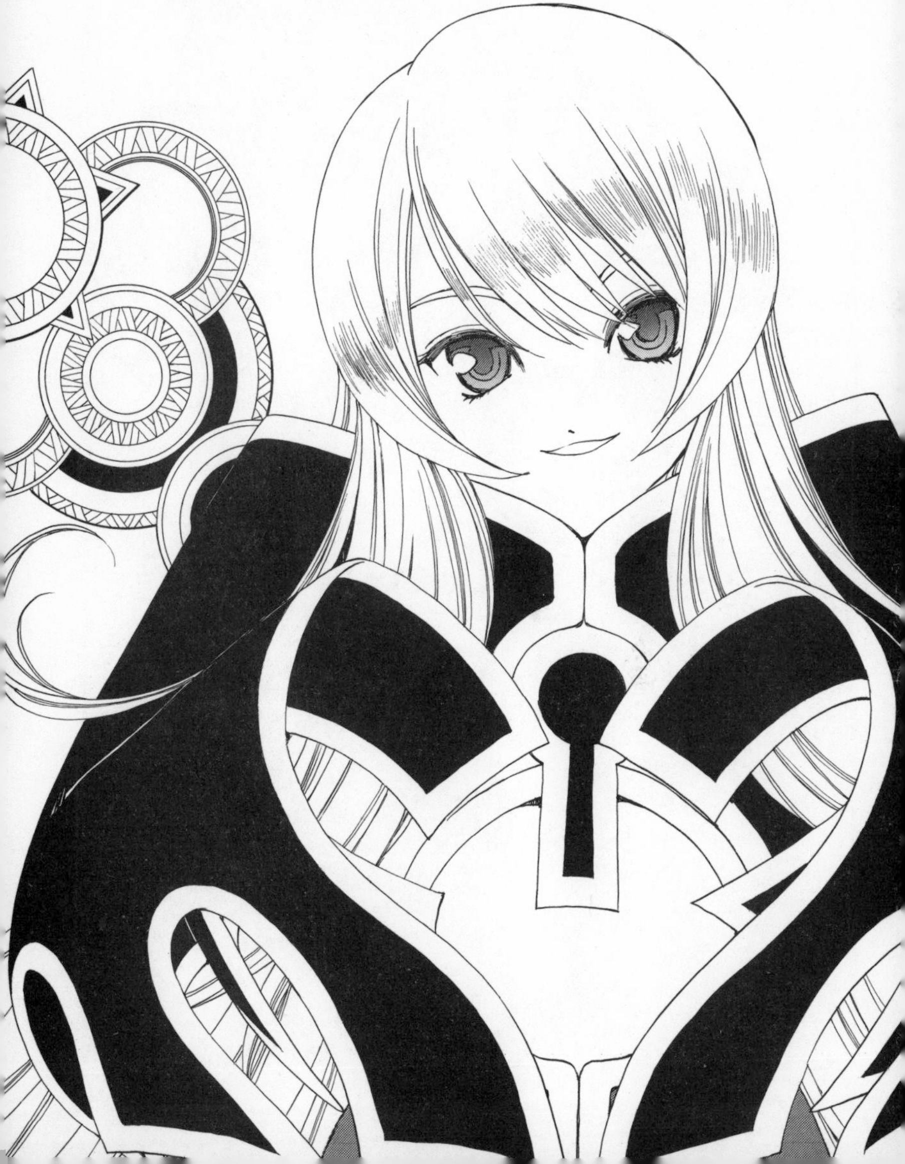

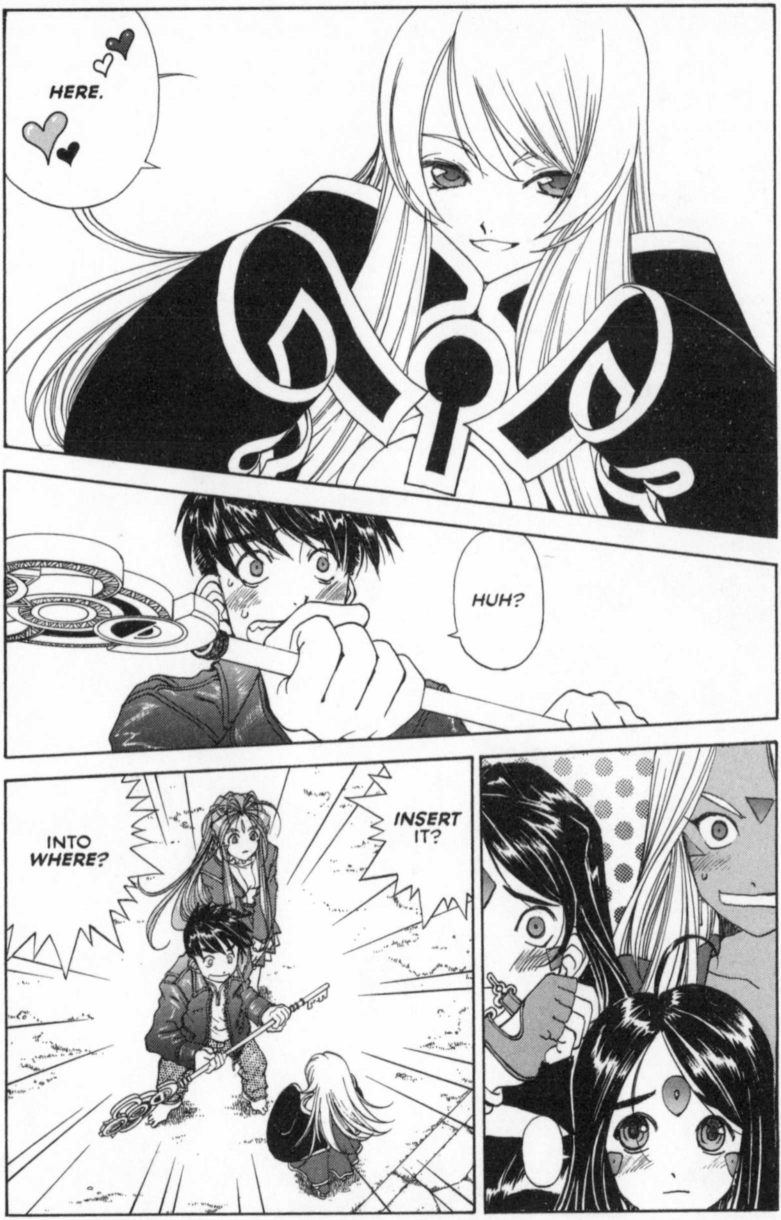
HERE.
HUH?
INSERT IT?
INTO WHERE?

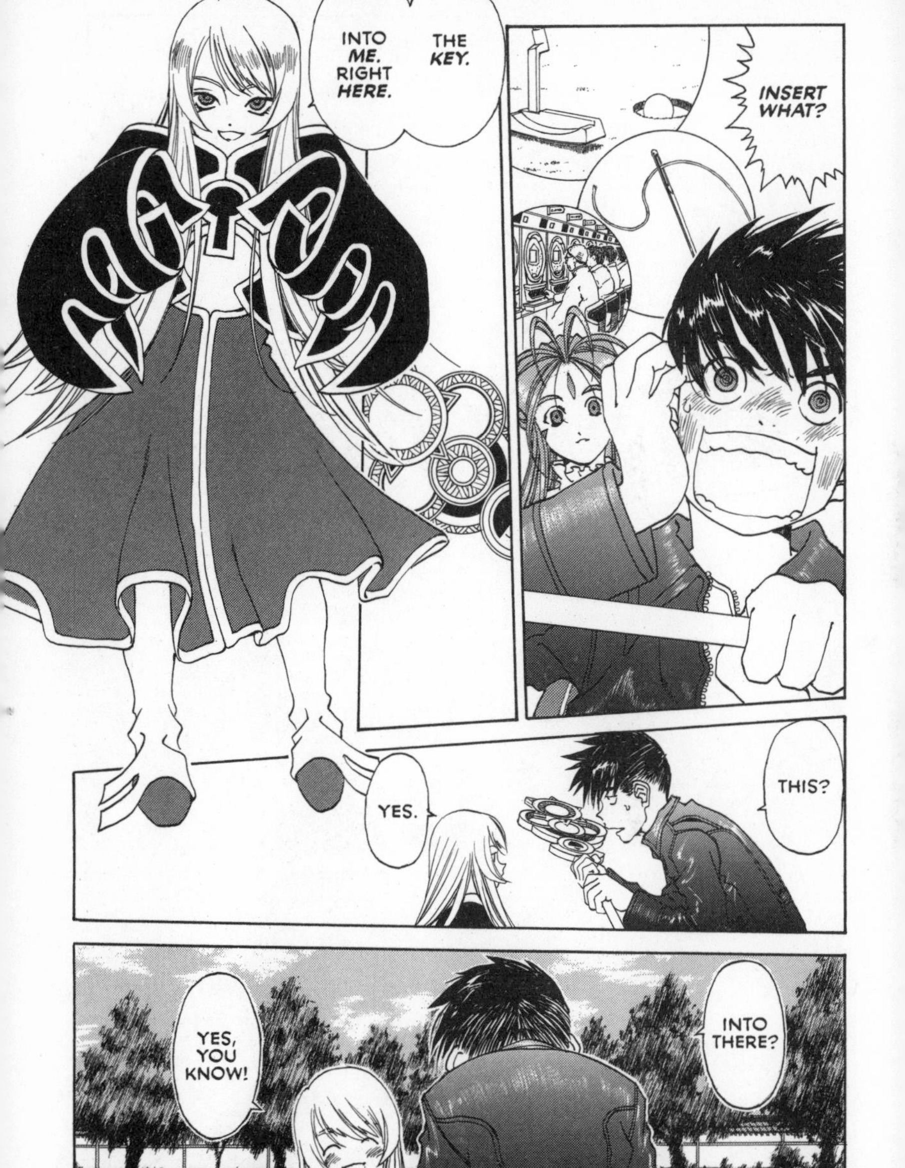

INSERT WHAT?
THE KEY.
INTO ME. RIGHT HERE.
THIS?
YES.
INTO THERE?
YES, YOU KNOW!

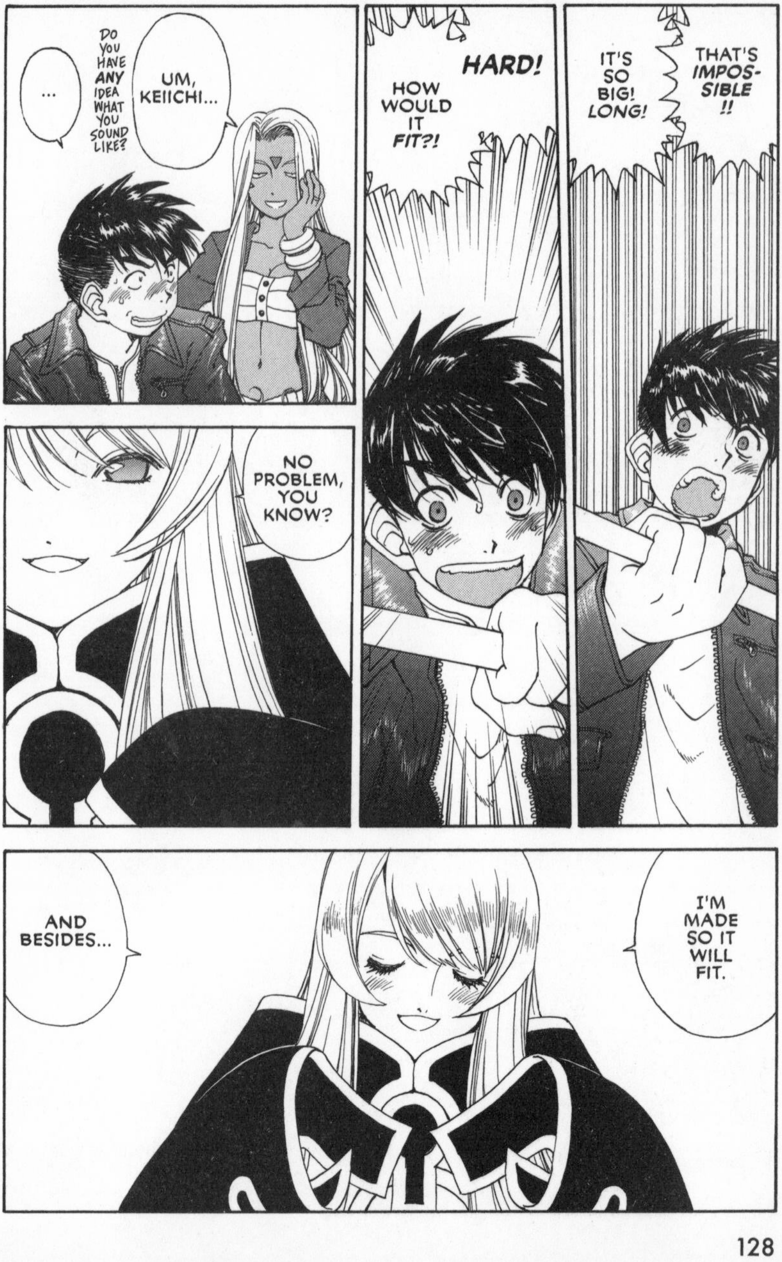
THAT'S IMPOSSIBLE!!
IT'S SO BIG! LONG!
HARD!
HOW WOULD IT FIT?!
UM, KEIICHI...
DO YOU HAVE ANY IDEA WHAT YOU SOUND LIKE?
...
NO PROBLEM, YOU KNOW?
I'M MADE SO IT WILL FIT.
AND BESIDES...

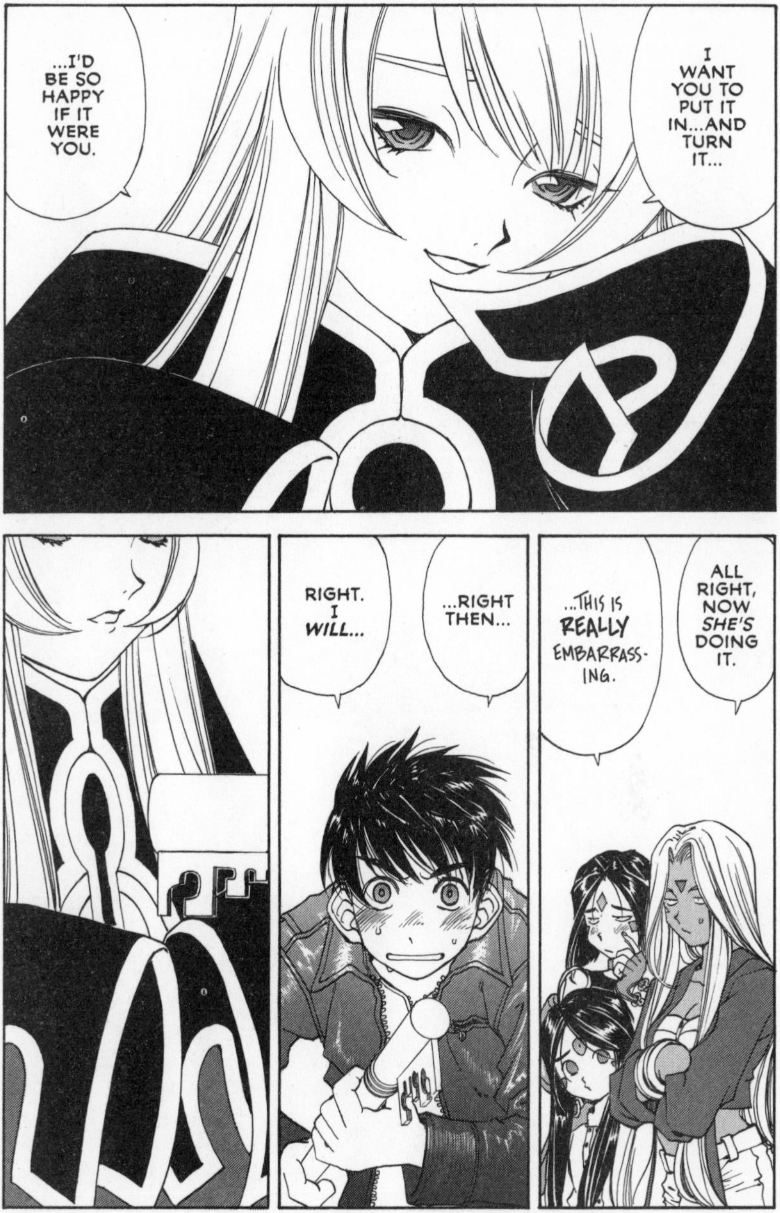
I WANT YOU TO PUT IT IN...AND TURN IT...
...I'D BE SO HAPPY IF IT WERE YOU.
ALL RIGHT, NOW *SHE'S* DOING IT.
...THIS IS **REALLY** EMBARRASS-ING.
...RIGHT THEN...
RIGHT. I *WILL*...

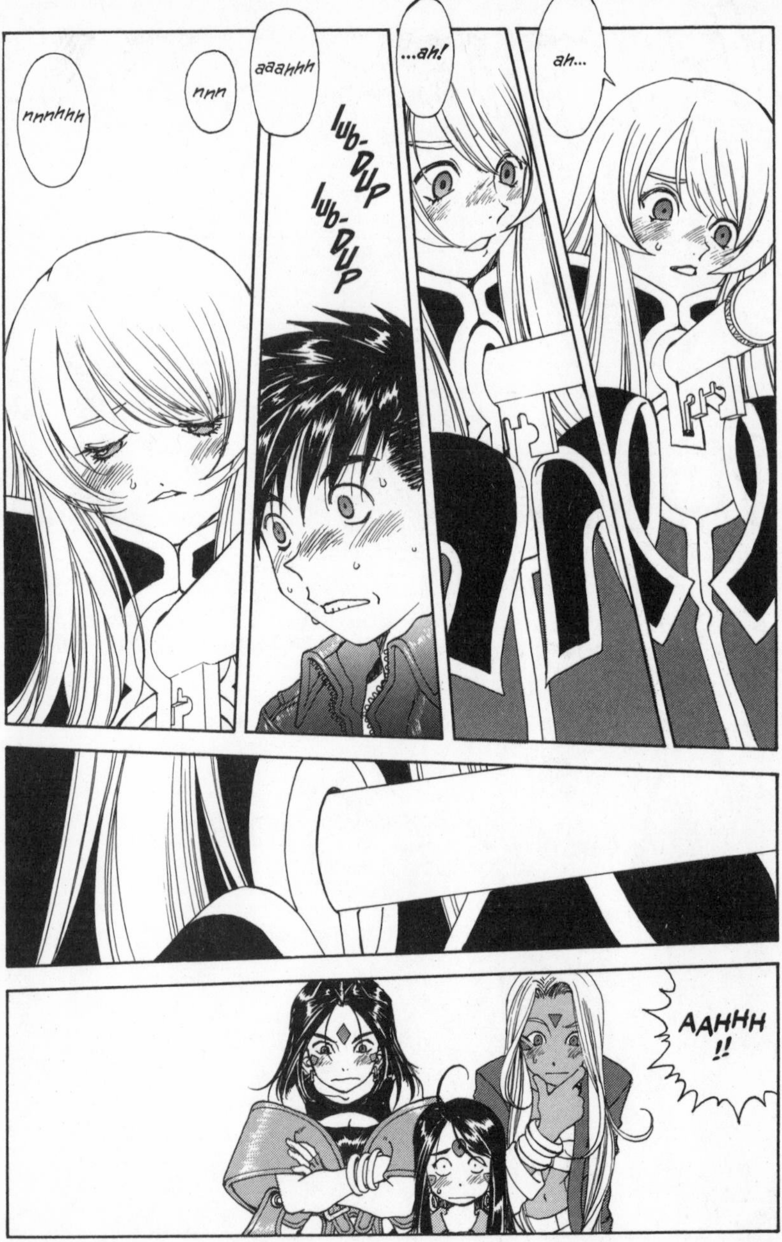

ah...
...ah!
aaahhh
lub-DUP lub-DUP
nnn
nnnhhh
AAHHH !!

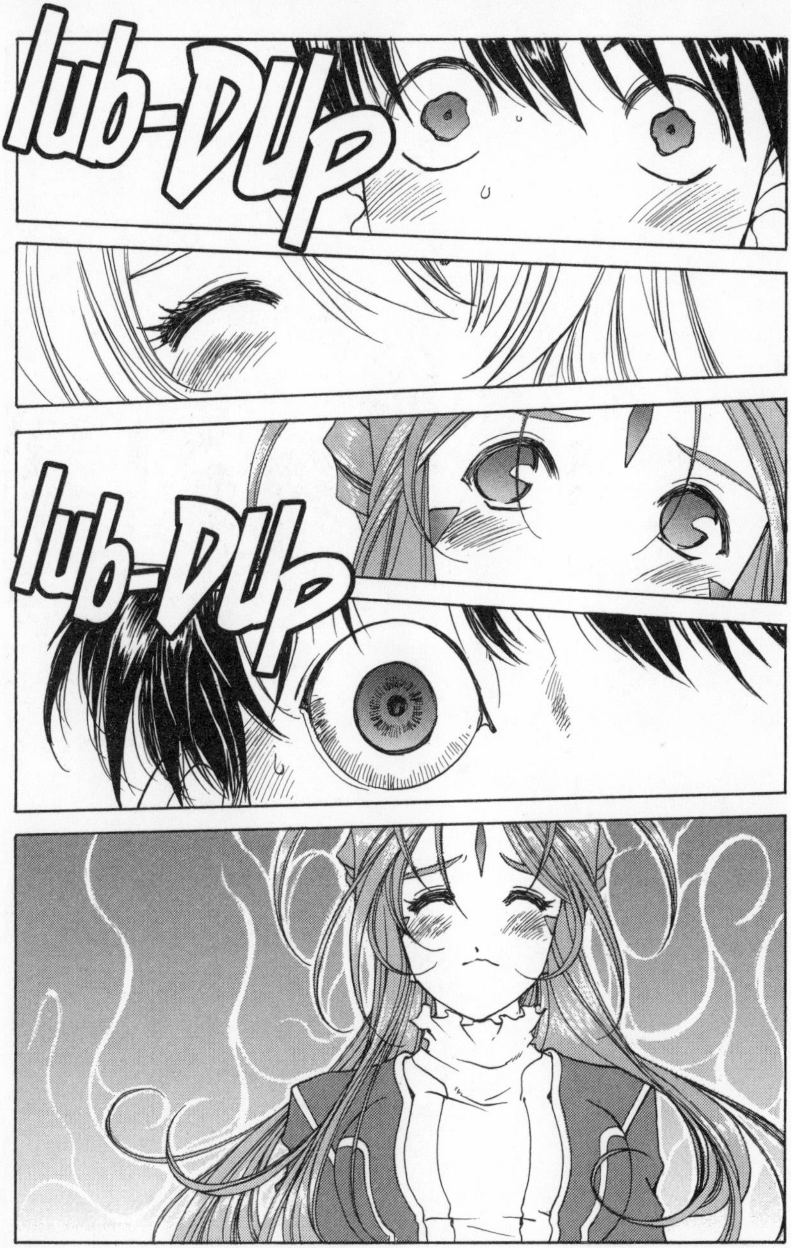
lub-DUP
lub-DUP

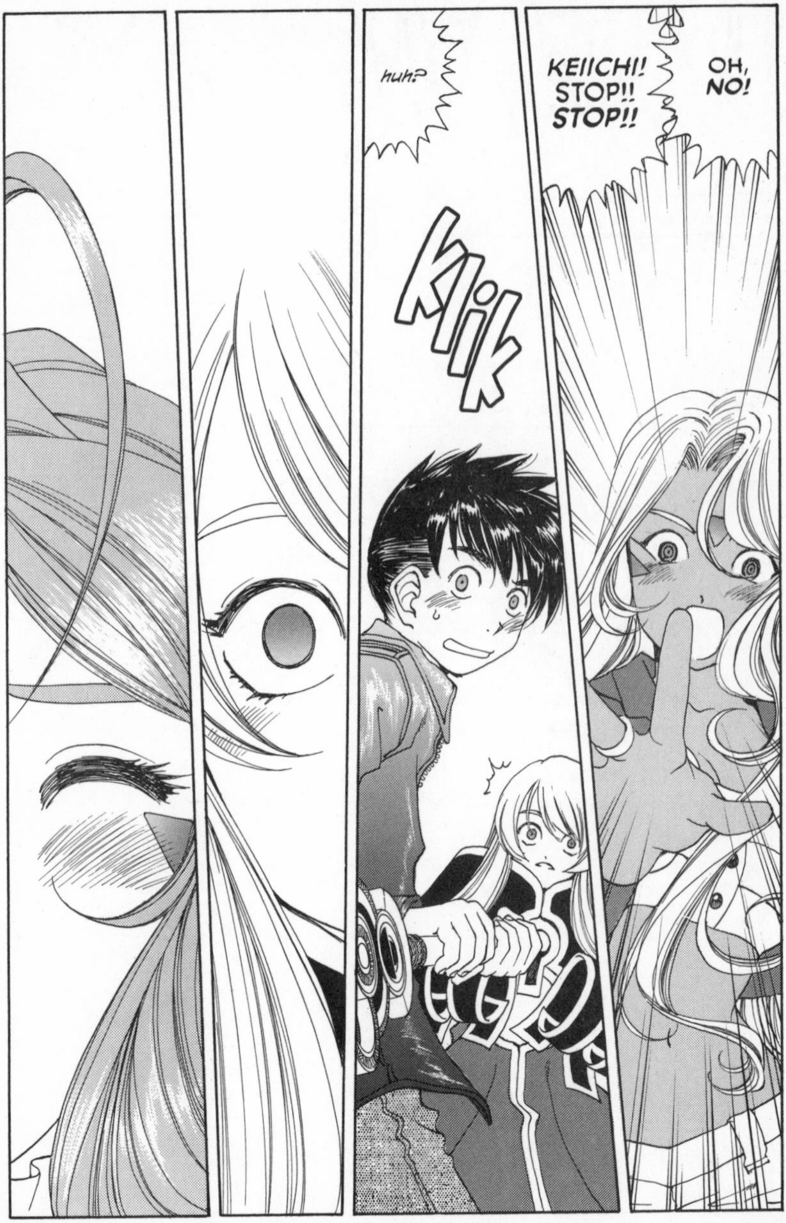
OH, NO!
KEIICHI! STOP!! STOP!!
huh?
klik

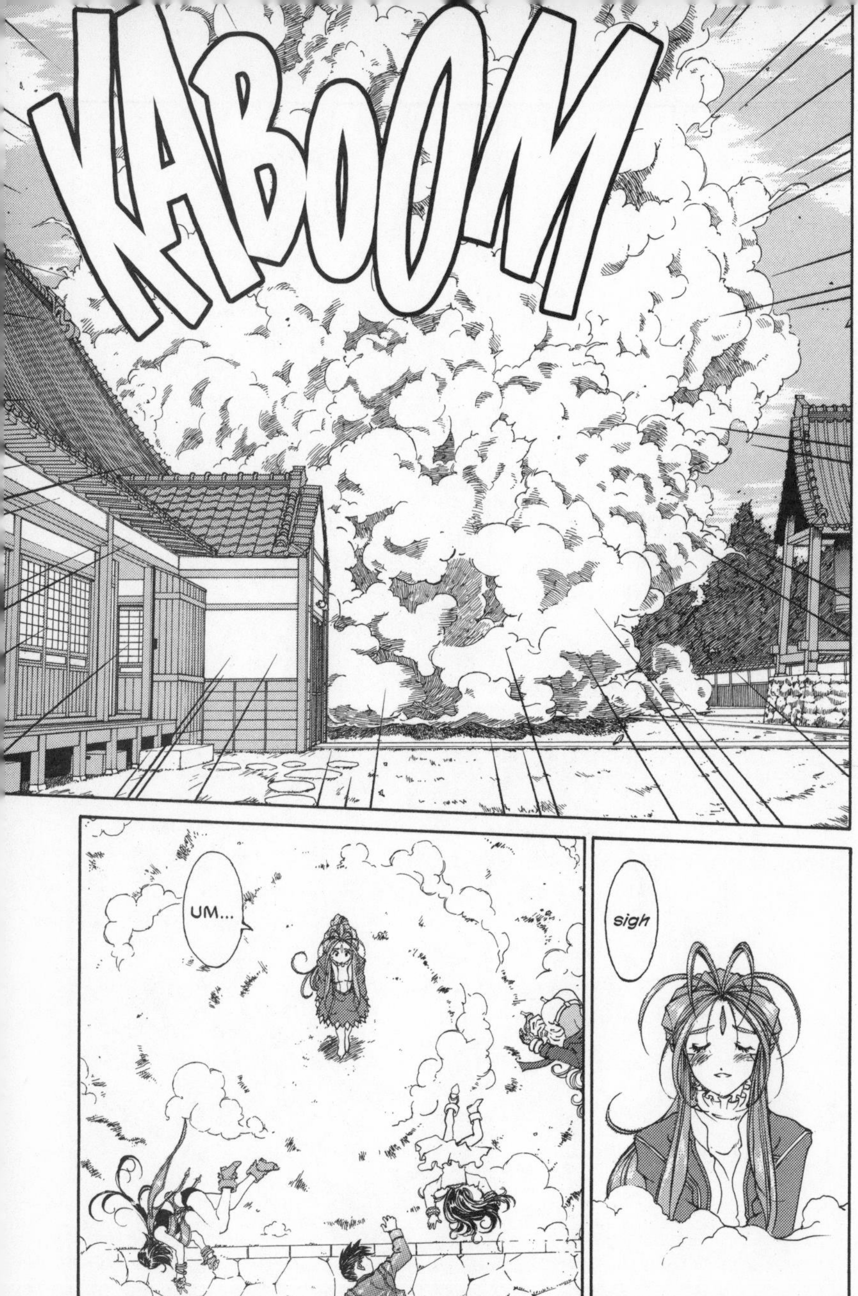
KABOOM
sigh
UM...

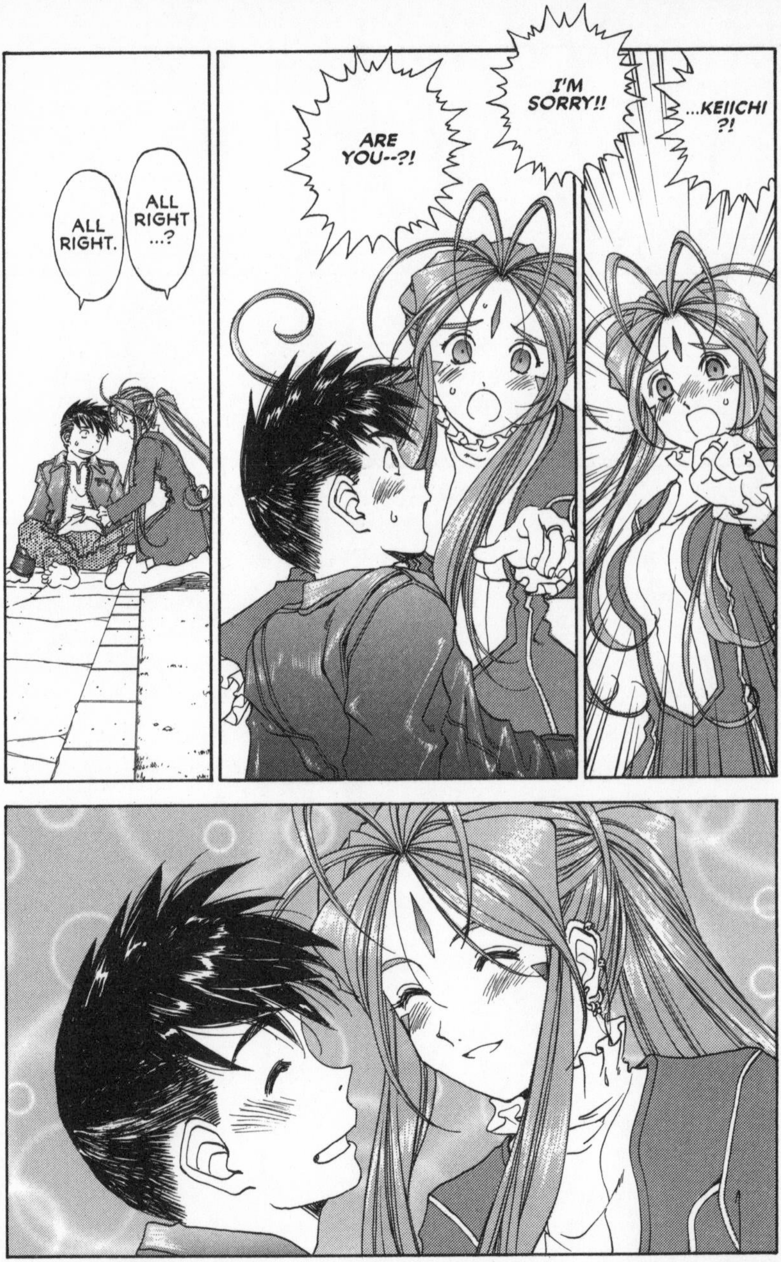
...KEIICHI ?!
I'M SORRY!!
ARE YOU--?!
ALL RIGHT ...?
ALL RIGHT.

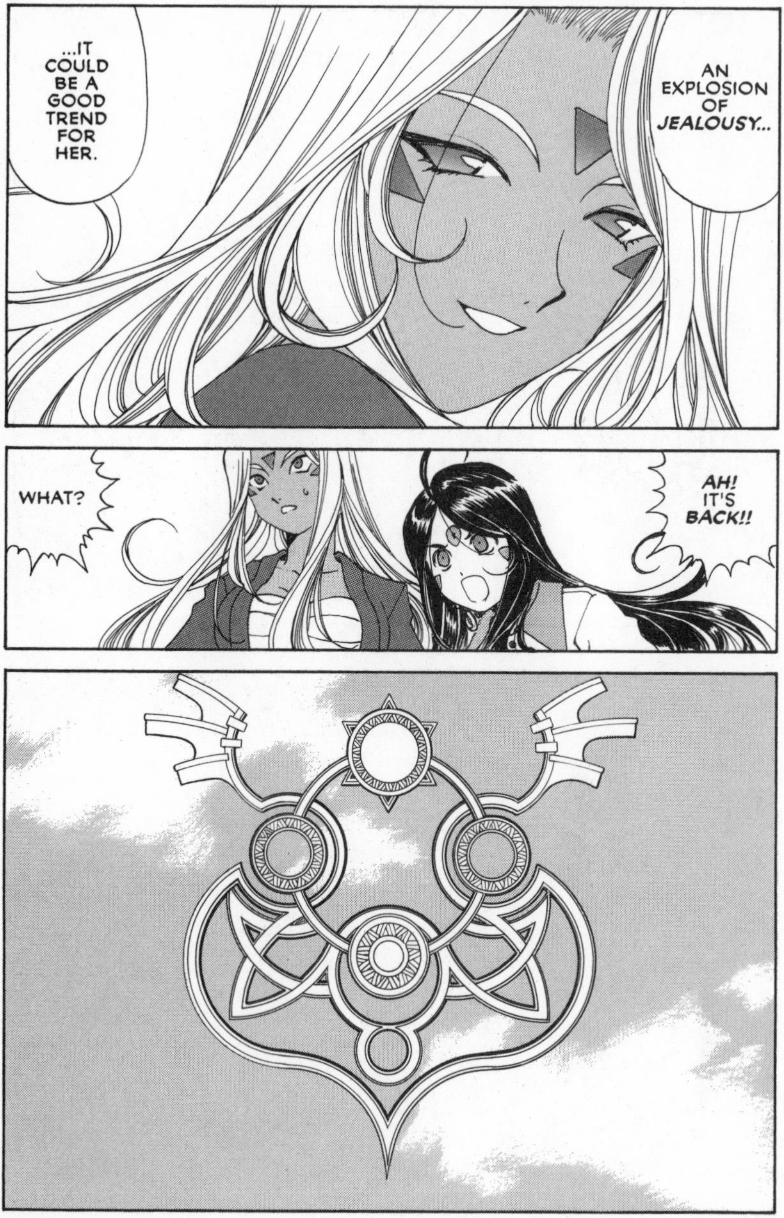
AN EXPLOSION OF *JEALOUSY...*
...IT COULD BE A GOOD TREND FOR HER.
AH! IT'S *BACK!!*
WHAT?

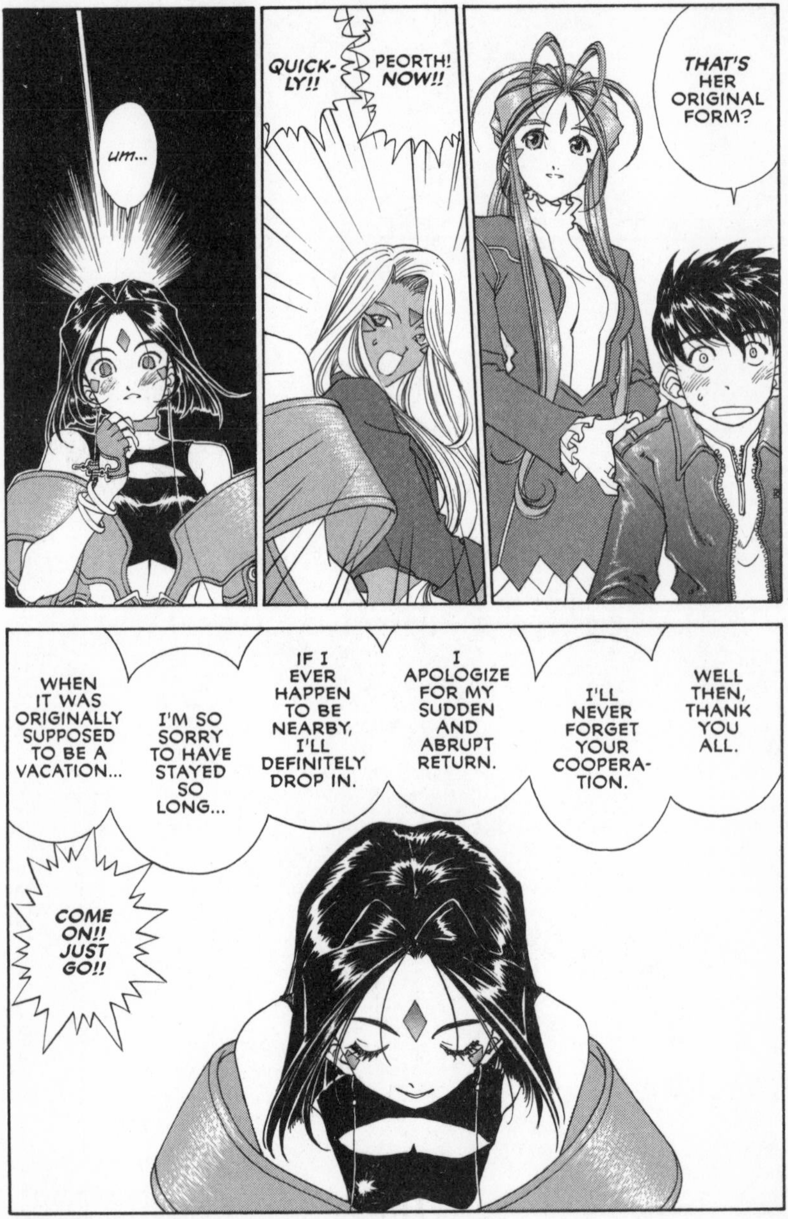
THAT'S HER ORIGINAL FORM?
PEORTH! NOW!!
QUICK-LY!!
um...
WELL THEN, THANK YOU ALL.
I'LL NEVER FORGET YOUR COOPERA-TION.
I APOLOGIZE FOR MY SUDDEN AND ABRUPT RETURN.
IF I EVER HAPPEN TO BE NEARBY, I'LL DEFINITELY DROP IN.
I'M SO SORRY TO HAVE STAYED SO LONG...
WHEN IT WAS ORIGINALLY SUPPOSED TO BE A VACATION...
COME ON!! JUST GO!!

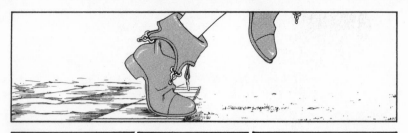

FARE-
WELL.

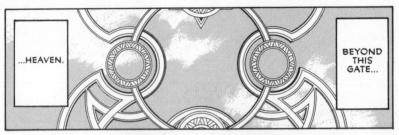

...HEAVEN.

BEYOND THIS GATE...

LET'S MEET AGAIN.

...SORRY, YOU KNOW?

OH...

oops?

um

uh

WHACK

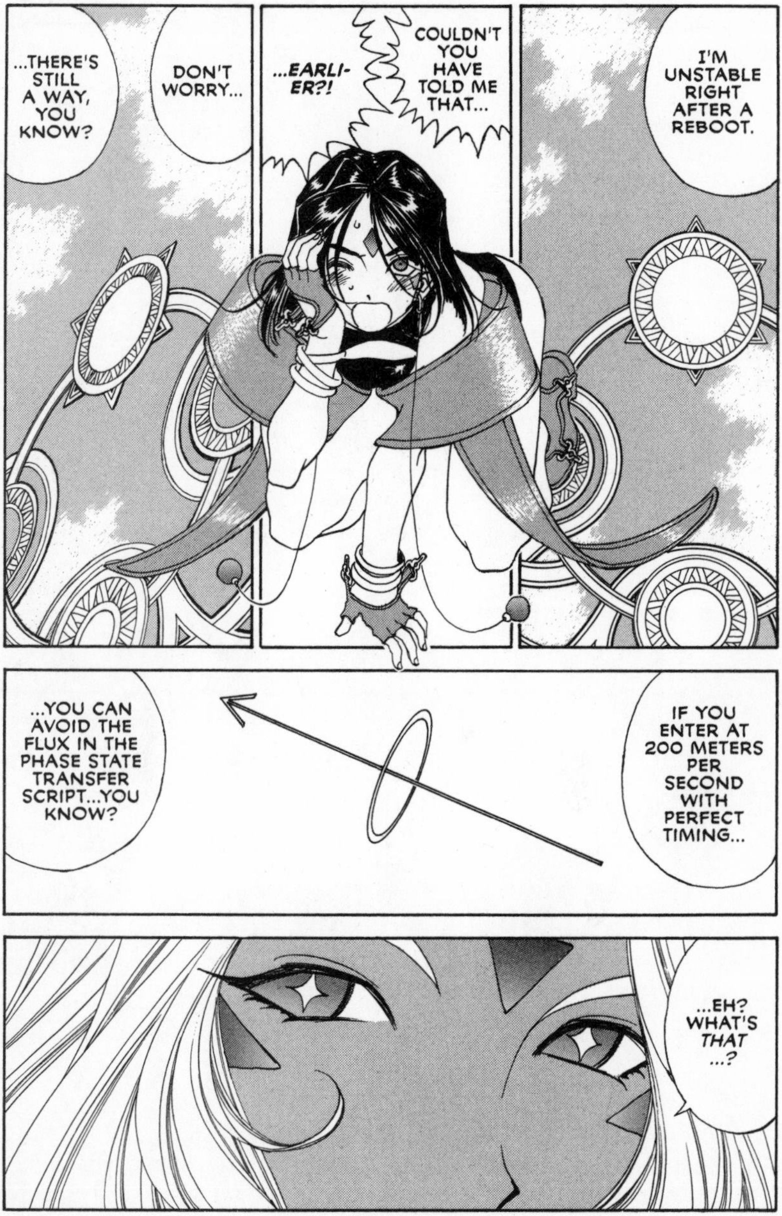
I'M UNSTABLE RIGHT AFTER A REBOOT.
COULDN'T YOU HAVE TOLD ME THAT...
...EARLI-ER?!
DON'T WORRY...
...THERE'S STILL A WAY, YOU KNOW?
IF YOU ENTER AT 200 METERS PER SECOND WITH PERFECT TIMING...
...YOU CAN AVOID THE FLUX IN THE PHASE STATE TRANSFER SCRIPT...YOU KNOW?
...EH? WHAT'S *THAT* ...?

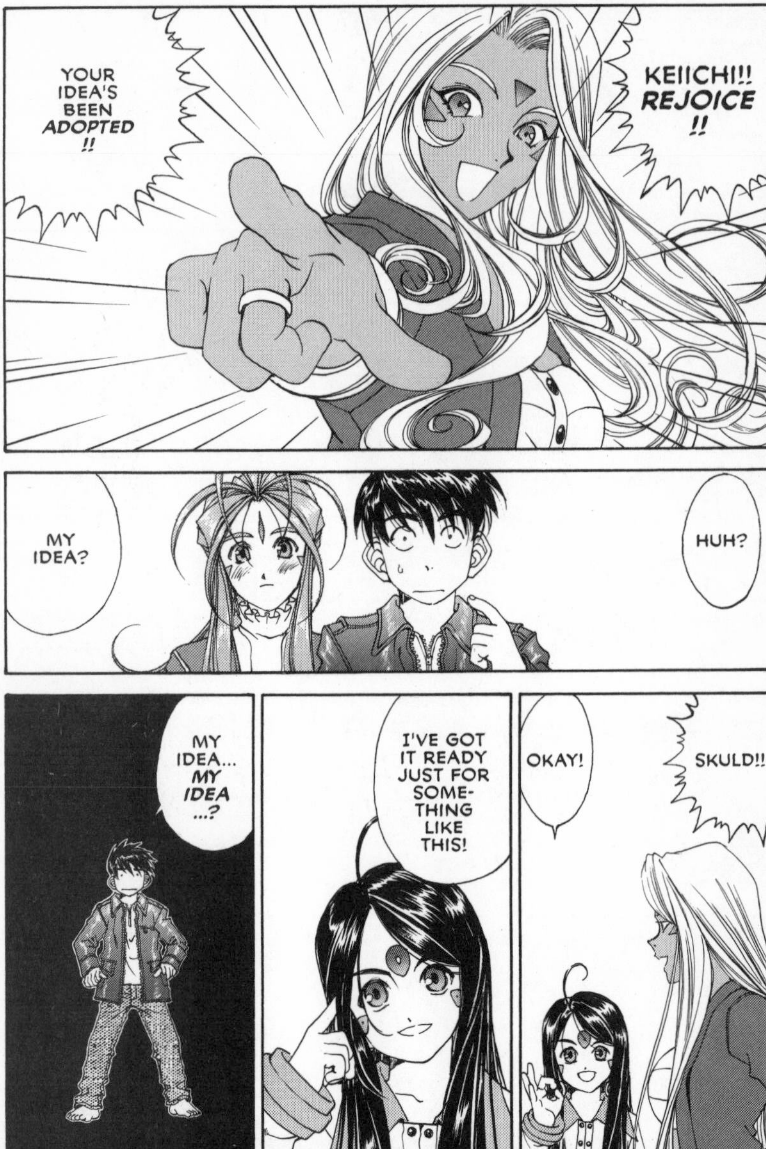
KEIICHI!! REJOICE !!
YOUR IDEA'S BEEN ADOPTED !!
HUH?
MY IDEA?
SKULD!!
OKAY!
I'VE GOT IT READY JUST FOR SOME-THING LIKE THIS!
MY IDEA... MY IDEA ...?

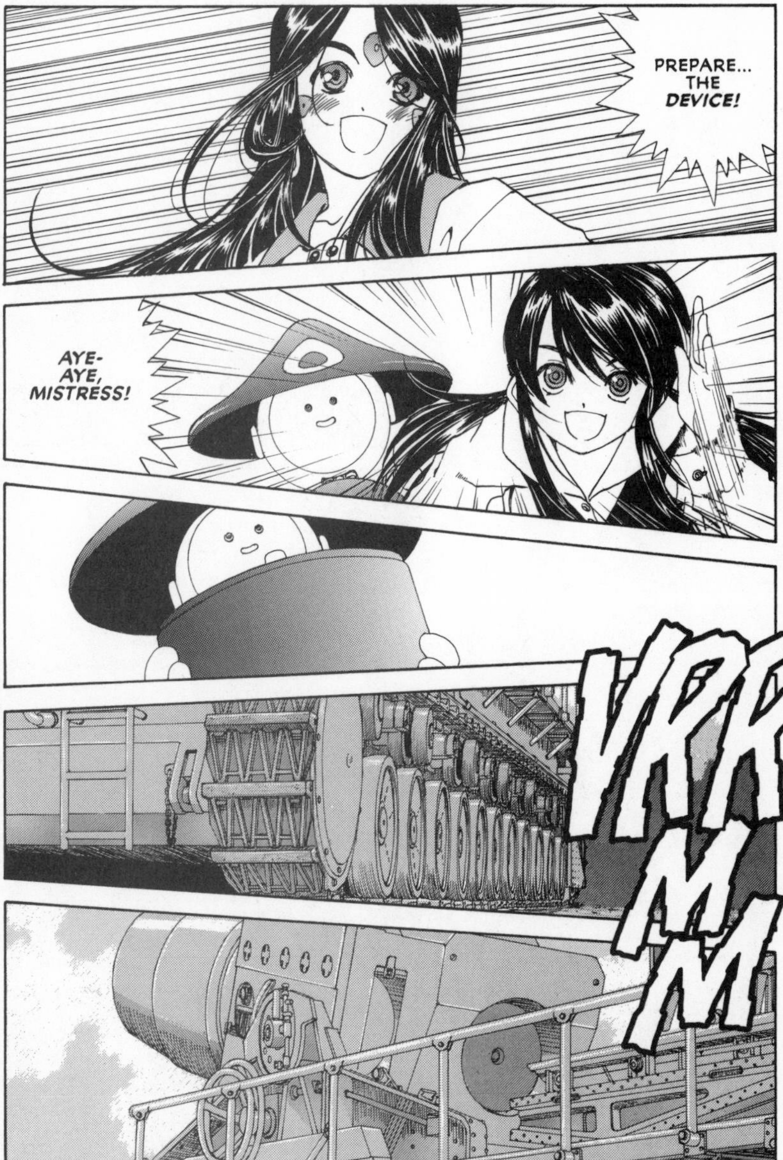
PREPARE... THE DEVICE!
AYE-AYE, MISTRESS!
VRRMMM

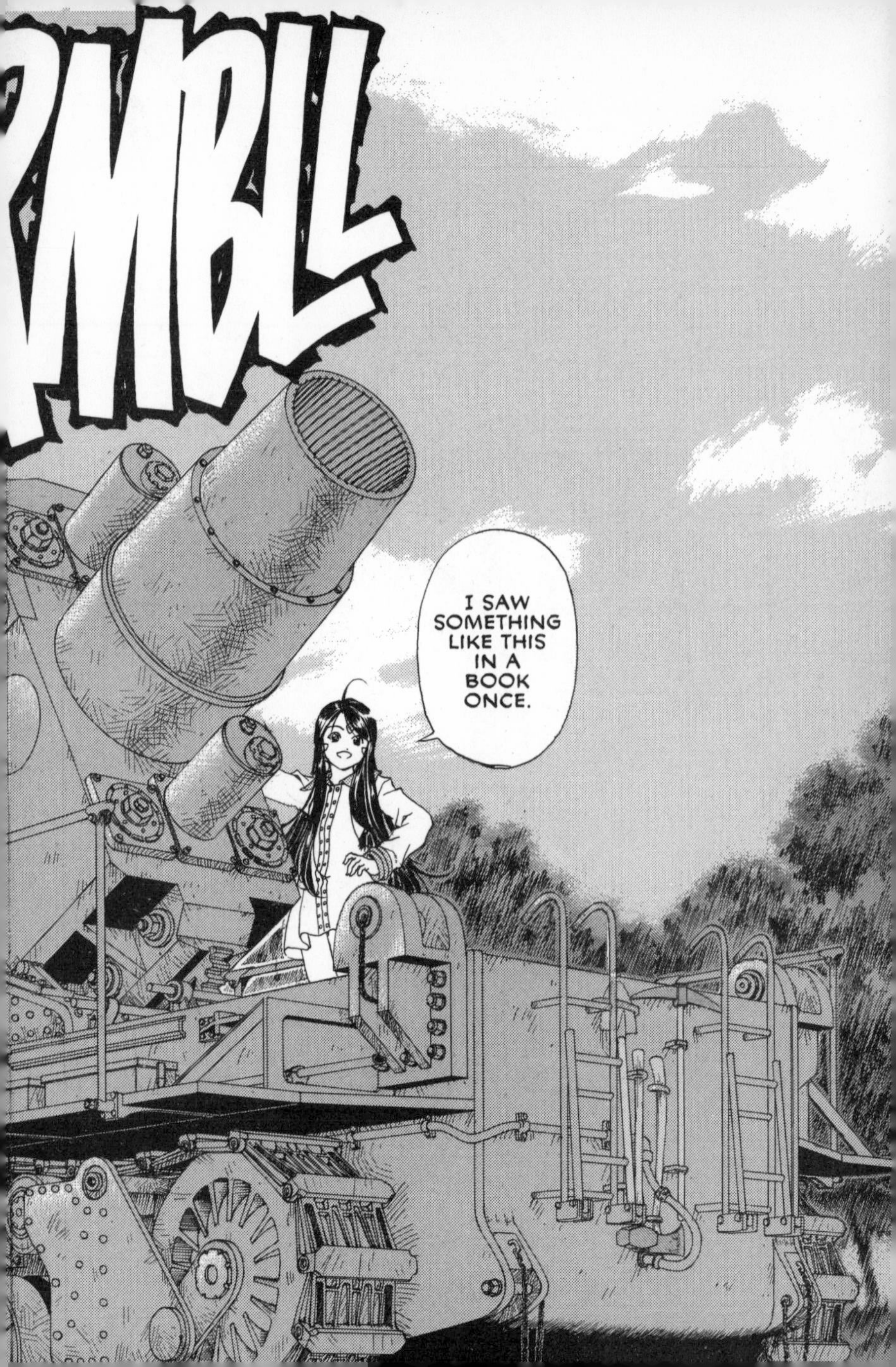
I SAW SOMETHING LIKE THIS IN A BOOK ONCE.

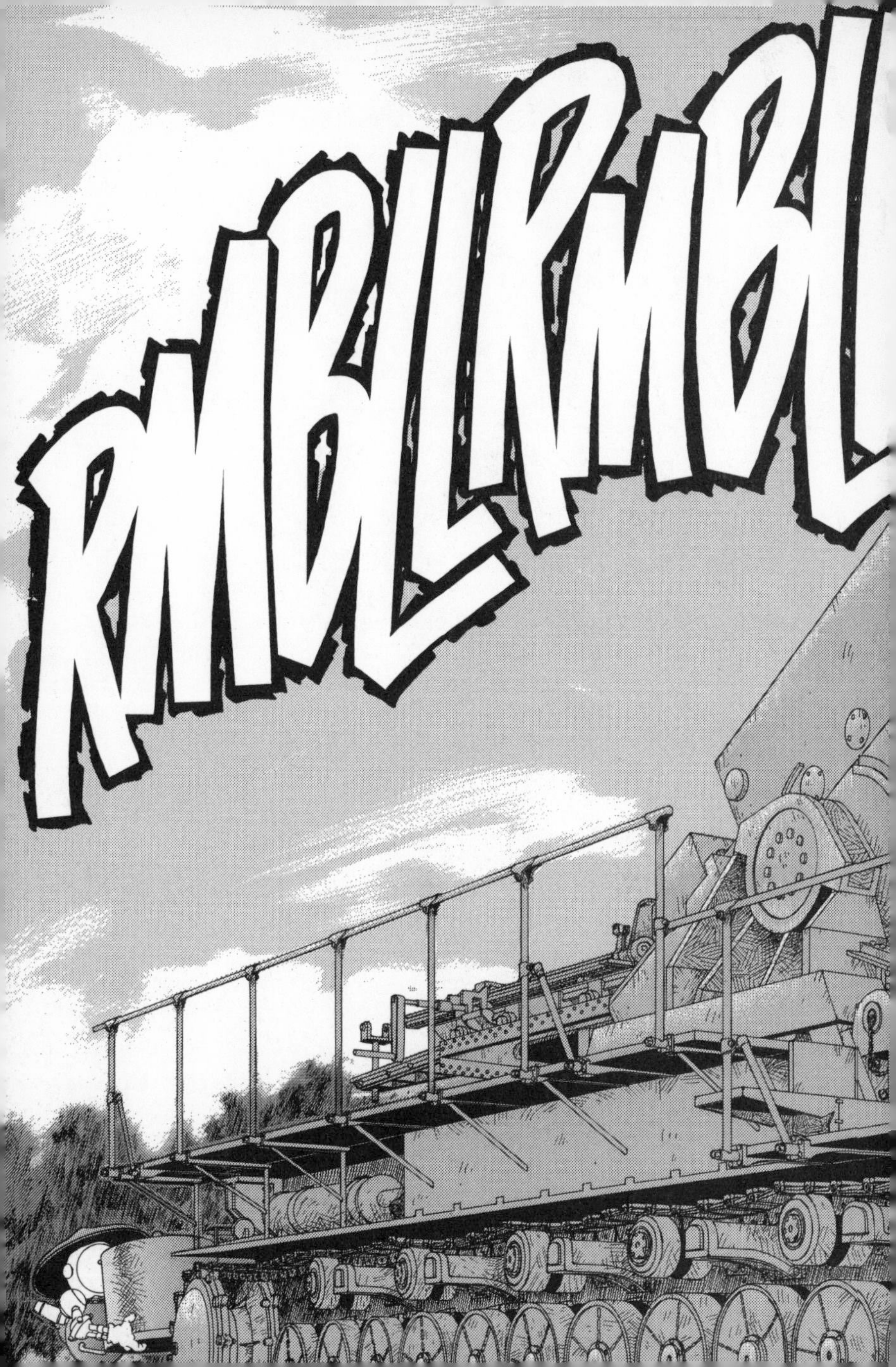
RMBLRMBL

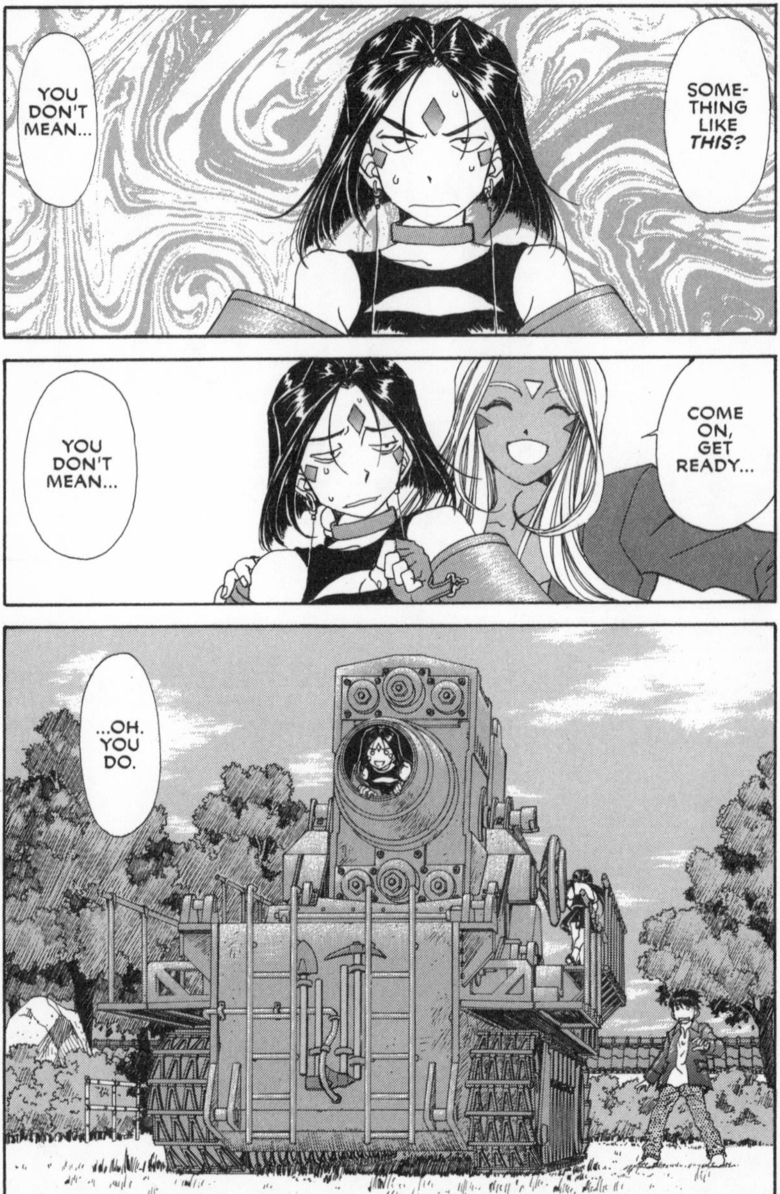
SOME-THING LIKE *THIS?*
YOU DON'T MEAN...
COME ON, GET READY...
YOU DON'T MEAN...
...OH. YOU DO.

EDITOR
Carl Gustav Horn

DESIGNER
Scott Cook

ART DIRECTOR
Lia Ribacchi

PUBLISHER
Mike Richardson

English-language version
produced by Dark Horse Comics

Published by Dark Horse Manga
a division of Dark Horse Comics, Inc.
10956 SE Main Street
Milwaukie, OR 97222
www.darkhorse.com

To find a comics shop in your area,
call the Comic Shop Locator Service
toll-free at 1-888-266-4226

First edition: January 2009
ISBN 978-1-59582-233-8

1 3 5 7 9 10 8 6 4 2

Printed in Canada

letters to the

ENCHANTRESS

10956 SE Main Street, Milwaukie, Oregon 97222
omg@darkhorse.com • www.darkhorse.com

NOTE: Full addresses and e-mail addresses will not be printed, unless you ask! All fan artwork, letters, and e-mails submitted become the property of Dark Horse Comics.

Wait! I've just printed the full address and e-mail of this volume's contributor even *without* asking, because I failed to realize the contributor is *me!* That's right, this is the editor's very first bit of *Oh My Goddess!* fan art.

I *could* simply say it was drawn in desperation (that much is obvious) over not having received any not-drawn-by-the-actual-editor-of-the-manga fan art or letters recently. But then I said to myself (prompting worried glances from passers-by), "Carl, it's easy to make *complaints*, but have *you* ever tried drawing a piece of *Oh My Goddess!* fan art?" "Uh, why . . . no . . . I haven't . . ." I said shamefacedly, and not with that cute manga shame, either.

So while I was waiting for some *OMG!* Vol. 31 pages to upload (in the unlikely event you didn't know, we switch off between doing an "old" volume like this and a new one like Vol. 31 every two months), I drew the piece you see on the next page. There is no un-heaped and -piled flat space on my desk large enough for even an 8.5 x 11" sheet of paper (Hammermill 24lb, pulled from the color printer), so I used

my copy of CLAMP's artbook *North Side* to press on. Fortunately, the ink didn't bleed through.

Anyway, I chose this particular person, jacket, pose, and bike, because they all match my own sister, who is a motorcycle otaku: her Icon jacket (rideicon.com; I didn't know until she told me that they were from Portland, much less that they were in my part of town), and her 1986 Harley XL Sportster 1250 (bored out from its original 1100, I understand). To confirm these details, I heard a great deal over the phone about the Evolution engine, not to mention opinions on the '73 Honda Elsinore 125 (and 250), the 2008 Ducati 1100S Hyper Motard (and why it would be great to have two of them), and the 1978 Norton 850 Commando chopped and bobbed ("which no one has done yet").

I just kept nodding politely like I understood, no doubt the same way she would have done for me, if I had said, "Don't you think that if you watch both *Kannagi* and *Golgo 13*, they effectively cancel each other out?"

Moral of the story? If you want to see better fan art than this, it's up to you! ^_^

—CGH

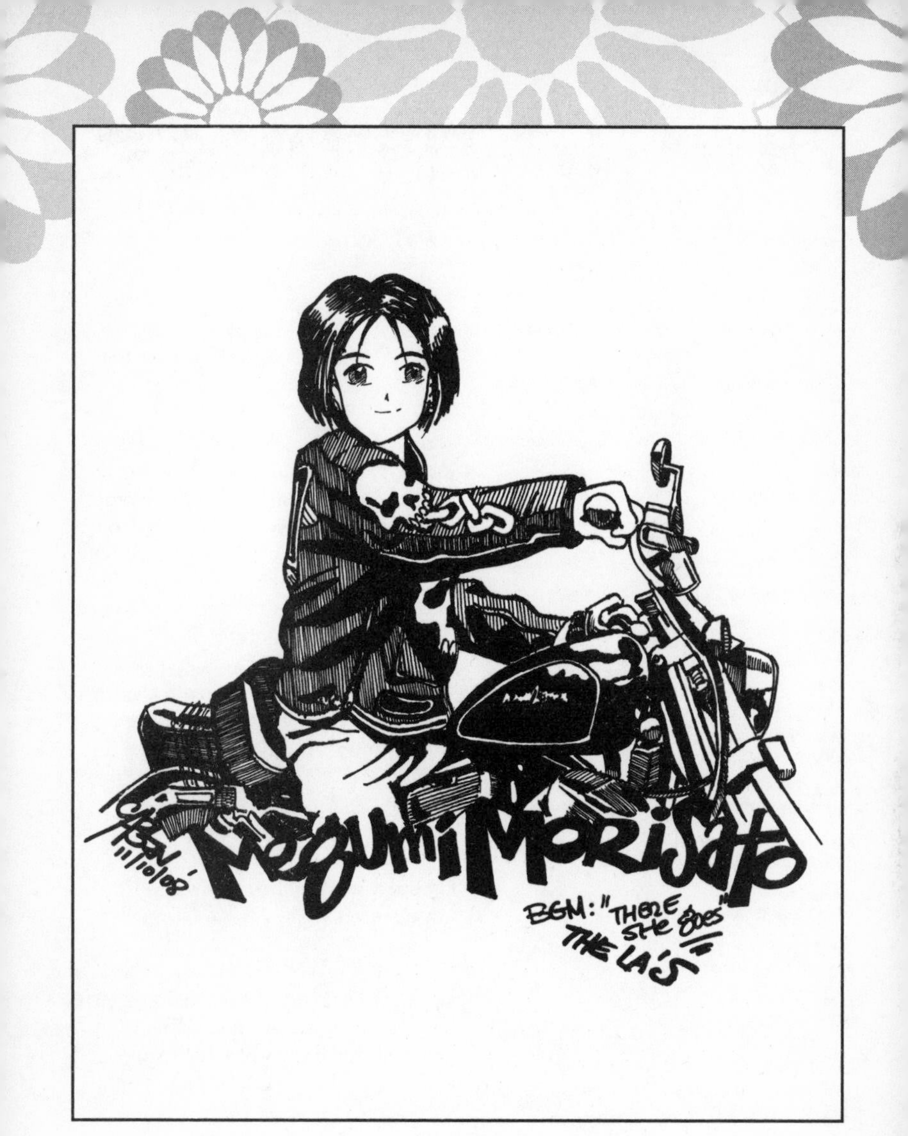
Megumi Morisato
11/10/08
BGM: "THERE SHE GOES" THE LA'S

Kosuke Fujishima's

Oh My Goddess!

Dark Horse is proud to re-present *Oh My Goddess!* in the much-requested, affordable, Japanese-reading, right-to-left format, complete with color sections, informative bonus notes, and your letters!

Volume 1
ISBN 978-1-59307-387-9

Volume 2
ISBN 978-1-59307-457-9

Volume 3
ISBN 978-1-59307-539-2

Volume 4
ISBN 978-1-59307-623-8

Volume 5
ISBN 978-1-59307-708-2

Volume 6
ISBN 978-1-59307-772-3

Volume 7
ISBN 978-1-59307-850-8

Volume 8
ISBN 978-1-59307-889-8

Volume 22
ISBN 978-1-59307-400-5

Volume 23
ISBN 978-1-59307-463-0

Volume 24
ISBN 978-1-59307-545-3

Volume 25
ISBN 978-1-59307-644-3

Volume 26
ISBN 978-1-59307-715-0

Volume 27
ISBN 978-1-59307-788-4

Volume 28
ISBN 978-1-59307-857-7

Volume 29
ISBN 978-1-59307-912-3

Volume 30
ISBN 978-1-59307-979-6

Volume 31
ISBN 978-1-59582-233-8

$10.95 each!

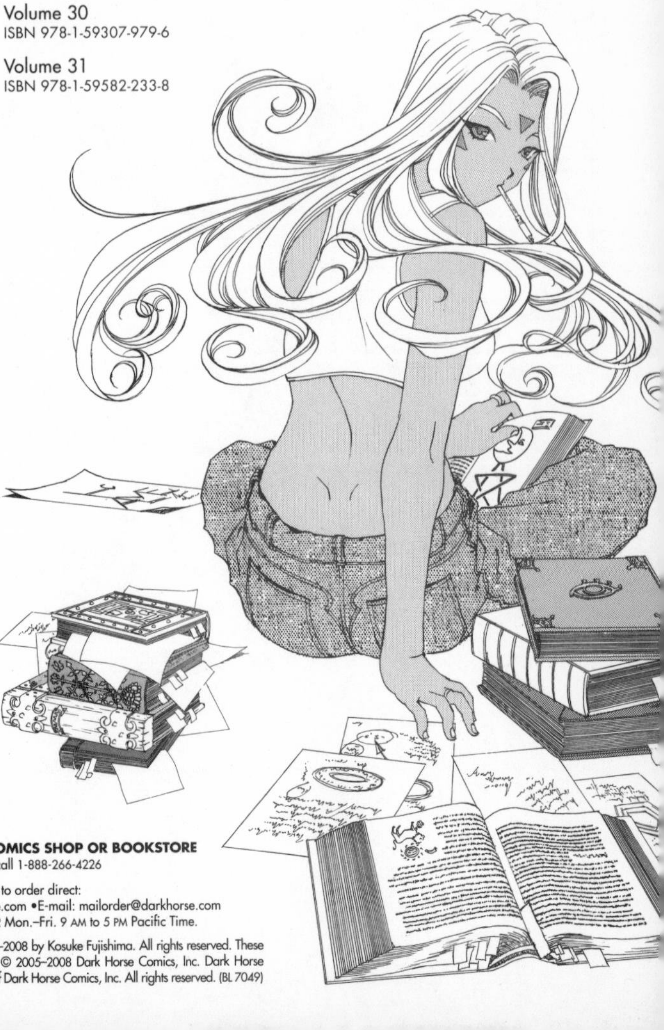

AVAILABLE AT YOUR LOCAL COMICS SHOP OR BOOKSTORE
*To find a comics shop in your area, call 1-888-266-4226

For more information or to order direct:
•On the web: darkhorse.com •E-mail: mailorder@darkhorse.com
•Phone: 1-800-862-0052 Mon.–Fri. 9 AM to 5 PM Pacific Time.

DARK HORSE MANGA

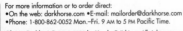

Kosuke Fujishima's **Oh My Goddess!**

Can't wait on the Goddesses? Change directions!

Just gotten into the new unflopped editions of *Oh My Goddess!*, and found you can't wait to see what happens next? Have no fear! The first **20 volumes** of *Oh My Goddess!* are available **right now** in Western-style editions! Released between 1994 and 2005, our *OMG!* Western-style volumes feature premium paper, and pages 40% larger than those of the unflopped editions! If you've already got some of the unflopped volumes and want to know which Western-style ones to get to catch up, check out http://www.darkhorse.com/Zones/Manga for a complete breakdown of how the editions compare!

Vol. 1: Wrong Number
ISBN 1-56971-669-2 / $13.95

Vol. 2: Leader of the Pack
ISBN 1-56971-764-8 / $13.95

Vol. 3: Final Exam
ISBN 1-56971-765-6 / $13.95

Vol. 4: Love Potion No. 9
ISBN 1-56971-252-2 / $14.95

Vol. 5: Sympathy for the Devil
ISBN 1-56971-329-4 / $13.95

Vol. 6: Terrible Master Urd
ISBN 1-56971-369-3 / $14.95

Vol. 7: The Queen of Vengeance
ISBN 1-56971-431-2 / $13.95

Vol. 8: Mara Strikes Back!
ISBN 1-56971-449-5 / $14.95

Vol. 9: Ninja Master
ISBN 1-56971-474-6 / $13.95

Vol. 10: Miss Keiichi
ISBN 1-56971-522-X / $16.95

Vol. 11: The Devil in Miss Urd
ISBN 1-56971-540-8 / $14.95

Vol. 12: The Fourth Goddess
ISBN 1-56971-551-3 / $18.95

Vol. 13: Childhood's End
ISBN 1-56971-685-4/ $15.95

Vol. 14: Queen Sayoko
ISBN 1-56971-766-4 / $16.95

Vol. 15: Hand in Hand
ISBN 1-56971-921-7 / $17.95

Vol. 16: Mystery Child
ISBN 1-56971-950-0 / $18.95

Vol. 17: Traveler
ISBN 1-56971-986-1 / $17.95

Vol. 18: The Phantom Racer
ISBN 1-59307-217-1 / $17.95

Vol. 19/20: Sora Unchained
ISBN 1-59307-316-X / $18.95

Adventures of the Mini-Goddesses
ISBN 1-56971-421-5 / $9.95

AVAILABLE AT YOUR LOCAL COMICS SHOP OR BOOKSTORE
*To find a comics shop in your area, call 1-888-266-4226
For more information or to order direct:
•On the web: darkhorse.com
•E-mail: mailorder@darkhorse.com
•Phone: 1-800-862-0052 Mon.-Fri. 9 A.M. to 5 P.M. Pacific Time.

AN ALL-NEW NOVEL BASED ON THE HIT MANGA AND ANIME!

OH MY GODDESS!

—FIRST END—

WRITTEN BY

YUMI TOHMA

WITH ILLUSTRATIONS BY

KOSUKE FUJISHIMA AND **HIDENORI MATSUBARA**

Keiichi Morisato was a typical college student—a failure with women, he was struggling to get through his classes and in general living a pretty nondescript life. That is, until he dialed a wrong number and accidentally summoned the goddess Belldandy. Not believing Belldandy was a goddess and that she could grant his every wish, Keiichi wished for her to stay with him forever. As they say, be careful what you wish for! Now bound to Earth and at Keiichi's side for life, the lives of this goddess and human will never be the same again!

ISBN 978-1-59582-137-9 | $14.95

AVAILABLE AT YOUR LOCAL COMICS SHOP OR BOOKSTORE
To find a comics shop in your area, call 1.888.266.4226. For more information or to order direct: •On the web: darkhorse.com •E-mail: mailorder@darkhorse.com •Phone: 1.800.862.0052 Mon.–Fri. 9 AM to 5 PM Pacific Time.

darkhorse.com

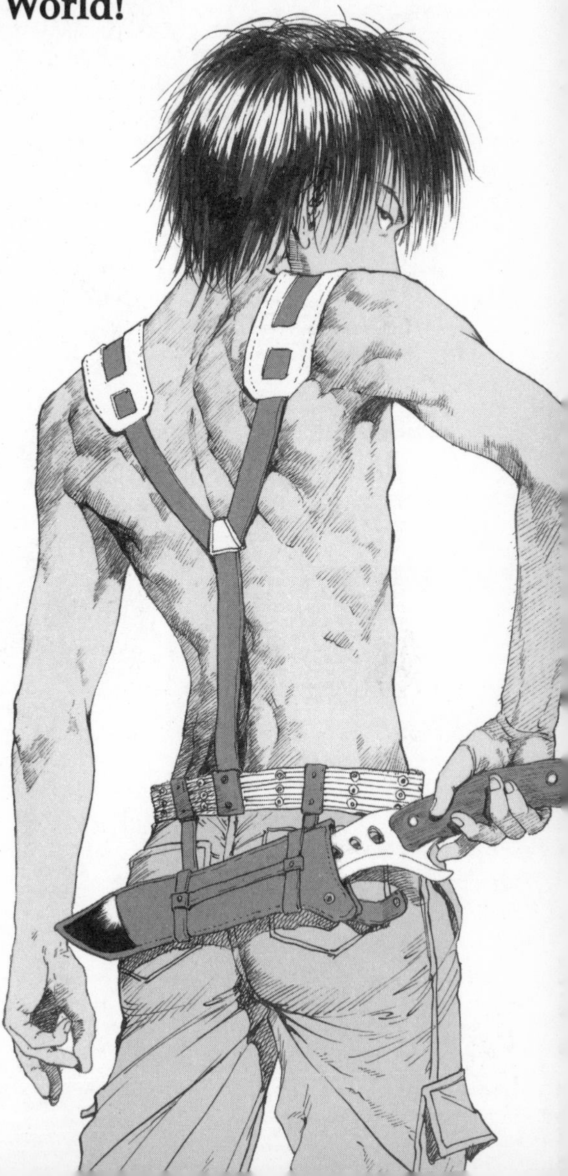

STOP! This is the back of the book!

This manga collection is translated into English, but arranged in right-to-left reading format to maintain the artwork's visual orientation as originally drawn and published in Japan. If you've never read comics this way before, take a look at the diagram below to give yourself an idea of how to go about it. Basically, you'll be starting in the upper right-hand corner, and will read each word balloon and panel moving right-to-left. It may take a little getting used to, but you should get the hang of it very quickly. Have fun! If this is the millionth manga you've read this way, never mind. ^_^

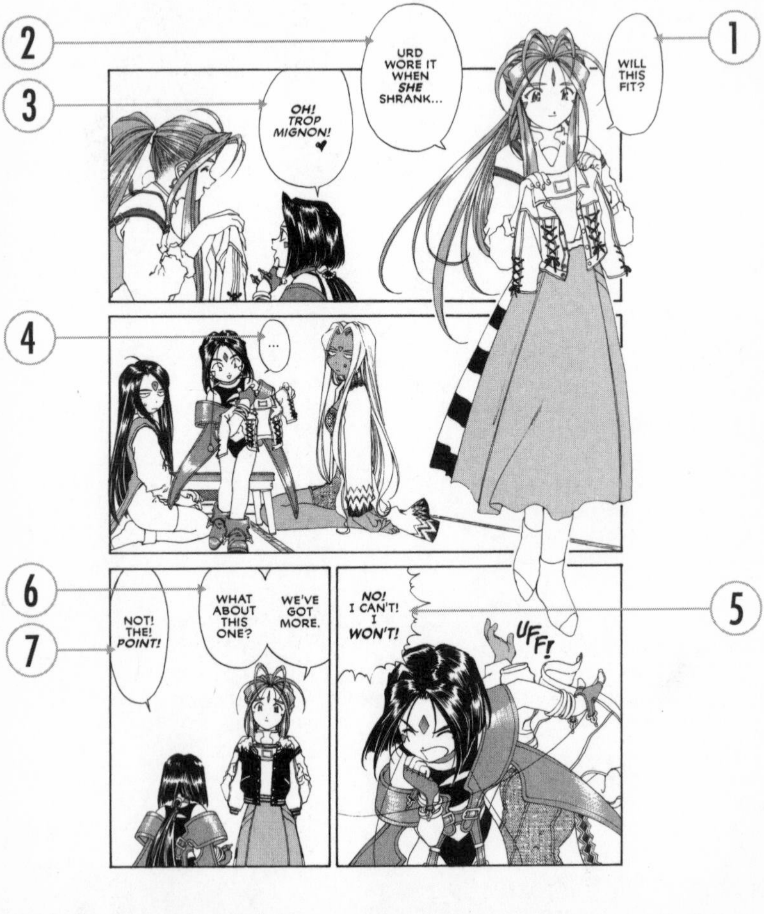
1
WILL THIS FIT?
2
URD WORE IT WHEN SHE SHRANK...
3
OH! TROP MIGNON!
4
...
5
NO! I CAN'T! I WON'T!
UFF!
WE'VE GOT MORE.
6
WHAT ABOUT THIS ONE?
7
NOT! THE! POINT!